Giving in Time

Giving in Time

Temporal Considerations in Philanthropy

Edited by
Ray Madoff and Benjamin Soskis

COPUBLISHED
WITH THE URBAN INSTITUTE PRESS

ROWMAN & LITTLEFIELD
Lanham • Boulder • New York • London

Copublished with the Urban Institute Press

Published by Rowman & Littlefield
An imprint of The Rowman & Littlefield Publishing Group, Inc.
4501 Forbes Boulevard, Suite 200, Lanham, Maryland 20706
www.rowman.com

86-90 Paul Street, London EC2A 4NE

British Library Cataloguing in Publication Information Available

Library of Congress Cataloging-in-Publication Data Available

ISBN 9781538131763 (cloth) | ISBN 9781538131770 (pbk.)
| ISBN 9781538131787 (ebook)

Contents

PART III: PRACTICE   **175**

Chapter 1

Introduction

A Brief History of Giving in Time

Stanley N. Katz and Benjamin Soskis

All gifts are oriented in time, just as they are oriented in space. Just as any donor must specify *where* a gift will be given, so too the donor must decide *when* a gift will be given. And just as donors must consider their responsibilities to potential beneficiaries who are geographically proximate against those who are more distant, donors must also balance the moral imperatives issued by the past, present, and future—the pull of traditions and founding charters, of current exigencies, and of future needs. Deliberations about the pacing, timeframe, and duration of gifts represent some of the more consequential and complex decisions that donors face and that the public can assess. Yet there are certain moments when these temporal considerations become especially salient, in public, scholarly, and practice-based discourse.

As this introductory chapter will explain, we are now in the midst of such a moment. Questions surrounding the timing of gifts, the proper "timely" response to crises, the legitimacy and the social value of endowments and perpetuity, and the obligations of the donor to the present or to the future, are now some of the most fiercely debated within the philanthropic and nonprofit sectors. Moreover, these questions do much to frame how the public and policymakers understand philanthropy—the good it can do, the challenges it confronts, and the dangers it poses.

This volume highlights some of the most exciting thinking on "giving in time" from a range of academic disciplines—history, political science, law, and philosophy. This chapter will offer a brief introduction to that thinking and will situate it within the broader history of how the temporal aspects of giving have been understood, with a particular emphasis on giving in the United States. It will also outline some of the primary reasons why recent years have brought increased attention to this constellation of issues we call "giving in time."

The dominant time-based orientation of gift-giving for much of human history was dictated by the immediacy of the tug of human sympathy and fellow-feeling. Men, women, and children responded to pressing needs as they encountered them. But for millennia, individuals have also extended the scope of ethical responsibility into the future. "Even before the right to make wills and testaments developed," scholar Marion Fremont-Smith has noted, "the practice of leaving property in perpetuity to other than paternal heirs was encouraged for religious purposes in both Egypt and Chaldea." Scholars have pointed to the funding of the Oracle at Delphi and the Library of Alexandria as early precedents for endowments, which allowed individuals to contribute to future needs. The practice developed by early Romans of bequeathing money or property to individuals to maintain burial sites and memorial services in perpetuity ultimately encouraged the endowment of larger corporate bodies, such as neighborhood associations, guilds and *collegia* to perform these and similar functions. In many of these cases, ideas regarding the immortality of the soul, *sub specie aeternitatis*, promoted an orientation toward giving in which the needs of the future were granted an equal or greater weight than the needs of the present.[1]

After the rule of Emperor Constantine, the church became the primary means through which social needs of the Roman Empire were met, and a large proportion of its institutions were funded through endowments. In Europe, the Middle Ages brought a significant expansion of permanently endowed institutions, as the practice of dedicating land to ecclesiastical institutions in perpetuity became more widespread, as did late-in-life or deathbed contributions, under the guidance of a priest. A form of perpetual foundation, the *waqf*, was established in Islamic societies by the ninth century and soon became "the premier institutional mechanism for philanthropic activity" in the Islamic world, allowing for "ongoing charity," even after the death of the donor. Some scholars have argued that waqfs served as the inspiration for some of the earliest European foundations.[2]

In 1601, endowed charities in England were granted legal codification through the Elizabethan Statute of Charitable Uses, which among other policies established charity commissioners to review disputed trusts. Such legal sanction further encouraged the spread of charitable trusts. Yet as Rob Reich demonstrates in this volume, the growth of endowments provoked a strong critique from Enlightenment thinkers; the fear of "mortmain," the "dead hand" of the past extending its grip into the present and future, which had shaped legal attitudes toward trusts in general since medieval times, spread to charitable trusts as well. For instance, in the 1736 Mortmain Act—spurred in part by anticlerical sentiment—Parliament prohibited charitable bequests in land and interests in land as well as charitable giving within twelve months of the death of the donor.[3]

Fears about the hold of the past on the present were in turn amplified by the emerging discipline of political economy, whose adherents reveled in tracing the unintended consequences of benevolent action. In the Victorian era, critics increasingly warned against the persistence of obsolete charitable trusts, designated by the donor to a purpose that had become outmoded or redundant with the passage of time, but which continued to grow nonetheless (funds dedicated to ransoming Christian captives from the Barbary pirates was one favorite example). The controversy prompted a wave of scholarship and essays on the dangers of endowments, which tended to affirm the estimation of one author in an 1880 prize-winning essay: "Whilst charity tends to do good, perpetual Charities tend to do evil." The concern became so acute that Parliament intervened and granted the charity commissioners even greater powers to redirect charitable funds away from outdated trusts. By the final decades of the century, temporality had become a central category of normative analysis for philanthropy critics.[4]

These concerns took their own distinctive form in the early days of the United States. Principles of English law, including the statutes allowing perpetual charitable trusts, largely governed during the colonial period. However, post-Revolution charitable trusts fell under increased suspicion because of their association with the privileges, concentrated wealth, and corrupting influence of Crown and Church and the threat they posed to republican ideology. Courts were generally suspicious of allowing "every private citizen the right to create a perpetuity for such purposes as to him seem good," and restrictive policies toward charitable trusts spread. States from New York to Virginia limited the amount of money that could be bequeathed to charitable institutions and the amount of property an incorporated charity could accumulate.[5]

However, the intensity of debates regarding philanthropic temporality in the United States was muted by the fact that until the second half of the nineteenth century, the surplus wealth in the hands of the nation's richest citizens was generally modest and most gifts were directed to current uses. However, the tremendous growth of industrial fortunes in the final decades of the nineteenth century spurred an increased engagement with the ethics of "giving in time." These new fortunes swelled the endowments of charitable institutions across the nation. After a flurry of large donations in the preceding decade, by 1900, endowments in higher education had reached a value of somewhere between $165 million to $200 million. Moreover, in the early decades of the century, the legal definition attached to an endowment began to assume its current form, "a fund which shall be maintained inviolate, the income of which shall alone be used." A growing endowment increasingly became a mechanism for elite educational institutions to signal exclusive status, which in turn both attracted increased philanthropic investment in endowments and helped to validate perpetuity more broadly as an institutional ethic.[6]

But there were also counter-pressures that encouraged spending for current needs. During these years, Catholic leaders often defined their distinctive sectarian approach to charity against the establishment of large endowments and the sequestering of funds within them that otherwise could be applied to the human needs of the moment. Catholic charity appeals at the end of the century insisted that "every penny raised will go toward the work which it should be given to, not to drawing large sums in interest." Not only did the urgent social needs of Catholic communities make diverting charitable funds to endowments seem callous, but, as historian of Catholic charity Mary Oates has noted, Catholic leaders worried that "if charities were routinely endowed, parishioners might neglect to give and thus lose the spiritual merits that accompany benevolence." In other words, it was not merely the needs of present-day beneficiaries that called for spending now, but also the spiritual needs of present-day benefactors. As Lila Corwin Berman relates in this volume, a similar model was also favored in the early decades of the twentieth century by Jewish civic leaders, who endorsed a money-in, money-out approach to charitable institutions, in which funds collected were almost immediately distributed, while legacies and endowment-building were discouraged.[7]

In the Gilded Age, the legal system faced increased pressure to loosen regulations of charitable trusts to allow for the newly created fortunes to be tapped to address pressing social problems. In 1893, after the New York Supreme Court invalidated a bequest to the New York City public library from former governor Samuel Tilden, because "New York law recognized as valid only those charitable trusts of which the beneficiaries were immediately ascertainable persons," the state assembly passed a law which allowed for charitable bequests with indefinite ends, in part out of a recognition that these could be given more precise delineation by each subsequent generation of trustees. The ruling opened a greatly expanded temporal vista for organized philanthropy.[8]

This does not mean that the fear of the "dead hand" had been banished at the turn of the twentieth century, when the institutions that would define the US philanthropic landscape for the rest of the century began to take shape. As a Cleveland trust lawyer, Frederick Goff, who would establish the nation's first community foundation in the city in 1914, witnessed numerous charitable trusts that had been committed to obsolete causes. He talked so frequently and menacingly about the perils of the "dead hand" that his daughter feared walking the halls of their own home at night, lest "the dead hand . . . reach out and grab her." He designed the community foundation to allow a wider pool of the city's residents, including donors large and small, to avoid the clutches of the "dead hand" and make use of a corps of respectable trustees, who could be relied on to direct philanthropic funds to worthy ends, now and in the future.[9]

Yet for all the fear that it inspired in the Goff household, it's clear that the "dead hand" was less a bogeyman among US charitable leaders than it had been in Britain. It was neutralized by the main features that would come to define the grant-making philanthropic foundation in the United States: the self-perpetuating board of trustees (bolstered by the above-mentioned Tilden Act) which could continually interpret donor intent in light of contemporary needs, and the general-purpose charter.

Both were promoted with temporal considerations in mind. When John D. Rockefeller sought to secure a federal charter for his eponymous foundation, his lawyers highlighted both features as guarantors of a fit between the gift and the time in which it was made. "The charities of the fourteenth century are not the charities of the twentieth century," Rockefeller's lawyer Starr Murphy told a Senate committee. "The charities of the twentieth century will not be the charities of the twenty-first century." It is "eminently desirable," Murphy explained, "that the power to determine to what specific objects [charitable bequests] should be applied should be left in the hands of living men, who can judge of the necessities and of the needs in the light of the knowledge which they have as contemporaries. . . . The wisdom of living men will always exceed the wisdom of any man, however wise, who has been long since dead." The indefiniteness and the "elasticity" of the foundation's purposes, far from being a legal liability, would allow it to be governed by living men (although it would also channel funds to charitable institutions which might outlive them) and to adapt to changing times.[10]

The temporal considerations that would preoccupy philanthropic leaders and their critics in the coming decades hinged less on concerns about the hold of the past on the present and more on what Sears, Roebuck president Julius Rosenwald termed the issue of "timeliness"—that is, the question of the relative responsibilities of donors to their own day and to the future. If the fear of the "dead hand" was a largely admonitory ethic, timeliness, as Rosenwald understood it, was an affirmative one. Most often, it took shape as a focus on the appropriate payout or disbursement of philanthropic funds.[11]

The first generation of modern philanthropic leaders demonstrated a range of attitudes toward "timeliness" and toward how those considerations should inform a foundation's life span. At one end stood Andrew Carnegie, the Scots-born steel magnate and the leading devotee of perpetuity. Perpetuity was, as one early historian noted, a "characteristic basal to Mr. Carnegie's concept of philanthropy" and a feature of all the philanthropic institutions he established. "My desire is that the work which I hav been carrying on . . . shall continue during this and future generations," Carnegie wrote in his 1911 letter of gift to the Carnegie Corporation, using his distinctive phonetic spelling. "My chief happiness as I write these lines lies in the thot that even after I pass away the welth that came to me to administer as a sacred trust for the good of my fellow men is to continue to benefit humanity for generations untold."[12]

What principles supported Carnegie's embrace of perpetuity? We cannot ignore the egoistic lure of immortality since Carnegie's benevolent impulses were deeply intertwined with his compulsive self-promotion. But we must also consider his general liberal faith in human progress, captured in his personal motto: "All is well since all grows better." A perpetual foundation would be carried along this gradual unspooling of human adaptability and perfectibility. So, in 1919, when Carnegie created the Carnegie Endowment for International Peace as a perpetual institution, he did so with a startlingly hopeful proviso, given the bloodshed that had just swept over the Western world. "When . . . war is discarded as disgraceful to civilized men . . . the trustees will please then consider what is the next most degrading remaining evil or evils whose banishment . . . would most advance the progress, eleva- tion, and happiness of man, and so on from century to century without end." In that "and so on" lies the kernel of this attitude toward foundation life span; unlike many of his contemporaries, he did not harbor millennial notions in which contemporary crises represented some distinctive and decisive epoch. He held the long, incremental—and progressive—view of human uplift.[13]

Related to this faith in human progress was his faith in human reason—or at least, his faith in the good sense and perspicacity of the trustees who would lead his philanthropic institutions in the future. Carnegie's understanding of time was dominated by both a sense of flux and of constancy. "Conditions upon the Erth inevitably change," he insisted, but the decency and judicious- ness of those who would lead his institutions in the future would not. As Henry Pritchett, the long-serving president of the Carnegie Foundation for the Advancement of Teaching, explained, Carnegie "decided in favor of the perpetual trust, influenced in large measure by his faith in his fellow men." According to Pritchett, Carnegie "created permanent endowments in the pro- motion of various great causes not because he believed these agencies would always function at the maximum efficiency; all human organisms, he was wont to say, have their periods of activity and of commonplace performance. But taking the long view, looking to generation after generation, he had con- fidence that successive groups of trustees would deal wisely and justly with their responsibilities."[14]

At the other pole, there was Sears, Roebuck's Rosenwald, who became the nation's preeminent critic of endowments and leading champion of limited- life philanthropy. The Rosenwald Fund, established in 1917 and best known for its funding of thousands of elementary schools for African Americans in the South, became in 1948 the first private foundation to spend all its funds and go out of existence in accordance with the expressed wishes of its founder. In a 1949 retrospective, the former director of the fund and a coauthor explained some of the benefits of spending down the fund:

> [The foundation's] officers and trustees were not preoccupied with saving funds and conserving capital. They did not have time to grow stale nor to build themselves into a routinized bureaucracy. They were able to throw their full resources into the work that needed to be done. Most important of all, because its life was short, the Fund was constantly striving to build all its effort into the continuing forces of society. The educational programs were created from the very beginning as parts of the public systems of schools and colleges or as institutions with a constituency so wide as to assure continued support.[15]

Here we find an early articulation of the basic claims that would be made on behalf of limited-life philanthropy for the next half-century: that it promotes a more vital, flexible style of giving; that it directs additional funds toward urgent problems; that it prevents the development of bureaucracy; that it is better attuned to the importance of grantee self-sufficiency.

In a pair of 1929 articles for the *Atlantic Monthly* and the *Saturday Evening Post*, Rosenwald laid out an explicit defense of "timeliness" as his defining philanthropic ethic, what he called the "warp and woof" of his foundation. His advocacy of limited-life philanthropy was rooted not only in the traditional cautionary rationale of the danger of the "dead hand," the fear that extending the moral preferences and priorities of one generation into the next brought inefficiency and waste, but in an insistence on an affinity and a responsibility between a donor and the age in which he or she lived. On a practical—and epistemic—level, this was simply a function of a temporal orbit of familiarity and intelligibility that extended only a generation or two into the future. As Rosenwald wrote, "Contemporary needs are the only needs of which we can be certain, and it is those needs that we must seek to serve."[16]

But there was also a deeper, more organic bond that Rosenwald suggested connected the donor and his age. "The generation which has contributed to the making of a millionaire," he wrote in the *Saturday Evening Post*, "should also be the one to profit by his generosity." The giver should be driven by the crises of the present moment, confident that those to come would find their own benefactors. "The crying demands of Negro schools and colleges are reasons for throwing all available resources into these present needs," he wrote in the *Atlantic*, "and leaving to coming generations the meeting of future requirements, which are certain to be different from those of to-day." Indeed, Rosenwald insisted that philanthropy should be extended to its beneficiaries like biblical manna, which fell to the Children of Israel to sate their hunger, and then "melted at the close of each day."[17]

Rosenwald could regard philanthropy's evanescence as a virtue because of his faith in its regeneration. If Carnegie's progressive orientation toward the future bolstered his commitment to perpetuity, for Rosenwald it did the opposite. He remained confident, as he argued, "that the generations that will follow us will be every bit as humane and enlightened, energetic and able, as we are, and that the needs of the future can safely be left to be met by the generations of the future." This belief translated as well to a reluctance to give to charitable endowments. So, when he attached a condition to a significant gift to the University of Chicago that every year all of the interest and some of the principal be spent until the full amount was exhausted, he admitted that "money disbursed now will not yield income to the University fifty years hence," but added reassuringly that "fifty years hence other contributors can be found to supply the current needs of that generation."[18]

If Carnegie promoted perpetuity and Rosenwald championed limited-life philanthropy, somewhere in the middle sat John D. Rockefeller, whose various philanthropic boards, and the leaders that directed them, exhibited a range of attitudes toward philanthropic life spans and corresponding payout practices, as opposed to a single uniform position on one or the other pole. In 1909, Rockefeller, for instance, released the trustees of the General Education Board (GEB), the first of the foundations he created, from any commitment to maintaining perpetual life, and the foundation closed its doors in 1964. As a final report issued by the GEB on its dissolution states, "the Trustees deliberately chose to meet the challenge of worthy causes rather than preserve the funds at their disposal for some indefinite future." In doing so, they balanced "the needs and uncertainties of the years ahead . . . against the concrete opportunities afforded by the first half of the twentieth century."[19]

Rockefeller did not insist on the spend-down model, though he was willing to accept a lifetime limit of one hundred years for the Rockefeller Foundation as a concession to receive a federal charter (the offer was ultimately rejected).[20] Instead, he left decisions on life span and payout up to the trustees of the foundations he established. There was in fact an indeterminateness toward the question of foundation life span that governed much of the first half-century of Rockefeller philanthropy. At any given moment, the urgency of a particular crisis or opportunity—the aftermath of World War I, for instance—might goad foundation leaders into spending from principal. But they continued to put off a decisive resolution to the question of philanthropic time frame.

That does not mean they ignored the question; to the contrary, it loomed large over much of their work. They just never settled it. In 1946, when the Rockefeller Foundation board was polled, a majority expressed support for terminating the Foundation within the next quarter-century, and all the trustees were willing to tap the principal fund "if opportunities develop for meeting needs and wants of importance and urgency." In the next decades, the board continued discussing the issue, pushing aside the possibility of a total spend-down but remaining open to the spending of principal. The matter of life span, they stated in 1964, "should be reviewed frequently in the light of changing financial conditions and world needs."[21]

The Rockefeller Foundation's open-ended approach to the question of life span reflected broader trends among foundations at mid-century. A 1952 congressional investigation of foundations determined that a majority of the larger foundations it probed had charters featuring "optional" or "discretionary" perpetuity. A survey conducted in the early 1960s by the Foundation Library Center confirmed this finding. Of the thirty-two responses it received from foundations regarding life-span decisions, thirteen reported a commitment to perpetual life, while another seventeen reported a status of some version of discretionary perpetuity (eight of which wrote that a substantial amount of capital had already been expended). Only one foundation reported an explicit commitment to limited life, with an actual date of termination set by the donor.[22]

The prominence of "discretionary" perpetuities and their open-ended temporal status ensured that questions about timeliness, and particularly about life span, remained at the forefront of discussions about philanthropic practice. As McGeorge Bundy declared in his first annual report as Ford Foundation president in 1966, "A foundation should regularly ask itself if it could do more good dead than alive." The significance of these questions was reinforced in the 1950s and 1960s by a series of congressional investigations of philanthropic foundations that culminated in the Tax Reform Act of 1969, which set the terms of the foundation regulatory regime for the next half century (including mandatory payout rates).[23]

By the 1950s, and throughout the 1960s, as concerns about a host of foundation abuses mounted, the betrayal of an ethic of philanthropic "timeliness" served as one framework through which congressional critics could express their belief that foundations had abrogated their responsibilities to the public. Calls for foundation time limits, which had risen during the Progressive era, did so again at mid-century. The special committee led by Tennessee congressman B. Carroll Reece to investigate foundation practice recommended a twenty-five-year limit, for instance. When Texas congressman Wright Patman took up the cudgel and began his investigation of foundations in 1962, he also advocated for a lifetime limit of twenty-five years.[24]

Patman's investigation into foundation abuses compelled the Treasury Department to begin one of its own, the culmination of which was a report on private foundations published in 1965. Treasury considered the question of foundation time limits but decided against endorsing them. It did identify, among the various critiques that had fueled the push for time limits, the one that seemed to be both most legitimate and amenable to specific remedy. "It has been contended that the interposition of the foundation between the donor and active charitable pursuits entails undue delay in the transmission of the benefits which society should derive from charitable contributions," the report stated.[25]

This was, of course, an articulation of a violated ethic of timeliness, highlighting the "undue delay" between the donation and the operationalized charitable benefits. Yet another way in which this delay was understood during this period was through a fiscal framework—between the conferral of a tax benefit to the donor and the benefits that accrued to the public that had, in effect, subsidized the donation, through charitable dollars reaching operating charities. This fiscalized understanding of timeliness grew in prominence during the 1960s as concerns about philanthropic abuses became increasingly entwined with the issues of tax avoidance and evasion.

After the publication of the Treasury Report, the momentum toward philanthropic reform stalled. But it picked up in the decade's final years, through a convergence of reports of foundation abuse, real and imagined, and as Congress began to consider tax reform. Once again, the ethic of philanthropic timeliness emerged as central to the effort. Foundation time limits did not make it into the House bill that would ultimately become the Tax Reform Act of 1969, which borrowed heavily from the Treasury report. But the issue was raised in the Senate, where an amendment was added by Sen. Al Gore, Sr. that would impose a forty-year limit on the tax-exemption on income, estate, and gift tax for private foundations (Gore had originally proposed a straight-up twenty-five-year life-limit). Debate about the proposal represented one of the most direct legislative engagements with questions surrounding "giving in time."[26]

To justify the time limit, Gore and his allies raised both the specter of the "dead hand," as well as the troubling temporal distance between when donors who gave to foundations took their tax breaks and when those funds actually reached charities. Gore's allies cited research that the majority of nonprofits at the time were facing budgetary crises and that increased foundation payout was one of the best means of guaranteeing them more fiscal security. Yet opponents of time-limits, led by Sens. Walter Mondale (D-MN) and Charles Percy (R-IL), had ready answers to these challenges, based on an alternative theory of "giving in time."[27]

The time-limit provision, a "wholesale and indiscriminate 40-year death sentence," as Mondale termed it, would "destroy" foundations, which were "one of the most creative and dynamic and unique institutions in American life." On the Senate floor, Mondale and his allies dismissed fears of the "dead hand," insisting that foundations, especially the vast majority that had been endowed with an expansive general charter, were in fact exceptionally responsive to the times (and Mondale added that courts' willingness to utilize the doctrine of *cy près* made fears about funds restricted to serve an outmoded purpose outmoded themselves). The record of foundations, he argued, demonstrated that the vast majority "are run by vital, modern, responsive, living, continuously changing trustees, who reflect the guiding interests of the founding donors only to the extent that they were truly visionary or wise enough to foster evolution in the foundation's activities and purposes." In other words, most foundations, he asserted, already followed an ethic of "timeliness."

But Mondale offered another argument that reframed such an ethic. He reminded his colleagues that they were not merely citizens of the current moment, but were the future generation and legatees that had previously been imagined by Carnegie and Rockefeller at the time of the founding of their foundations, just as other citizens to come would be the future beneficiaries of foundations established in the current moment. If the Rockefeller Foundation had been granted only forty years of tax-exempt life and had been forced to shut its doors in 1952, Mondale pointed out, it would not have been able to spark the Green Revolution. And if the Carnegie Corporation had closed after forty years, in 1951, it would not have had the opportunity to fund its work on preschool education and public television programming for children.[28]

These arguments carried the day, and the time-limit provision was defeated handily on the Senate floor, 69-15.[29] One factor that likely helped to guarantee its failure was another provision of the Tax Reform Act, a minimum annual distribution rate imposed on foundation assets (initially set at 6 percent, then, in 1975, lowered to 5 percent), that effectively addressed many of the concerns raised by perpetuity's congressional adversaries. (As Lila Corwin Berman details in this volume, the disparity thereby established between private foundations that carried a payout requirement and public charities, which did not, provided the opening for the growth of donor-advised funds [DAFs].) As a privately funded commission that initially proposed the policy noted, a reasonable payout percentage that would allow a well-managed foundation portfolio to maintain its size, while making productive contributions to society, represented "a balancing of priorities between the present and the future."[30]

That balance ultimately quelled some of the intensity of the discussions and debates surrounding "giving in time." The payout rate translated many of those discussions into more technical, administrative, and legalistic terms. Indeed, the foundation regulations passed as part of the Tax Reform Act of 1969 empowered tax lawyers and accountants—foundations' legal and accounting expenses nearly doubled between 1968 and 1970—who often regarded the prudent stewardship of philanthropic resources as their chief professional responsibility and deferred to an unspoken presumption of perpetuity, often without an elaboration of a strong theory of timeliness. Of course, this presumption of perpetuity served some private interests as fees for trustees and financial managers were typically based on endowment size.[31]

This is not to suggest that "giving in time" disappeared as a theme in philanthropic discourse. In the following decades, occasional efforts to reform the payout requirements led to renewed defenses of perpetuity and reminders of the importance of foundations as "island[s] of long-term thinking in a turbulent sea of short-term culture," in the words of one advocate. Economic downturns, which cut into the assets of many foundations, led to both internal and external reconsiderations of responsibilities to the present and to the future. A rising corps of conservative donors who worried that, over the decades, foundations tended to drift away from the intent of their founders—almost always in a progressive direction—led to an elevation of issues of timeliness among some donors and organizations, and even a commitment from some of them to spend down their foundations.[32]

Yet in the final decades of the century, temporal considerations were no longer as prominent and contentious topics of analysis and debate as they were during the deliberations over the Tax Reform Act of 1969. It was not until the opening decades of the new millennium that they would begin to approach, and perhaps even to surpass, that level.

Given the ways in which the salience of time-based considerations has ebbed and flowed over the course of the last half century, we can speak now of two definitions of "timeliness," both of which have grown more pronounced in contemporary philanthropic discourse and practice over the last decade.[33] First, timeliness can denote the elevation of temporality as a mode of analysis with respect to philanthropy, without favoring any one particular relationship between giving and time. High-profile debates about philanthropy increasingly center around the legitimacy and purpose of endowments; the benefits of spending down or embracing a commitment to perpetuity; the merits of disbursing philanthropic funds now or later; and the tug of intergenerational ethics, including the proper weight to assign to our responsibility to the near and distant future. In its second definition, timeliness can designate a particular relation between giving and time, one which insists upon the giver's responsibilities to their particular moment, an imperative that stakes donors more closely to contemporary needs and exigencies.

What explains the increased prominence of timeliness, both as a category of analysis and as a particular temporal orientation? There are several overlapping and likely mutually reinforcing reasons. Below we outline several of them.

THE SENSE OF CRISIS

One important booster of philanthropic timeliness is a pervasive sense of urgent social crisis, which has been building for several decades, fueled by real-world dangers but also stoked by media outlets incentivized to raise constant alarm. This sense of crisis has attached especially to the existential peril posed by climate change but extends more broadly to cover a host of other harms and has most recently been amplified by the coronavirus pandemic and by protests over police brutality toward African Americans.

The experience of crisis often demands a reweighting of attention and resources toward the present. Such a temporal reorientation is recognizable in the charitable giving that surges in response to natural disasters, military conflicts, epidemics, and political upheavals. It has also been characteristic of many funders dedicated to addressing climate change. "Given the state of the environment and global warming coming at us like a freight train," the founder of the Beldon Fund explained regarding his decision to spend down his foundation, "it was unethical to retain money for the future when who knows what the future might look like." Even climate funders who appreciate philanthropy's need to maintain a broad time horizon often invoke an ethic of timeliness when developing a response to climate change. Larry Kramer, president of the Hewlett Foundation, has sought to galvanize giving to the cause by invoking the "problem" of time. Although he has defended the merits of perpetuity, he also insists that time is running out to prevent irreversible damage and avoid a doom loop that would undermine nearly all the good work that philanthropy hopes to achieve. "It's time to stop fiddling and help put out the fire," he has insisted to other philanthropies, urging them to dramatically increase their funding to address climate change.[34]

How philanthropy has defined and delimited what constitutes an actionable crisis has also come under increased scrutiny. Looking beyond a temporally circumscribed calamity or disaster, some funders have begun to understand the consequences of longer-lasting, more general systems of oppression or domination as crises that demand immediate attention. The recent increased focus of some philanthropies on economic precarity and racial injustice has prompted a reconsideration of time-based philanthropic norms, challenging a high valuation on deliberateness and patience in favor of distributive immediacy.[35] This imperative does not merely give greater weight to the present but regards as its highest priority getting money into the hands of beneficiaries as quickly as possible.

The dictate of an ethic of distributive immediacy has led some major donors, such as MacKenzie Scott, former wife of Amazon founder Jeff Bezos, to increase giving rates to unprecedented levels (although these so far have largely failed to keep pace with the even more explosive rates at which their wealth is growing). "I have no doubt that tremendous value comes when people act quickly on the impulse to give," Scott has declared. A similar attitude has also led to the spread of rapid-response funds, constructed with minimal bureaucratic processes for grant-making, whose aim is to get money in the hands of charities and individuals as quickly as possible, and to the increased prominence of direct cash transfers, which also hold out the possibility of speedy disbursement and immediate assistance.[36]

THE RISE OF THE ENGAGED LIVING MAJOR DONOR

Another factor that has heightened the salience of timeliness has been the rise of the engaged living major donor, and, as Benjamin Soskis outlines in his chapter in this volume, a concomitant rise in an ethic of "Giving While Living".

For much of the twentieth century, the nation's wealthiest citizens often turned to philanthropy late in life. In the 1990s, however, attitudes toward the timing of major donors' giving began to shift, as they began to engage in philanthropy more systematically, and earlier in their careers. Yet as late as 1999, a notable philanthropy scholar could write in the *Washington Post*, with a hint of surprise, "Philanthropy has become a controversial matter these days, particularly when donors make their own decisions about how and when to spend their money rather than leaving those details to professionals in the foundations they have set up."[37]

That trend continued in the new millennium, as those who made enormous fortunes in the tech and finance industries at relatively young ages gave away significant parts of those fortunes in the non-twilight portion of their lives—in what one commentator termed a repudiation of the "earn now, figure out the giving later" approach.[38] These living mega-donors began to rival, and in many respects dominate, the nonprofit landscape, where legacy foundations once presided. Of course, legacy foundations also "give in time." But individuals operate with a different temporal framework than do institutions and so their rise has brought a shift in—and often increased attention to—temporality.

Most significantly, the living donor has boosted the significance of time frames associated with a lifetime. In this context, deliberations over the wisdom of spending now versus spending later translate into decisions about when in a donor's life they should initiate or intensify a philanthropic program, with the bounds of human mortality establishing an assumed temporal terminal point. Additionally, given that major donors are now encouraged to begin their philanthropic careers earlier in their lives, their giving intersects with a novel constellation of major life events; Mark Zuckerberg and Priscilla

Chan, for instance, pledged to spend 99 percent of their fortune on philanthropy after their first daughter was born, while MacKenzie Scott developed her distinctive approach to giving in the aftermath of her divorce from Jeff Bezos.[39]

Starting earlier in their lives means that large-scale philanthropists face much longer horizons of giving, offering more room for deliberate experimentation and risk-taking. Indeed, when Zuckerberg and Chan pledged to spend the vast majority of Zuckerberg's Facebook fortune on philanthropy "during our lives," they also made clear that their giving would be done over decades, stressing the importance of maintaining "long time horizons" and highlighting the dangers of "short term thinking."[40]

This wider temporal vista means that the giving of engaged living major donors often combines some of the virtues associated with perpetuity (such as patience) within a delimited time frame. It also ensures continued debate over the means of fulfilling the dictates of timeliness, since a commitment to give during one's lifetime leaves open a range of possible opportunities for fulfillment and does not necessarily entail a close tethering of philanthropic response to the exigencies of the particular moment. Indeed, when Bill and Melinda Gates and Warren Buffett were debating the terms of the Giving Pledge, the campaign they led to convince the world's billionaires to make a public commitment to direct half their wealth to philanthropy in their lifetimes, they discussed whether one of its founding principles should be the imperative to "Give Now." The suggestion, however, was ultimately dismissed. The Pledge would not insist on a strong weighting of the present over the future, at least as defined within an individual lifetime.[41]

The origins of the wealth of many engaged living donors in finance and technology has also fueled a more "strategic" approach to philanthropy which has sought to determine donations' "return on investment." Such an ROI framing has underscored temporal dimensions of philanthropy by directing attention to the "ripple effects" that current grants can have over time (as Tony Proscio discusses in his chapter), such that a gift today can produce compounding social value over future years.[42]

CHALLENGES TO PERPETUITY

The rise of the engaged living mega-donor has coincided with a surge in challenges to the perpetual foundation, another development which has increased the attention directed to time-based philanthropic considerations. As Joel Fleishman, director of Duke University's Center for Strategy Philanthropy and Civil Society and former president of Atlantic Philanthropies, has noted, "The single most important change that has taken place since 1990" is that "prospective donors appear to be favoring either the creation of a time-limited foundation with a lifespan roughly concurrent with their own or the direct disposition of substantial gifts during their lifetimes without the involvement of a foundation at all. That is a seismic shift in philanthropic practice."[43]

It is important to note that a commitment to Giving While Living does not necessarily entail a concomitant commitment to limited-life philanthropy; in fact, the two can sometimes be in tension, since an imperative to give during one's lifetime can lead donors to channel funds to foundations with perpetual life, and the drive to spend down a foundation can require the enlargement of a philanthropic bureaucracy that can potentially sideline an engaged living donor.[44] And yet, as Fleishman suggests, there is an unmistakable consonance between the two, and it should not be surprising that support for an ethic of Giving While Living and for limited-life philanthropy have grown in tandem.

Since at least the late 1990s, philanthropy analysts had claimed they detected the stirrings of increased support for limited-life philanthropy, yet a wholesale transformation in giving norms never materialized and perpetuity continued to be the dominant temporal orientation among those who led existing private foundations. In the 2010s, the presumption of perpetuity was increasingly challenged, as major donors such as Bill and Melinda Gates and Mark Zuckerberg and Priscilla Chan expressed support for limited-life philanthropy. The rationales offered for such support often were grounded in the more exacting definition of philanthropic timeliness, which insisted on the responsibility of the donor to their own age. Chuck Feeney, whose Atlantic Philanthropies became the largest limited-life foundation to close its doors in September 2020 and who became a vocal opponent of perpetuity, explained that his decision to "spend-down during my lifetime" was based on his recognition that "today's needs are pressing," and on his confidence that "the future will bring a new generation of philanthropists" to address future needs.[45]

By the second decade of the twenty-first century, the dominance of perpetuity as a model of temporality had eroded even further, such that it was impossible to consider it any longer the default for philanthropic institutions. A 2020 report analyzing a survey of private foundations from Rockefeller Philanthropy Advisors and NORC at the University of Chicago noted that "nearly half of the organizations established in the 2010s were founded as time-limited vehicles," whereas for foundations established in the 1980s, the proportion was closer to 20 percent.[46]

The report also noted that more attention is being paid to timeliness, regardless of the decisions about time frames philanthropic institutions end up making. While foundation leaders in the final decades of the twentieth century rarely "intentionally discussed or planned their institutional philanthropic timeframes," its authors note, in recent years, "in part due to innovations driven by shifting social norms and the rise of strategic philanthropy, organizations are considering the length of time over which they want to operate as a core component of their strategy." Yet whereas limited-life philanthropy has been publicly championed as an alternative philanthropic norm by some of the wealthiest, most prominent living donors (those likeliest to draw the most attention to discussions of timeliness), few living donors have defended the model of perpetuity. What defenses have been made have most often come from the heads of legacy foundations, who often have less power to shape public discourse outside the bounds of the philanthropic sector.[47]

RISE OF DONOR-ADVISED-FUNDS

The astronomical growth of DAFs must also be counted as a reason for increased attention toward considerations of "timeliness." Much as the expansion of private foundations in the 1940s and 1950s sparked congressional investigation of foundation abuses and prompted inquiries into foundation time-spans and spending rates, the growth of DAFs, private philanthropic accounts held at sponsoring charities that (unlike private foundations) carry no mandated payout rate but allow donors to claim an immediate tax deduction, have renewed debates about the responsibility of donors to the present moment and the need for public policies which incentivize the disbursement of philanthropic funds into the hands of operating charities.

Propelled by the explosion of DAFs at commercial sponsoring organizations (first authorized in 1991) the growth of DAFs has been astronomical, vastly outpacing the rate of growth of charitable giving more generally. Donations to DAFs increased from $7.1 billion in 2008 to $47.9 billion in 2020. In fact, between 2010 and 2020, the share of giving to DAFs as a percentage of total individual giving in the United States more than tripled from 4.4 percent to 14.8 percent. In 2016, for the first time in the quarter of a century since the *Chronicle of Philanthropy* began tracking the charities that received the most donations each year, a DAF sponsoring organization, the Fidelity Charitable Gift Fund, occupied the top spot of the rankings, pushing aside United Way. The following year, 6 of the top 10 charities in the *Chronicle*'s rankings were DAF sponsors. Commercial DAF sponsoring organizations have in recent years also ranked as some of the nation's largest grant-makers measured by dollars out-the-door.[48]

The regulation of DAFs has become one of the most contentious policy issues relating to charitable giving. Debates surrounding DAFs have elevated timeliness as a dominant theme within the public discourse surrounding philanthropic practice. Those advocating for regulatory reform accuse DAFs of facilitating the irresponsible warehousing of funds and point to the gap between when DAF holders receive a tax break for giving to them, subsidized by the public, and when the public actually benefits from those funds, when donations reach nonprofit grantees. Particularly concerning for those advocating reform is the fact that DAFs also effectively negate the 5 percent payout rule applicable to private foundations since (as discussed by Galle and Madoff in this volume) private foundations are able to meet the letter if not the spirit of the payout rule by making distributions to DAFs. Defenders of the status quo focus on the fact that the overall payout rates of DAFs are higher than the 5 percent required payout rate imposed on private foundations and argue that they allow donors and private foundations to take their time in determining how they want to disburse the funds they have allocated toward philanthropy. In June 2021, bipartisan legislation was introduced in Congress that would generally require DAFs to disburse funds within fifteen years to receive an immediate tax deduction and which would incentivize even faster disbursement. Supporters of the legislation promoted it as a means of challenging "the slow-moving philanthropic status-quo" and of guaranteeing that "today's dollars [are] being used to confront today's challenges."[49]

This is by no means an exhaustive accounting of all the factors that have led to increased attention to questions of "giving in time." Among the additional developments that have contributed is the growth of the effective altruism movement, an approach toward philanthropy which seeks to apply strict rationality to questions involving how to do the most good. Effective altruism has promoted the ethical imperative of "long-termism," which advocates for time horizons extending into future centuries, and even millennia, and directs attention to contemporary donors' responsibility to the billions, even trillions of humans yet born.[50]

The heightened attention given to issues of economic inequality has intensified journalistic and legislative scrutiny of large nonprofit endowments and amplified the charge that they are warehousing funds that should be disbursed to address current needs.[51] The increased focus many funders have given to issues surrounding racial justice and racial equity has also cast a light on the racialized politics of philanthropic time frames, raising important questions about who has the power to make time-based decisions. Additionally, demands over reparations for slavery and other forms of injustice and dispossession have confronted philanthropy with questions surrounding "giving in time" that involve donors' responsibilities to the past.[52]

The Covid-19 crisis, and the protests over racial violence that erupted in the summer of 2020, stoked pre-existing debates around the issue of philanthropic timeliness. In the first months of the pandemic, a host of funders adopted rapid-response grant-making, prioritizing the need to get money out the door to grantees and recipients as quickly as possible.[53] Advocates within the philanthropic sector called for foundations to increase payout rates, insisting that the urgency of present-day needs trumped the imperatives of endowment preservation. In this context, advocates sought to reframe the desire to save for future crises as a socially irresponsible form of resource hoarding. "The strength of a funder's grantees at the end of this crisis will be a much better measure of the significance of a foundation than the size of its endowment," a consortium of philanthropy-serving organizations declared. (According to a June 2021 survey from Candid, 43 percent of private foundations, and 59 percent of those awarding $50 million or more, did increase payout.) But the prominence of these exhortations also prompted renewed defenses of perpetuity, an explicit engagement with the ethical underpinnings of what had often been treated as an unspoken default. Ultimately, the pandemic called forth more deliberate and sustained discussions of philanthropic temporality than any other moment in the last several decades.[54]

The experience of the Covid-19 pandemic affirmed and amplified a conviction that had been mounting among many philanthropy analysts of the previous decade: that temporality is one of the most important vectors along which philanthropic giving must be analyzed and assessed. That conviction had been the impetus for a meeting of scholars and practitioners at Stanford University in May 2016, on "Giving in Time: Perpetuities, Limited Life, and the Responsibility of Philanthropy to the Present and the Future" and then for a follow-up conference of scholars at Boston College Law School four months later. Those conferences planted the seeds for this volume; much of the material published here was first presented at the scholars' conference.

Those gatherings made clear the vibrancy of the work currently being done on questions related to "giving in time," as well as the value of approaching that work from a variety of disciplinary perspectives. Those perspectives are organized in the chapters that follow around the axes of history, theory, and practice.

In his chapter, historian Benjamin Soskis provides an historical perspective on the notion of "Giving While Living." Although it has roots that go back as far as the teachings of medieval Christian moralists, the idea that philanthropy should not begin at the death of the donor, or indeed, even be deferred until old age, reached an early peak with the emergence of scientific philanthropy, more than a century ago. As mentioned earlier, Julius Rosenwald was the best known, but by no means the only, advocate for the idea that those who accumulated great wealth should actively engage in distributing their wealth while they could use the talents and proclivities that had generated the wealth in the first place.

Soskis argues that the idea of Giving While Living emerged from the convergence of three imperatives: the duty to commit one's wealth to charity before death; the duty of the donor actively to oversee the distribution of charitable funds; and the duty of the donor to perform charity publicly in order to create a model for others. Versions of these ideas emerged throughout Europe in the wake of the Reformation, as charity's focus shifted from salvation to repair of the terrestrial world, and capitalism provided means for donors to do so. But a variety of traditional legal mechanisms for creating perpetuities created barriers to inter vivos charitable wealth distribution by the nineteenth century, and these outmoded legal forms had to be transformed in order to free up donors to act at the time, late in the century, when truly massive fortunes enabled potential donors to think about making large charitable gifts for expansive purposes during their lifetimes.

Andrew Carnegie was the best known of the early philanthropists to articulate what Giving While Living might mean. In his 1889 *Gospel of Wealth*, Carnegie invoked all three charitable imperatives for the wealthy to take an active role in distributing their resources while they were still in command of the talents that had enabled them to create such extraordinary wealth. Carnegie's essay, and his personal example, have reemerged as a leading exemplar of how today's mega-wealthy should behave, inspiring some of our biggest contemporary fortune-creators to become philanthropists at ages much younger than Carnegie himself. Carnegie has become, Soskis contends, the "archetype of the engaged, living donor" at a time when, until recently, such a philanthropic stance was a rarity. Philanthropy has become a much-admired behavior for young capitalist accumulators at the peak of their powers rather than the capstone of a long career of accumulation.

The political philosopher *Rob Reich* sets out a theoretical case against the use of perpetuity as a philanthropic strategy. Reich frames the issue of "a perpetual time horizon" by reference to the experience of the Rockefeller family more than a century ago. John D. Rockefeller Sr. very badly wanted a congressional charter for his proposed foundation, and his representatives offered a number of concessions to Congress in the hope of securing one. The most important concession was to forgo perpetuity for the proposed philanthropic foundation, and instead agree to spend down the assets of the foundation within one hundred years. But Congress was unmoved and refused to grant the charter, so the Rockefeller family quickly obtained a charter from New York state—creating a foundation without limit of time. And indeed, by the early twentieth century, the majority of foundations created under state law were incorporated as perpetuities. This meant that their donors (and the trustees who succeeded to the control of donors) were under no time pressure to distribute the corpus of the foundation, and for the most part trustees managed the assets of their foundations so as to limit their annual expenditures so that they did not decrease the net value of the foundation endowment over time.

Reich considers this a bad practice and explains why he disapproves of the perpetuity of philanthropic foundations by going back even further into the history of philanthropic thought, explicating the case against perpetuity made by the English utilitarian philosopher John Stuart Mill, the most famous opponent of perpetuity in the nineteenth century. Mill was following in the footsteps of the eighteenth-century French Enlightenment thinker, Anne-Robert Turgot and the German philosopher Immanuel Kant, both of whom condemned what they considered the objectionable control of the "dead hand" over concentrations of wealth. Mill was not opposed in principle to foundations, but he saw no reason for the state to permit perpetual foundations and he felt very strongly that the state should reserve the right to intervene in defense of the public interest in the expenditure of foundation assets. Mill believed it appropriate for the donor of endowed funds to be able to designate the purpose of his gift during his lifetime, but no longer, since the donor should not be allowed to control resources from his grave. Mill did not believe a prohibition on perpetuities violated the property rights of the donor, since in his view the endowed funds were really the property of the intended beneficiaries of the endowment—and in the long run, the only acceptable rationale for the distribution of endowed funds was that they were socially useful.

Reich accepts Mill's argument and contends that perpetuity serves no useful social function in a democratic society, and he argues that social utility is the only acceptable rationale for the existence of endowments. At this point, Reich summarizes the argument he has made so strongly that the best reasons for philanthropy he poses are that it decentralizes the production of public goods, that it facilitates the power of minority opinion in a democracy, and that it incentivizes innovation in public life. Foundations, Reich asserts, would not exist without the privileges created for them by law, and those privileges can only be justified by the use of philanthropic funds to create public goods. Perpetuity, hence, has no appropriate role in the governance of philanthropic foundations.

Historian Lila Corwin Berman addresses the question of how the American Jewish community dealt with the problem of temporality in its philanthropic policies. She analyzes the historical development of what she terms the "contest between perpetual philanthropic accumulation and timely philanthropic distribution" for American Jews. This was an important and long-standing contest in a community with a very long history of both religious commitment to charity and social commitment to community. Philanthropy is where those two commitments intersect, and Berman's topic is the emergence of a long-term American Jewish shift from preferences for "timely distribution" to perpetual philanthropic accumulation.

By the twentieth century, the American Jewish community had become larger, wealthier, and better established in this country. The principal organizational device for modern philanthropy had become the Jewish federation system, which provided a central collection and distribution system for charitable funds to support Jewish community organizations. The federation was really a sort of ethnically defined community chest structure, which in theory relieved individual charitable organization of the burden of raising their own funds through its annual appeals to the entire Jewish community. By mid-century, every town of any size in the United States had its local Jewish federation, which generally proved effective in soliciting Jewish residents for charitable contributions and distributing them to local Jewish charities.

The Jewish federations were explicitly opposed to the creation of endowments to support their work, since they were committed to the redistribution of charitable contributions just as soon as they were received. They bragged to potential donors that they were not "charity trusts" accumulating capital in order to amass philanthropic power, unlike the large national philanthropic foundations that jealously guarded their endowments. While this was probably a sensible and understandable strategy in the early twentieth century, the animus toward perpetual endowments made less sense as the Jewish community grew wealthier, especially following World War II. By then, Jewish charity seemed less necessary for the provision of basic community needs and more important "as a purveyor of [Jewish] culture or identity." This coincided with the professionalization of Jewish charity and led to the idea that endowment-building was an appropriate mechanism for leveraging the size and effectiveness of Jewish philanthropy.

Berman explains that, largely thanks to the ingenuity of the Cleveland lawyer Norman Sugarman, Jewish federations avoided being characterized as private foundations—a classification which would have subjected them to payout requirements, as well as greater oversight and reporting obligations—and took advantage of the freedom and tax benefits of the "public charity" form to attract donations (including funds that had previously been set aside in private foundations), enlarge their assets and expand their philanthropic mandate. They thus created what amounted to a Jewish community foundation, engaged in using private gifts to fund public goods for the Jewish community. A variety of charitable entities of this type were formed, New York's Jewish Communal Fund being the largest. Like other community foundations, the Jewish charities created DAFs to attract philanthropic investment by wealthy Jews, and in the process built hugely endowed institutions.

Theodore Lechterman, a political theorist, addresses the problem of charitable trusts. He points out that intergenerational charitable transfers (ICTs) are part of a very long tradition in philanthropy, but they pose the problem of the "dead hand" (*mortmain*, in English law), or the control of charitable property beyond the lifetime of a donor. Is it appropriate for a charitable donor to control the use of his donation from the grave, as it were, by establishing a perpetual trust to carry out his wishes in perpetuity?

Lechterman asks if this is, in principle, a good thing for a liberal democratic society to permit. Is it fair to future generations? To current ones? Thomas Jefferson, writing to James Madison in 1789, remarked that no law of nature permits persons to control property after death, since it is "self-evident 'that the earth belongs in usufruct to the living'; that the dead have neither powers nor rights over it." This is a powerful statement, and yet American law, within a century after Jefferson's death, came to accept and even encourage perpetual charitable trusts. That means, observes Lechterman, that ICTs "unilaterally impose past persons' conceptions of the public benefit upon future generations."

How can a democratic polity accept (indeed, encourage) such a facially undemocratic process? There are several theoretical possibilities, but they all have problems, Lechterman argues. The first is that while there is no natural right to testation, the state has found it convenient to establish the universal capacity to transfer property through bequest. Second, ICTs seem contrary to the democratic notion of equality of opportunity. This would not be so if they were a mode of democratic redistribution of wealth, but that is seldom how ICTs are used. Finally, ICTs seem in tension with the Rawlsian principle of "just savings," which compels generations to share the burden of just institutions over time. So there are difficulties, but it is possible for a democratic society to structure ICTs in such a way that they benefit both current and future generations.

Lechterman then explores ways in which future generations can have a stake in the continued existence of ICTs—so that current generations are not prevented from exercising control over the distribution of ICT property. The need is to screen out ICTs whose philanthropic purposes have become obsolete and ensure that ICTs continue to act over time in ways that conduce to the public benefit. Lechterman would support the right of donors to specify the general uses for which their ICT funds would be distributed, subject to periodic review by public authorities. The doctrine of *cy près* has traditionally been used by Anglo-American law to ensure that outmoded trust purposes do not prevent the charitable use of endowed funds, but Lechterman thinks that all trusts should undergo periodic review ("audit and adjustment") as a regulatory mechanism for ensuring that ICTs are benefitting the public as well as carrying out the wishes of donors. This sort of trust regulation can eliminate obsolescence "while also leveraging the unique wisdom of the past."

The legal scholar Miranda Perry Fleischer offers a philosophical analysis of charitable giving and intergenerational justice from a libertarian point of view. She argues that most commentators on charity base their views on either welfarist or egalitarian principles; Fleischer, on the other hand, pushes for those concerned with philanthropy to take a more rights-based approach that focuses on the interests and rights of donors. The welfarist thinker asks who should benefit from charity, current or future generations? This often leads to a preference for current benefits, on the assumption that future generations will be better off than the present, so spending current dollars will be more efficient than deferring charitable expenditures. This, of course, is a powerful argument against the employment of endowments established to facilitate future charitable giving.

Alternatively, Fleischer suggests, we should employ libertarianism, a rights-based theory of justice, to inform our views of charity. Libertarians believe, following John Locke, that the right to property is the basic social right, and in general that the state should not interfere with a person's right to use his or her property. The state therefore should not prohibit a person from considering the needs of future generations, since such a decision is integral to property rights. Thus libertarians do not believe that the state should prohibit the creation of perpetuities or endowments for specific purposes.

Nevertheless, most libertarians consider that some minimal interference with the right to control one's property, and thus some minimal degree of redistributive taxation, is compatible with justice. Such interference can be justified for purposes of rectification or for providing a minimal safety net. Accordingly, tax law can provide limited subsidies to incentivize charitable giving. Fleischer is concerned with characterizing charitable preference in taxation as what lawyers call "tax expenditures" so that the charitable deductions can be analyzed similarly to other forms of state spending. Tax benefits for social purposes result from state coercion, and redistribute property from some taxpayers to others, so they must be limited just as all state spending is limited.

Fleischer explains that, for the libertarian, property rights are not absolute, but subject to the "Lockean proviso," that one may accumulate natural resources only if "enough and as good" is left for others. The state should not interfere with the freedom of the person to do what he or she wishes with his or her property, except that it can tax individuals to protect his or her property (establishment of courts and police) and to ensure that the Lockean proviso can be met (rectification).

There is room for disagreement among libertarians as to limitations on charitable giving, since the right to property is not absolute, and since the state has a clear but limited power to tax property-owning individuals. In principle there is no libertarian objection to perpetual endowments, although some libertarians object to intergenerational control over property. Whether the usage of endowed funds to provide for the welfare needs of future generations can be justified is a difficult question for libertarians, so questions of temporality in philanthropic practice remain controversial.

Philosopher Will MacAskill addresses the concerns of the newly emerging group of philanthropists who describe themselves as "effective altruists." The group has been deeply influenced by the utilitarian philosopher Peter Singer who has outlined the analysis of consequentialist thinking for philanthropy. Following Singer, MacAskill defines effective altruism as "the use of evidence and careful reasoning to work out how to maximize positive impact on others with a given unit of resources, and the taking of action on that basis."

As MacAskill explains, the issue of timing is critical for effective philanthropists. Although they are committed to change in the present, they recognize that there may be circumstances in which immediate charitable investment might not be the most cost-effective approach. MacAskill outlines the considerations the effective altruist needs to evaluate the timing of charitable giving. Some considerations, he thinks, are minor. These include tax considerations, future weakness of will (you might spend on yourself if you wait), uncertainty, and self-interest. Major considerations include valuing the present generation more highly, changing opportunities, getting better knowledge, values changes and investment returns.

All of the major considerations require deep analysis. For instance, we all place at least some extra weight on the interests of those with whom we have special relationships—so we might want to give to them now. It is also the case that the world is getting richer, and so delay makes giving more expensive in the future and possibly less necessary. On the other hand, if we wait there may be new philanthropic opportunities available to us, and new charitable organizations may come into existence. And there is bound to be more and better information available if we delay giving until later. The general approach to effective altruism is empirical and susceptible to quantitative analysis, but MacAskill also outlines a complex framework for evaluating qualitative approaches to effective altruism. He provides a matrix to assign values to evaluate special relationships, changing opportunities, knowledge, values, movement growth, and the amount of money to donate.

Scholar Lucy Bernholz broadens the understanding of the problem of perpetuity for philanthropic foundations beyond the distribution of monetary funds. She contends that while historically financial resources were the basis for foundation philanthropy, in the twenty-first century, digital resources have moved to the fore. One of the major problems for foundations is to manage (and preserve) their digital resources in ways consistent with their missions. Digital resources come in many different forms, among them records of foundation activity, publications, and communications records. Utilizing and managing these resources is now a major task for every foundation. Bernholz suggests that there now exists the possibility of new philanthropic institutions "purpose-built for managing digital resources for public benefit," "the 21st century, digitally-assumptive equivalent of the 20th century modern foundation."

Bernholz believes that foundations must come to terms with the ways in which digitized information opens up new philanthropic opportunities. She highlights the nonrival character of digitized network data—using the economist's conception of a resource that can be used by anyone without limiting anyone else's access to it. Digital data inevitably has multiple creators who possess multiple claims to ownership of the data. These attributes bring both new opportunities and new limitations for foundations—not least of the limitations being the quickly evolving nature of the law of intellectual property. Digital data also bring with their opportunities important obligations on foundations for management and preservation.

One of the most significant impacts of digital resources has been their broadening of access for the range of potential data users. This has created great opportunity, especially in an era dominated by notions of open access, but it also creates problems for control, privacy, and ownership (in the domain of intellectual property). Digital data has, for one thing, made it possible for the public to learn much more about foundations themselves, and so has had the effect of increasing the transparency (up to a point) of foundation management. The big question, however, is how philanthropic digital resources can be managed so as to enhance the foundation's mission. Open access and open data are possible program strategies for foundations, but contemporary philanthropy is only just beginning to explore their potential.

Bernholz's conclusion is that the foundations have both an opportunity and a responsibility to manage data responsibly. She imagines data trusts, "virtual libraries of data, [protected by foundations] and making [data] available into the future." Her larger vision is one of creating the digital infrastructure for civil society, based on a "digital infrastructure for philanthropy." This would enable foundations to extend the life of data resources beyond particular funded programs, thus working for long-term public benefit, and creating a new and more productive form of philanthropic perpetuity.

Sociologist Helmut Anheier and Researcher Sandra Rau provide an internationally comparative context for thinking about time-limited philanthropy in their survey of European practices and attitudes. Anheier and Rau make the point that both United States and European philanthropic institutions are responding to similar recent pressures, especially the historically low interest rates in all countries following the 2008–2009 global financial crisis. But the institutional situations of philanthropy are quite different in Europe than in the United States. Only the United States requires philanthropic foundations to comply with a payout rule; a majority of European foundations are operating (rather than grant-making) institutions; strategic philanthropy has made a major impact on US foundation behavior, and encouraged spending down endowed assets, but "strategic" ideas have not had much impact in Europe, in part because there are fewer large grant-making foundations and in part because of the lower degree of professionalization in European philanthropy. Anheier and Rau argue that the institutional differences between European and American foundations have prevented European institutions from experiencing the pressures toward time limitation that American philanthropy is currently experiencing.

Anheier and Rau also explain how the very different historical experiences of Europe and the United States have produced very different philanthropic institutions, although there were and are significant differences across the national experiences in Europe as well. The result, however, has been that while general-purpose grant-making foundations have emerged as an independent force in the United States, their European counterparts have remained predominantly in the business of service delivery. The differences in the legal environment for philanthropy have also made a significant impact on the types of philanthropic institutions and philanthropic behaviors in the two regions—most significantly for limitations of time, the general European legal preference for the principle of asset protection came to imply that European foundations should be established in perpetuity.

Anheier and Rau conclude that there are no general European trends in the direction of time limitation for foundations, although the situation varies widely across Europe, and there are different situations in different countries across the continent. The policy environment for time limitation in philanthropy varies according to the economic size and the degree of politicization in each country. Europeans have by now accepted the institutional form of the philanthropic foundation, and current reforms, rather than imposing more rigorous state control of foundations, seem aimed at enabling rather than restricting philanthropy. For the moment, perpetuity is the norm for philanthropy in Europe.

Francie Ostrower, a sociologist, brings the research tools of social science to bear on the question of the importance of life span to foundations. Her chapter is based on three different research projects she has undertaken, each of which involved collecting information from the managers of philanthropic foundations. She asks a fundamental question with respect to giving in time: "How salient is life span to foundation attitudes and practice?" Ostrower contends that the importance of life span is an empirical as well as a theoretical problem, and her research provides much of the available evidence on the question.

Ostrower starts with the speculation that life span is not likely to be the most important factor in assessing the effectiveness of philanthropic foundations—asset size is likely to be more useful. But life span may well be an important reflection of the values and norms of the foundation managers who make decisions about life span. In fact, a recent survey indicates that life span was not considered by professionals in the field to be highly correlated with foundation effectiveness or as a factor in formulating grant-making goals or styles. Ostrower notes, however, that "sunsetting foundations" (those which have already made a decision to spend down their assets and terminate their grant-making at a date certain in the future) may well perform differently than time-limited foundations, especially in their attentiveness to donor intention.

And Ostrower finds that donor control is the crux of the debate over perpetuity, since limited-life foundations are more donor-centric. But even here, the donor's intent matters only up to a point, although the normal reason for sunsetting is to preserve donor intent. The fear is that perpetuity mitigates against donor intent insofar as over time the influence of a no-longer-living donor dissipates. But the preservation of donor intent is not the only argument for sunsetting or spending down, since many foundation managers fear the philanthropic institutionalization they assume perpetuity encourages. That is to say that a perpetual foundation tends to take on a life of its own, quite apart from the wishes of its founder. The preservation of the organization for its own sake is the logic of perpetuity. Managers of limited-life foundations "regard philanthropy in a more personalistic way and have an antipathy toward institutionalized philanthropy."

In sum, Ostrower finds that limitations on life are factors in the ongoing considerations that foundation managers take into account as they make decisions as to foundation policy. The impact of decisions regarding life span is not automatic but depends upon other values and strategies that managers employ. That means that longevity plans are not the best indicator of foundation practice, but only one factor in grant-making decisions.

Tony Proscio has an unusual position from which to consider the value of time-limited philanthropy. Proscio is a long-time philanthropic consultant who recently spent a decade analyzing Atlantic Philanthropies during its dramatic and well-publicized spend-down. Proscio relates the reasoning behind the decision to terminate the foundation, by far the largest spend-down to date, and provides two case studies of Atlantic philanthropic investment in order to illustrate the actual impact of the spend-down on particular grantees.

Chuck Feeney, a billionaire who became wealthy through the creation and management of duty-free shops around the world, became an advocate of "giving now" after he began to experience the problems and opportunities of philanthropic investing. His theory was simple: the social benefit of a foundation grant of a dollar today is greater than what can be generated by the same dollar (and investment returns on that dollar over time) in a few years. Proscio describes this as "a concentrated burst of near-term giving," which enables the donor to produce very large impacts if his timing is good and his investment objectives well-chosen. The analysis is a simple cost-benefit calculation, assuming that we can calculate the social value, and the return on our social investments compounds at a higher rate than financial assets would. It is a rational calculation that limited-life philanthropy can generate greater returns by paying out now than it could by preserving its assets indefinitely and spending more gradually. The assumption is that such big investments will have ripple effects over time, compounding the benefits of the original philanthropic investment.

Proscio points out that if Mr. Feeney's assumptions are correct, the challenge for a time-limited foundation is to choose the right intervention in the right field. He gives two examples of how this worked for Atlantic. The first is a project to improve youth services in Ireland, through a campaign to change the way that Irish public agencies chose to fund assistance for youth in poor or troubled families. The second was a project for increasing the supply of nurses in South Africa. In both cases, but especially in South Africa, the early returns are encouraging, although in both countries it will take years before it is clear whether and how the programs have succeeded. But it is already apparent that these two "big bets" by Atlantic have produced favorable responses from the governments of Ireland and South Africa and have had a major impact on related investments by other philanthropic foundations.

Proscio admits that "not everything that counts can be counted," but he argues that the Atlantic experience suggests some of the relevant questions be asked about time-limited mega-philanthropy. Perhaps the most interesting of these for readers of this volume is that "the decision about how and when to set a time limit on a philanthropic initiative is not a challenge exclusive to limited-life institutions." Timing, that is to say, is crucial to all philanthropic investments, and we need to learn more about it.

Brian Galle and Ray Madoff, both scholars of US tax law, address the need to reform payout rules. The "payout" rule for private philanthropic foundations first entered American law as part of the Tax Reform Act of 1969, which also created the distinction between "public charities" (supported by many donors) and "private" (supported by one or a few donors) foundations, and which, as discussed earlier, contained a 6 percent payout requirement (later reduced to 5 percent).

The 5 percent payout rule has become widely accepted and widely touted (by the foundation world, among others) as a reasonable compromise that allows private foundations to exist in perpetuity while ensuring that a portion of their funds be put to current charitable use. Even more importantly, the 5 percent payout rule has served to legitimate private foundations to the public by giving foundations a readily recognized role of providing steady sources of capital to charitable organizations. All of these rationales make it seem that the 5 percent payout rule is well established as both a practical and theoretical matter.

However, despite the apparently robust nature of the 5 percent payout rule, Galle and Madoff contend that the 5 percent payout rule operates more as a fig leaf than as a meaningful control on private foundation spending because: (1) unlimited administrative expenses can be counted as part of the payout; (2) unlimited contributions to DAFs qualify toward the payout requirement; and (3) certain investments in for-profit companies can also qualify. These permitted practices allow foundation trustees and managers to circumvent the intention of Congress with the passage of the Tax Reform Act to get money to operating charities, and Galle and Madoff argue that these are loopholes in the law that need to be closed.

The authors consider the arguments for eliminating the payout rule altogether, but find them unsupported and conclude that a payout rule is a necessary corrective to what they call the "natural tendencies" of foundation managers to hoard rather than spend. Congress, after all, created tax incentives for charitable contributions in the expectation that charity would enhance the public welfare, and in so doing relieve the public fisc of some portion of welfare cost. The loopholes in the payout requirement work against this basic purpose of charitable tax law, especially with respect to DAFs, which permit donors to take a full charitable deduction at the time of gift without imposing any legal obligation to payout (make charitable gifts) within a definite period of time.

The scholars and researchers in this volume address fundamental questions relating to "giving in time." What is the responsibility of donors to the present relative to the future? When in one's lifetime should one give? How should donors balance speed and responsiveness with reflection and deliberation? The volume does not make any claim to reaching conclusive answers to any of these questions, nor to represent a comprehensive survey of the current work being done on these issues. The gaps and absences are themselves worthy of scrutiny and will hopefully draw attention to current scholarship and scholarship that has not yet been initiated but should be. Taken as a whole, however, these chapters establish how essential temporality is as a category of analysis with respect to philanthropy, such that any work that does not engage with it is, by definition, inadequate to the times.

NOTES

1. Marion R. Fremont-Smith, *Governing Nonprofit Organizations: Federal and State Law and Regulation* (Cambridge, MA: Belknap Press of Harvard University

Press, 2004), 14–16, 20–21; Kevin C. Robbins, "The Nonprofit Sector in Historical Perspective: Traditions of Philanthropy in the West," in *The Nonprofit Handbook* 2nd ed., eds. Walter W. Powell and Richard Steinberg (New Haven, CT: Yale University Press, 2006), 18.

2. Peter Brown, *Through the Eye of a Needle*: Wealth, the Fall of Rome, and the Making of Christianity in the West, 350–550 AD (Princeton, NJ: Princeton University Press, 2012), 62–64; Evelyn Brody, "Charitable Endowments and the Democratization of Dynasty," *Arizona Law Review* 39 (Fall 1997): 873–948; Suzanne Roberts, "Contexts of Charity in the Middle Ages: Religious, Social, and Civic," in *Giving: Western Ideas of Philanthropy*, ed. J.B. Schneewind (Bloomington: Indiana University Press, 1996), 37, 38; Khalil Abdur-Rashid, "Financing Kindness as a Society: The Rise and Fall of the Waqf as a Central Islamic Philanthropic Institution," *Journal of Muslim Philanthropy and Civil Society* 5, no. 1 (2021): 49–69 (quote on p. 50); Thomas Adam, "From Waqf to Foundation: The Case for a Global Integrated History of Philanthropy," *Journal of Muslim Philanthropy and Civil Society* 4, no. 1 (2020): 55–73.

3. A.H. Oosterhoff, "The Law of Mortmain: An Historical and Comparative Review," *The University of Toronto Law Journal* 27, no. 3 (Summer 1977): 279–88.

4. Rhodri Davies, *Public Good by Private Means: How Philanthropy Shapes Britain* (London: Alliance Publishing Trust, 2015), 168; Ray D. Madoff, *Immortality and the Law: The Rising Power of the American Dead* (New Haven, CT: Yale University Press, 2010), 91; Brody, "Charitable Endowments and the Democratization of Dynasty," 903–5; John Stuart Mill, *Dissertations and Discussions: Political, Philosophical, and Historical*, vol. 1 (New York: Henry Holt and Company, 1874), 32–33.

5. Peter Dobkin Hall, *Inventing the Nonprofit Sector and other essays on Philanthropy, Voluntarism, and Nonprofit Organization* (Baltimore, MD: Johns Hopkins University Press, 1992), 30–31; Ruth H. Bloch and Naomi R. Lamoreaux, "Voluntary Associations, Corporate Rights, and the State: Legal Constraints on the Development of American Civil Society, 1750–1900," in *Organizations, Civil Society, and the Roots of Development*, eds. Naomi R. Lamoreaux and John Joseph Wallis (Chicago: University of Chicago Press, 2017), 241–46; Irvin Wyllie, "The Search for an American Law of Charities, 1776–1844," *The Mississippi Valley Historical Review* 46, no. 2 (1959): 203–21; Bascom v. Albertson, 34 N.Y. 584, 614–15 (1866); Stanley M. Katz, Barry Sullivan, and C. Paul Beach, "Legal Change and Legal Autonomy: Charitable Trusts in New York, 1777–1893," *Law and History Review* 3, no. 1 (Spring 1985): 51–89.

6. Bruce Kimball and Benjamin Johnson, "The Inception of the Meaning and Significance of Endowment in American Higher Education, 1890–1930," *Teachers College Record* 114 (October 2012): 4, 5; Horace Coon, *Money to Burn: What the Great American Philanthropic Foundations Do with their Money* (New York: Longmans & Green and Co., 1938), 138.

7. Mary J. Oates, *The Catholic Philanthropic Tradition in America* (Bloomington: Indiana University Press, 1995), 133; Lila Corwin Berman, *The American Jewish Philanthropic Complex* (Princeton, NJ: Princeton University Press, 2021), 34.

8. Olivia Zunz, *Philanthropy in America: A History* (Princeton, Princeton University Press, 2012), 14–16; J. Frederick Taylor, "New Chapter in the New York Law of Charitable Corporations," *Cornell Law Review* 25 (1940): 382.

9. Zunz, *Philanthropy in America*, 54–55; Waldemar A. Nielsen, *The Golden Donors: A New Anatomy of the Great Foundations* (New York: E.P. Dutton, 1985), 244.

10. "Incorporation of the Rockefeller Foundation," 61st Cong., 2nd sess., 1910, S Rep. 405, 12–16; Frederick T. Gates to John D. Rockefeller, June 22, 1912, Box 3, Folder 57, Frederick T. Gates Collection, Rockefeller Archive Center, Tarrytown, New York.

11. Julius Rosenwald, "The Burden of Wealth," *Saturday Evening Post* (January 5, 1929), 12.

12. Howard J. Savage, *Fruit of an Impulse: Forty-Five Years of the Carnegie Foundation, 1905–1950* (New York: Harcourt, Brace and Co., 1953), 27; Andrew Carnegie to the Trustees of the Carnegie Corporation of New York, November 10, 1911, in *A Manual of the Public Benefactions of Andrew Carnegie* (Washington, DC: The Carnegie Endowment for International Peace, 1919), 206–7.

13. David Nasaw, *Andrew Carnegie* (New York: Penguin Press, 2006), 646; Joseph Frazier Wall, *Andrew Carnegie* (New York: Oxford University Press, 1970), 365.

14. Carnegie to the Trustees of the Carnegie Corporation, November 10, 1911, in *A Manual of the Public Benefactions of Andrew Carnegie,* 207; Pritchett quoted in Savage, *Fruit of an Impulse*, 29, 350; Henry S. Pritchett, "The Use and Abuse of Endowments," *The Atlantic Monthly* 144, no. 4 (October 1929): 523.

15. Peter M. Ascoli, *Julius Rosenwald: The Man who Built Sears, Roebuck and Advanced the Cause of Black Education in the American South* (Bloomington: Indiana University Press, 2006), 395; Edwin Embree quoted in John R. Thelin and Richard W. Trollinger, *Time is of the Essence: Foundations and the Policies of Limited Life and Endowment Spend-Down* (Washington, DC: Aspen Institute Program on Philanthropy and Social Innovation, 2009), 6. See also Hasia Diner, *Julius Rosenwald: Repairing the World* (New Haven, CT: Yale University Press, 2017).

16. Rosenwald, "The Burden of Wealth," *Saturday Evening Post* (January 5, 1929), 12; Julius Rosenwald, "Principles of Public Giving," *The Atlantic Monthly* (May 1929), 603.

17. Rosenwald, "Burden of Wealth," 12; Rosenwald, "Principles of Public Giving," 603; Ascoli, *Julius Rosenwald*, 318.

18. Ascoli, *Julius Rosenwald*, 282–88; Diner, *Julius Rosenwald*, 61; Rosenwald, "Burden of Wealth," 12; Rosenwald, "Principles of Public Giving," 603.

19. *The General Education Board: An Account of its Activities, 1902–1914* (New York: General Education Board, 1915), 15–16, 221; Eric John Abrahamson, *Beyond Charity: A Century of Philanthropic Innovation* (Rockefeller Foundation, 2013), 281, https://www.rockefellerfoundation.org/app/uploads/Beyond-Charity.pdf; *General Education Board: Review and Final Report, 1902–1964* (New York, 1964), vii.

20. Abrahamson, *Beyond Charity*, 20.

21. Abrahamson, *Beyond Charity*, 294, 295, 296.

22. Shelby Harrison and F. Emerson Andrews, *American Foundations for Social Welfare* (New York: Russell Sage Foundation, 1946), 70; Andrews, *Philanthropic Foundations* (New York: Russell Sage Foundation, 1956), 95, 101, 105; Warren Weaver, *U.S. Philanthropy Foundations* (New York: Harper & Row, 1967), 96.

23. Bundy quoted in "Ford Foundation Program Directions: Historical, Recent, Present." Catalogued Reports (FA 739E) report #012169 (1982), Ford Foundation Records, Rockefeller Archive Center; Zunz, *Philanthropy in America*, 193–96, 202–6; Eleanor L. Brilliant, *Private Charity and Public Inquiry: A History of the Filer and Peterson Commissions* (Bloomington: Indiana University Press, 2000); John Lankford, *Congress and the Foundations in the Twentieth Century* (River Falls, WI: Wisconsin State University, 1964).

24. Hall, *Inventing the Nonprofit Sector*, 66–71.

25. The Treasury Department suggested the establishment of an independent non-governmental body, which would "examine a foundation after it has had a reasonable period of time within which to prove itself." If the review led to a conclusion that the foundation could not justify its continued existence, the report suggested that the non-governmental body should have the power to "wind up [the foundation's] affairs, distribute its assets in accordance with its purposes, and dissolve it." *Treasury Department Report on Private Foundations* (Washington, DC: Government Printing Office, 1965), 5.

26. James J. Fishman, "The Private Foundation Rules at 50: How Did We Get Them and Do They Meet Current Needs?" *Pittsburgh Tax Review* 17, no. 2 (2020): 247–75; Brilliant, *Private Charity*, 83; U.S. Congress, *Congressional Record* 115 (December 5, 1969): S 37199.

27. U.S. Congress, *Congressional Record* 115 (December 5, 1969): S 37197.

28. U.S. Congress, *Congressional Record* 115 (December 5, 1969): S 37197, 37198; (December 4, 1969): S 37084.

29. Sen. Gore grew increasingly distraught that his ideological peers were not lining up beside him. "One of the strangest anomalies in our history," he lamented, "is that my liberal friends somehow think this [defense of perpetuity] is a liberal cause for which they are fighting. They are fighting for the vested interests of this country, for the vested wealth of this country, to be tied up in perpetuity for the descendants of a few people who have waxed rich." U.S. Congress, *Congressional Record* 115 (December 5, 1969): S 37200, 37304–37205.

30. Brilliant, *Private Charity*, 84; Commission on Foundations and Private Philanthropy, *Foundations, Private Giving and Public Policy* (Chicago: University of Chicago Press, 1970), 148; Berman, *American Jewish Philanthropic Complex*, 126–32.

31. Peter Frumkin, "The long recoil from regulation: private philanthropic foundations and the Tax Reform Act of 1969," *The American Review of Public Administration* 28, no. 3 (1998/9): 269–70.

32. Vincent Stehle, "Payout Proposal Doesn't Consider the Long Haul," *Chronicle of Philanthropy*, August 7, 2003; John J. Miller, *A Gift of Freedom: How the John M. Olin Foundation Changed America* (San Francisco, CA: Encounter Books, 2006).

33. Parts of the following section are adapted from Benjamin Soskis, "Norms and Narratives that Shape US Charitable and Philanthropic Giving," *Urban Institute*

Research Report (March 2021): 26–38, and is reprinted with permission from the Urban Institute.

34. Concerns about environmental degradation have heightened attention to intergenerational ethics, including the "social rate of time discount," used to compare the well-being of those alive today with future generations. Neil Buchanan, "What kind of environment do we owe future generations?" *Lewis & Clark Law Review* 15, no. 2 (2011): 339–67; Hal R. Varian, "Recalculating the Costs of Global Climate Change," *The New York Times*, December 14, 2006. Shelly Banjo, "Philanthropists Set Spending Deadlines," *Wall Street Journal*, May 21, 2009; Larry Kramer, "Philanthropy Must Stop Fiddling While the World Burns," *Chronicle of Philanthropy*, January 7, 2020.

35. There is a historical precedent to this. Among the founding principles of the Garland Fund, incorporated in 1922 and one of the leading funders of economic justice and civil rights in the following decades, was "that the money should be distributed as fast as it can be put into reliable hands." Megan Ming Francis, "The Price of Civil Rights: Black Lives, White Funding, and Movement Capture," *Law and Society Review* 53, no. 1 (2019): 284.

36. Deniz Çam, "How MacKenzie Scott Gave Away Nearly $6 Billion Last Year—and Ended Up Richer," *Forbes.com*, April 6, 2021, https://www.forbes.com/sites/denizcam/2021/04/06/how-mackenzie-scott-gave-away-nearly-6-billion-last-year-and-ended-up-richer/?sh=679251aa68cc; MacKenzie Scott Giving Pledge letter, May 25, 2019, https://givingpledge.org/Pledger.aspx?id=393; Soskis, "Norms and Narratives that Shape," 21–26, 34–35; Rebecca Koenig, "New Funds Offers Speedy Grants in Response to Trump Victory," *Chronicle of Philanthropy*, December 22, 2016; James Ferguson, *Give a Man a Fish: Reflections on the New Politics of Distribution* (Durham, NC: Duke University Press, 2015); Annie Lowrey, *Give People Money: How a Universal Basic Income Would End Poverty, Revolutionize Work, and Remake the World* (New York, Crown, 2018); Marc Gunter, "The new new thing in philanthropy? Cash," *Nonprofit Chronicles*, April 14, 2020, https://medium.com/nonprofit-chronicles/the-new-new-thing-in-philanthropy-cash-f33d4cf72401.

37. Peter Frumkin, "He Who's Got It Gets to Give It," *Washington Post,* October 3, 1999.

38. Theodore Schleifer, "Inside Jack Dorsey's radical experiment for billionaires to give away their money," *Vox*, June 11, 2020, https://www.vox.com/recode/2020/6/11/21287395/jack-dorsey-start-small-billionaire-philanthropy-coronavirus-twitter-square-kaepernick-rihanna.

39. Benjamin Soskis," To Be Young, Rich, and Philanthropic," *HistPhil*, January 11, 2016, https://histphil.org/2016/01/11/to-be-young-rich-and-philanthropic; Vindu Goel and Nick Wingfield, "Mark Zuckerberg Vows to Donate 99% of Hist Facebook Shares for Charity," *The New York Times*, December 1, 2015; Nicholas Kulish, "Giving Billions Fast, MacKenzie Scott Upends Philanthropy," *The New York Times*, December 20, 2020.

40. Mark Zuckerberg and Priscilla Chan, "A Letter to Our Daughter," *Facebook* post, https://www.facebook.com/notes/770757020443898/?pnref=story.

41. Marc Gunther and Drew Lindsay, "Has the Giving Pledge Changed Giving?" *The Chronicle of Philanthropy*, June 4, 2019.

42. Paul Brest and Hal Harvey, *Money Well Spent: A Strategic Plan for Smart Philanthropy*, 2nd ed. (Stanford, CA: Stanford Business Books, 2018); Paul J. Jansen and David M. Katz, "For nonprofits, time is money," *McKinsey Quarterly* (February 2002): 124–33; Michael Klausner, "When time isn't money: Foundation Payouts and the Time Value of Money," *Stanford Social Innovation Review* (Spring 2003): 51–59.

43. Joel L. Fleishman, *Putting Wealth to Work: Philanthropy for Today or Investing for Tomorrow?* (New York: PublicAffairs, 2017), xix.

44. When, for instance, Atlantic Philanthropies officially initiated its spend-down in January 2002, as per the wishes of its founder Chuck Feeney, it led to increased professionalization and bureaucratization, an expanded board and a more formal and systematic approach to grant-making and program evaluation. This in turn strained against the entrepreneurial, "start-up" culture that privileged the intuition and judgments of a few key individuals, and lead to conflict between Feeney and Atlantic's board. See Conor O'Clery, *The Billionaire Who Wasn't: How Chuck Feeney Secretly Made and Gave Away a Fortune* (New York: PublicAffairs, 2013), 332–70.

45. Elizabeth Boris, Carol J. De Vita, and Marcus Gaddy, *2015 Trends Study* (National Center for Family Philanthropy, November 2015), 20; Loren Renz and David Wolcheck, *Perpetuity or Limited Life: How do Family Foundations Decide?* (Foundation Center, 2009), 2–3, 9; Loren Renz and Steven Lawrence, *Foundation Grown and Giving Statistics: 2003 Preview* (Foundation Center, 2004), 10; "Foundation Trust," Bill & Melinda Gates Foundation, https://www.gatesfoundation.org /about/financials/foundation-trust; Charles [Chuck] Feeney, "Founder's Intent," July 28, 2004, Atlantic Philanthropies records; Steve Bartoni, "The Billionaire Who Wanted to Die Broke…Is Now Officially Broke," *Forbes*, September 15, 2020.

46. Rockefeller Philanthropy Advisors and NORC at the University of Chicago, *Strategic Time Horizons: A Global Snapshot of Foundation Approaches* (Rockefeller Philanthropy Advisors and NORC at the University of Chicago, 2020), 4.

47. See, for instance, Larry Kramer, "Foundation Payout Policy in Economic Crisis," *Stanford Social Innovation Review*, January 4, 2021. Rockefeller Philanthropy Advisors and NORC at the University of Chicago 2020, *Strategic Time Horizons*, 4–5.

48. Roger Colinvaux, "Donor Advised Funds: Charitable Spending Vehicles for 21st Century Philanthropy," *Washington Law Review* 92 (2017): 68; Molly F. Sherlock and Jane G. Gravelle, "An Analysis of Charitable Giving and Donor Advised Funds," *Congressional Research Service*, July 11, 2012; National Philanthropic Trust, *The 2021 DAF Report*, https://www.nptrust.org/reports/daf-report/; Chuck Collins, Helen Flannery, and Josh Hoxie, *Warehousing Wealth: Donor-Advised Charity Funds Sequestering Billions in the Face of Growing Inequality* (Institute for Policy Studies, 2018), 8, https://ips-dc.org/wp-content/uploads/2018/07/Warehousing -Wealth-IPS-Report-1.pdf.

49. The coeditor of this volume, Ray Madoff, was influential in securing the legislation's introduction. Alex Daniels, "Role of Donor-Advised Funds Prompts Heated

Debate," *Chronicle of Philanthropy*, October 23, 2015; Lewis B. Cullman and Ray Madoff, "The Undermining of American Charity," *New York Review of Books*, July 14, 2016; Dan Parks, "Sens. Grassley and King Push Measure to Accelerate DAF and Foundation Giving," *The Chronicle of Philanthropy*, June 9, 2021; Paul Major and Lora Smith, "Rural Community Foundations Support the ACE Act—you should too," *The Hill*, August 14, 2021; John Arnold, "The Slow-Moving Philanthropic Status Quo," *The Wall Street Journal*, December 22, 2020.

50. See Toby Ord, *The Precipice: Existential Risk and the Future of Humanity* (New York: Hachette Books, 2020) and Hilary Greaves and William MacAskill, *What We Owe the Future* (New York: Basic Books, 2002), https://globalprioritie sinstitute.org/wp-content/uploads/The-Case-for-Strong-Longtermism-GPI-Working -Paper-June-2021-2-2.pdf.

51. Ann Kim, "The Push for College Endowment Reform," *The Atlantic*, October 4, 2017.

52. Michael Kavate, "Inside the Foundation Payout Debate: How Crisis and Opportunity Are Forcing Change," *Inside Philanthropy*, June 19, 2020; Ellen Friedman, Glen Galaich, and Pia Infante, "There is No Better Time Than Now for Philanthropy to Spend Itself out of Existence," *Chronicle of Philanthropy*, July 27, 2020; William Foster and Darren Isorn, "Endow Black-led Nonprofits," *Stanford Social Innovation Review* (Winter 2021), https://ssir.org/articles/entry/endow_black _led_nonprofits; Edgar Villanueva, *Decolonizing Wealth: Indigenous Wisdom to Heal Divides and Restore Balance* (Oakland, CA: Berett-Koehler Publishers, 2018), 159–66.

53. Dan Parks, "Coronavirus 'Rapid Response' Funds Proliferate as Threat Grows," *Chronicle of Philanthropy*, March 11, 2020.

54. Alex Daniels, "Grant Maker Dilemma: Spend More Now or Protect Shrinking Endowments?" *The Chronicle of Philanthropy*, April 1, 2020; Alex Daniels, "9 Leading Nonprofit Groups Urge Foundations to Dig Into Endowments to Support Charities," *The Chronicle of Philanthropy*, April 2, 2020; Sarina Dayal and Grace Sato, "Did foundation giving and payout shift in 2020?" Candid blog, June 29, 2021, https://blog.candid.org/post/did-foundation-giving-and-payout-shift-in-2020/; Kramer, "Foundation Payout Policy," *Stanford Social Innovation Review*, January 4, 2021; Daniel Hemel and Joseph Bankman, "Should Foundations Give Now or Later? There is No Right Answer," *The Chronicle of Philanthropy*, June 17, 2020.

Part I

HISTORY

Chapter 2

"Giving While Living" in Historical Perspective

Benjamin Soskis

In June 2015, Sean Parker, the cofounder of Napster and the founding president of Facebook, published an op-ed in the *Wall Street Journal* that issued a call to arms on behalf of "hacker philanthropy." In it, he urged a new generation of tech entrepreneurs to apply their skill, ingenuity, and anti-institutional inclinations to their philanthropy. And Parker pushed his peers to do so *now*. "There's no better time to start than the present," he insisted.[1]

With that statement, Parker signaled his support for the Giving While Living movement. Yet it's a sign of the movement's capaciousness that one of its main champions over the last two decades has been an individual temperamentally far removed from the young Silicon Valley entrepreneurs to whom Parker was preaching. Chuck Feeney made his fortune in duty-free sales and, in 1984 at the age of fifty-three, transferred the entirety of it to establish Atlantic Philanthropies. For much of the final decades of the last century, Atlantic was one of the largest foundations in operation in the United States. In 2002, following Feeney's wishes, its trustees committed to spend down all its assets, and in 2020, it closed its doors for good. Preternaturally modest and wary of the spotlight, Feeney initially insisted on complete anonymity for his foundation. Ultimately, though, he brought Atlantic out of the shadows in order to spread the Giving While Living gospel, which, as he defined it, required "personally devot[ing] oneself to meaningful efforts to improve the human condition."[2]

If the fact that Parker and Feeney could both march under the banner of the Giving While Living movement points to its expansive, powerful appeal, it also signals the movement's definitional indeterminacy. The ambiguities within "Giving While Living" are worthy of scrutiny, because the movement represents one of the most prominent examples of how considerations of timeliness have been incorporated into contemporary philanthropic practice. Although its name highlights the obvious ontological distinction on which "Giving While Living" is premised—between being or not being alive—because of the limits imposed on us by our mortality, it also necessarily implies a temporal distinction.

This chapter highlights the three primary components that inform the Giving While Living ethic as it has developed over the last few decades and demonstrates how each reflects an engagement with "giving in time." It also examines the extent to which each of these engagements leaves key questions related to temporality unresolved, questions that hinge on the relationships between and relative status accorded to the three strains that comprise the ethic.

The Giving While Living ethic can suggest a range of attitudes toward the intersection of temporality and philanthropy. Chuck Feeney, for instance, has explained the ethic's attraction by affirming his belief "that money raised for philanthropy is to be spent at the time that it's raised, or close to it." For Feeney, "Giving While Living" combines both personal discomfort with holding onto a fortune for too long—a sort of "hot potato" theory of philanthropy—with the belief that the skills and temperament that helped generate a fortune should be tapped expeditiously and applied to that fortune's philanthropic disbursement. It is also staked to the belief that opportunities for learning and social investment compound over time. "Today's needs are so great and varied," Feeney once wrote, "that intelligent philanthropic support and positive interventions can have greater value and impact today than if they are delayed when the needs are greater."[3]

More generally, "Giving While Living" as a distinct philanthropic movement represents the convergence of three intertwined imperatives. At its most basic level, "Giving While Living" makes an absolute, transactional and temporal demand on the donor, requiring him or her to commit money to charitable causes before death. This condition can be satisfied and assessed quantitatively—with a bank account transfer and a pulse. Beyond this, there is also a qualitative dimension to "Giving While Living," requiring the *active* engagement of the donor in administering or overseeing the gift. Finally, the ethic carries with it a promotional, evangelical charge; "Giving While Living" must be performed in public in order to spark the giving of others. If the first imperative establishes an explicit relationship to temporal considerations, the other two do so more subtly. Active engagement with and active evangelization for philanthropy cannot be conducted postmortem; each must occur within the bounds of a lifetime. Yet donors have exhibited a range of views regarding the precise time frames that should govern engagement and promotion, and it is this variety that lies at the root of the movement's expansiveness—and indeterminacy.

The first fundamental strand of "Giving While Living" takes its place within a much broader history of decisions regarding the timing of charitable gifts. This history's two main poles have been the testamentary charitable transfer, taking effect at death, and the *inter vivos* gift, which can be overseen, administered, and enjoyed by a living donor.

Over time, it is difficult to say which has been responsible for more charitable giving. There is, of course, a vast tradition of quotidian small-scale almsgiving, the extension of material aid in response to an immediate encounter with suffering, which has largely passed unremarked through the sieve of historical accounting. Much large-scale *inter vivos* giving, on the other hand, has been recorded—public documentation and public regard being one of its primary aims. Classical Greek and Roman culture, for instance, encouraged a system of what scholars have termed civic *euergetism*, in which prominent citizens were expected to make frequent donations that glorified their cities—building public baths or putting on public games—and could expect in return public honor and enhanced social status. Such compensation was meant to be savored by the living.[4]

Of course, giving was also often undertaken with expectations of returns beyond one's own lifetime, extending into the realms of eternity itself, and in this capacity, bequests and legacies often served as instruments of charitable intent. Deathbed charity, prompted only when the giver faced the real prospect of no longer being counted among the living, and with no expectation of active superintendence over the gift, provided a particularly powerful opportunity for spiritual self-reckoning. The perils of damnation that awaited the unrepentant became prominent themes in early Christian teachings and testamentary gifts authorized in the final moments of one's life were held out as a means of averting that fate.[5]

In the medieval period, the practice of deathbed giving spread as the church encouraged Christians close to death to leave their property to ecclesiastical institutions in order to secure salvation, as with the establishment of a chantry, a Mass recited at an altar for the soul of the donor in Purgatory. Such gifts, with their intercessionary appeals and "*post mortem* provisions," reinforced what historian Jacques Le Goff called "the solidarity between the living and the dead" and intertwined the time frames associated with each, the mortal and the immortal.[6]

Indeed, by the close of the twelfth century, as one historian has noted, most wills "were rendered on the person's deathbed, with priests in attendance; the presence of the clergy strongly influenced the outcome. The priest's duty was to remind the testator of the needs of the parish and its poor; often the priest drew up the will himself." Because the poor were considered especially powerful intercessors, a bequest to a religious institution that performed works of mercy on their behalf could serve both a charitable function as well as the spiritual interests of the donor. On a more terrestrial level, commentators also appreciated that giving one's property away at death allowed the testator to make productive use of it during the course of his life; it was a less personally taxing system of redistribution. Salvian of Marseilles made this point tartly in a fifth-century tract, and its logic would hold for the next millennium and a half. He assumed that most Christians of the period lacked the ascetic zeal of the early saints, who had renounced all their wealth and given it to the church. Luckily, God had provided an "extremely soft" option for these less morally strenuous souls, in transferring their wealth at death.[7]

As hinted by the undercurrents of Salvian's commentary, even as individual religious leaders encouraged testamentary and deathbed giving, there was also a long-running counter-discourse that looked askance at such practices, especially in comparison to *inter vivos* corporeal works of mercy. There were two primary early critiques of testamentary giving that fed into what could be considered a pre-modern Giving While Living movement. The first was moral. Medieval and early modern texts, for instance, warned against "delayed giving" because it signaled an undue attachment to wealth and a diminished capacity for self-sacrifice and thus did little to inspire others. In one articulation of this view, an English gentleman wrote in 1690 that "to Defer our Charity till Death, is to lose much of the commendation that is inseparable from holy PRACTICE; because then it appears a work of necessity, to give that away, which we cannot longer possess."[8]

The other critique was largely prudential. Since the moment of death's arrival was unpredictable, in forestalling the settling of one's charitable commitments, the potential giver ran the risk of leaving his charitable affairs intestate. Such was the warning offered by the thirteenth-century French church reformer, Jacques de Vitry, who in a model sermon designed to be preached to hospital workers urged his audience not to put off their charity till their later years: "For he who delays today will perhaps not give or minister tomorrow, with death unexpectedly having arrived or grave illness." Testators also risked leaving their charitable bequests to unreliable executors. As English author John Stow wrote, "I wish men to make their own hands their executors . . . for/ 'Women be forgetfull, children be unkind,/ Executors be covetous, and take what they find."[9]

Over the last few centuries, variations on this prudential challenge to deathbed giving, applied to charitable bequests more generally, have proved the most powerful. In fact, the trend toward "Giving While Living" has tended to coincide with various movements that have periodically crested over the last five centuries to rationalize and impose greater discrimination on charitable giving. These efforts have linked a focusing of philanthropic time frames on the life of the donor with exertions of donor control. At different moments in history, charity reformers have worried about the waste, inefficiency, or lack of strategic focus evident in predominant modes of giving, and in response have urged philanthropists to become more actively involved in superintending their benefactions, a calling that cannot be undertaken from the grave—or even, at some level, with the declining faculties of old age.

The first wave of charity reform occurred after the Reformation, when Protestants sought to distance their own giving from the practices that had predominated under the Catholic Church. An emerging mercantile class began to forge philanthropy into an instrument directed less toward the giver's spiritual condition than toward the betterment of this world. In sixteenth-century England, this at first led to a wave of bequests, often celebrated as demonstrating the inherent generosity of Protestant culture, responding to the turmoil brought on by Henry VIII's dissolution of the monasteries, which had previously assumed responsibility for the care of the poor.[10]

Yet the eighteenth century witnessed a significant decline in posthumous giving, corresponding to mounting concerns about obsolete or superannuated legacies and the dangers of the "dead hand." As the historian Donna Andrew has written, "The charitable Christian was increasingly being advised to disburse his charity during his lifetime, in order to have greater control over its direction." She cites an injunction from a 1712 sermon on this subject. "[The Christian] is fearful lest his Legacie should be lost, or not dispos'd of according to his Mind and Intention. And therefore takes Care to distribute a good Part of his Charity with his own Hands." Given the predominance of this attitude, Andrew points out, it is not surprising that "Guy's Hospital, built in 1727, was the last major philanthropic venture to be erected by bequest in eighteenth-century London."[11]

Guy's generosity, far from meeting universal approbation, provoked a round of public attacks for "disinheriting kinfolk." Indeed, the eighteenth-century demotion of the bequest as the preferred mode of giving was reinforced by a prominent strain within the Anglo-American legal tradition that looked suspiciously on transfers of property at the time of death and that regarded the deathbed as the frequent scene of emotional manipulation on the part of ecclesiastical authorities. Aggrieved heirs who believed they had been robbed of their rightful legacy by conniving priests made up a powerful lobby to limit the scope of posthumous giving. Such sentiments helped push passage of the 1736 "Law of Mortmain," which sought to limit the "publick mischief" of "many large and improvident alienations or dispositions made by languishing or dying persons" that Parliament believed to be on the rise. The law therefore required, among other stipulations, that any charitable gift be made at least twelve months before the donor's death, a modest push toward "Giving While Living."[12]

Similar legal reasoning held an appeal for early Americans as well. It was bolstered by a leveling impulse in Puritan thought, especially pronounced in the first generations of settlement. Puritan communitarianism established a preference for the slow, steady application of private wealth to the public good as opposed to the grander gesture of the large bequest, which was premised on the accumulation of a substantial personal fortune. If early Puritans urged disciplined and productive labor in a calling (and thus could be said to sanction the accumulation of wealth), they also celebrated the ideal of steady self-impoverishment in service of the godly community. John Hull, a Puritan merchant, for instance, praised one Massachusetts Bay governor, John Endecott, for having "died poor, as most of our rulers do, having more attended the public than their own private interests." Nearly two centuries later, the corollary of such praise was invoked to cast doubts on the moral worth of the bequests of merchant and fur trader John Jacob Astor, who, when he died in 1848, was the wealthiest man in the United States. Astor had left $400,000 to establish a free library in New York, which, coming out of an estate valued at more than $20 million, many deemed too little and too late. Astor could have easily endowed the library "in his life time," sniffed one Boston newspaper, "but he would have lost the interest of the money in that case. Posthumous charity demands no self-sacrifice."[13]

In the first decades of the nineteenth century, the proliferation of voluntary associations, funded largely by subscription, provided opportunities for small-scale "Giving While Living." Most large-scale benefactions, on the other hand, still came through bequest. Yet these faced an inhospitable legal landscape in some jurisdictions. In the post-Revolutionary decades, several states, led by Virginia, passed mortmain statutes, fueled by Democratic-Republican suspicion of corporations and of the accumulation of property within ecclesiastic and eleemosynary institutions. These, as legal scholar Ray Madoff explains, "restricted charitable giving by either disallowing charitable bequests in wills made shortly before the donor's death or by prohibiting charitable gifts in excess of a designated fraction of the donor's estate." Even after the Supreme Court, in 1844, resolved some of the objections to the legal legitimacy of charitable bequests, several states maintained a restrictive position and continued to set them aside.[14]

Other states, such as Massachusetts, developed more permissive policies. Taken as a whole, both state law and Supreme Court jurisprudence could be said to exhibit a preference for *inter vivos* gifts, since fewer of the restrictions applied to them. Yet, until the final decades of the nineteenth century, only a handful of Americans accumulated enough surplus personal wealth to make large-scale "Giving While Living" practical. The proliferation of such transfers, and the unfolding of a modern movement based on the Giving While Living ethic, came about only with the massive industrial fortunes of the Gilded Age.

The pressures applied by those fortunes, as well as the mounting social challenges facing the nation in the final decades of the nineteenth century, encouraged a loosening of restrictive laws toward charitable trusts. Private fortunes represented reservoirs of financial resources that could be tapped to alleviate poverty, educate citizens, and bolster civic institutions. The debates over the proper balance between the regulation and encouragement of charitable trusts peaked with the tumult surrounding the Tilden Trust, the bequest made by former New York governor Samuel Tilden of more than $5 million to establish a free library in New York, as well as to promote other scientific and educational institutions. Tilden's heirs challenged the trust, and in 1891, the New York Court of Appeals invalidated it, citing, among other objections, the indefiniteness of its ends. The decision resulted in a storm of protest, and in 1893, the New York legislature passed the Tilden Act, which established a more permissive policy toward charitable trusts, including bequests. With greater legal sanction, large-scale charitable bequests flowered in the final decades of the nineteenth century and were closely parsed by the press. Indeed, at this point, there was no expectation, or even stated preference, for the wealthy to give while they were alive, so long as the public eventually received its due.[15]

At the same time, among these industrialists arose a new corps of philanthropists, committed to the cause of scientific charity and to the active *warm-blooded* management of their benefactions. Their prominence led the timing of philanthropic gifts to once again become the subject of sustained public discussion.

The classic articulation of this viewpoint was Andrew Carnegie's "Gospel of Wealth." Written in 1889, and first published as "Wealth" in the *North American Review* (its famous title was added when it was republished soon after in the *Pall Mall Gazette*), the essay represented the steel magnate's efforts to resolve the great problem of the age: the growing gap between the rich and the poor. Carnegie proposed actively engaged philanthropy as the solution; it would both justify great wealth to the public and would provide a channel for some (unspecified) part of that wealth to be returned to society, so as to prevent the accumulation of dynastic fortunes. Such giving would not eliminate the gap between the classes, since Carnegie determined great concentrations of wealth to be a salutary fact of nature. Instead, it would provide "ladders upon which the aspiring can rise." It would also legitimate great concentrations of wealth by allowing the millionaire to serve as "a trustee for the poor, intrusted for a season with a great part of the increased wealth of the community, but administering it for the community far better than it could or would have done for itself."[16]

Such a neat resolution depended upon wealthy citizens abandoning two traditional means of disposing of personal fortunes. First, they could not leave fortunes to their families; such an act merely spoiled the next generation. Nor could they bequeath them at death to some charitable cause, since too often this resulted in the money being used in ways that contravened the testator's intent. Carnegie held up a third possibility: surplus wealth should be "administered by its possessors during their lives." Only in this mode could those who had accumulated a fortune apply the talents that had brought them their wealth toward its redistribution. Only in this way could the man of wealth assume control of his giving and publicly affirm his trusteeship.

This view represented a change in the attitude toward "giving in time." When Philadelphia-based banker Stephen Girard died in 1831 and left much of his $10 million fortune to charity (his will was published and widely circulated in the *United States Gazette*), the bequest was roundly celebrated as the consummate act of stewardship. But for Carnegie, although he admired Girard, such timing was not commendable. As Carnegie memorably phrased it, "The man who dies thus rich dies disgraced."[17]

Carnegie's essay sparked a broader discussion in the transatlantic popular press regarding the responsibilities of wealth, though it did not necessarily affect a transformation in attitudes toward the charitable bequest. It can be argued, in fact, that Carnegie's influence over his fellow philanthropists' giving time frames was greater at the start of *this* century than it was at the turn of the last century. His "Gospel," for instance, shaped the thinking of Chuck Feeney, who kept a copy of it on his desk and frequently handed it out to associates as a window into his own thinking.[18]

Indeed, Carnegie's "Gospel" has in recent years attracted a wide range of disciples. It "is practically holy scripture for many of today's philanthrocapitalists," the class of entrepreneurs who see the market as the greatest force for social good, note the authors of *Philanthrocapitalism*, one of the more influential books on philanthropy of the past several decades. Before Warren Buffett pledged to turn over a large part of his fortune to the Bill and Melinda Gates Foundation, he gave Gates a copy of the essay. More recently, the president of the Ford Foundation, Darren Walker, has invoked the tract in calling for a "New Gospel of Wealth" for the twenty-first century.[19]

One reason for the contemporary revival of Carnegie's essay is its ability to express all three strands of the Giving While Living ethic. On one level, the "Gospel"—as well as the model presented by Carnegie himself—simply affirms the call for the nation's richest citizens to direct *more* of their wealth to philanthropy during their lifetimes, a quantitatively satisfiable imperative. At his death, when contemporaries tallied Carnegie's major benefactions, the amount reached over $350 million, more than any other living donor of the age. Carnegie left behind a fortune of a "mere" $30 million, two-thirds of which was bequeathed to the Carnegie Corporation, while another large chunk went to fund personal pensions for his close associates and employees.

He left no monetary bequest to his wife or daughter (though he did leave them considerable real-estate holdings).[20]

The "Gospel" also reflects his appreciation of the philanthropist's educative mission—the ethic's third strand. Carnegie's legacy dictates that the wealthy participate in the public discourse surrounding the responsibilities of wealth. As Carnegie once explained, "I do not wish to be remembered for what I have given, but for that which I have persuaded others to give." He refers here both to his public promotion of the responsibilities of great wealth and to his preference for matching gifts, which required communities to contribute to the upkeep of the libraries he donated. In both cases, he understood his contributions as a philanthropist to stem from the amplifying influence his example could exert on others' charitable commitments.[21]

Perhaps the most significant reason for a revived interest in Carnegie's "Gospel" is the powerful call it issued for the personal engagement of the wealthy in philanthropy. Those who accumulated money through their own discipline and ingenuity, Carnegie insisted, had a civic obligation to apply their talents toward their fortune's redistribution for the public good. In an age which celebrates the contributions of the heroic entrepreneur, this has proved an enticing imperative. Indeed, Carnegie's contemporary disciples have appreciated that his Gospel's dictates could not be satisfied through fulfillment of only the first strand, with a transfer of wealth and a passive act of dispossession. The "living" mandated by the ethic required *active* stewardship—although Carnegie left the precise threshold of donor engagement an open and pressing question.

This archetype of the engaged, living large-scale donor now casts such a powerful presence on the contemporary philanthropic scene that it is easy to forget that the figure has until recently been the exception. When Waldemar Nielsen, one of the twentieth century's most perceptive observers of the philanthropic sector, surveyed the largest foundations in the 1970s and 1980s, he was struck by how little thought many donors seemed to extend to their giving. "Far from being wise, farsighted, public-spirited, purposeful benefactors, many of the big donors set up their foundations if not in a fit of absentmindedness then simply as part of tidying up their affairs at the end of a lifetime devoted to business and the acquisition of wealth," he noted. "In moving from the profit-making to the not-for-profit sphere, they with few exceptions forgot their accumulated organizational skills entirely." In Silicon Valley, now a hotbed of engaged donorship, as late as the final decades of the twentieth century, most entrepreneurs turned to philanthropy late in life, if at all, and with little direct involvement. As Peter Hero, who led the region's largest community foundation, remarked, "The donor's role was to give away their money to the community foundation—and then, preferably, to die."[22]

These donors, even if they technically gave before death, violated the full tripartite Giving While Living ethic by neglecting its second strand, which demands active engagement. The relationship between that strand and the first is based on a relatively straightforward argument about "giving in time": because the energy, drive and ingenuity of an entrepreneurial donor are not inexhaustible resources in any given lifetime, a commitment to philanthropy should be initiated before they are significantly depleted. But if such logic discourages the indefinite postponement of philanthropic engagement, it does not mandate a particular starting time.

Given this indeterminacy, it is not surprising that the various historic junctures at which the Giving While Living ethic has been championed have also elicited a range of attitudes toward the proper moment at which philanthropic work should be initiated. One, with a long tradition behind it, suggests establishing strong lines of demarcation between the identities of wealth creator and wealth re-distributor. This approach mirrors the stark "normative and institutional" boundaries that were established at the close of the nineteenth century between nonprofit and for-profit corporations. It carried the assumption that giving away a fortune is a more noble vocation than the making of it, and thus, that the latter enterprise should be fully abdicated before the former can be embarked upon. It recommends philanthropy as a sort of valedictory—and at times redemptive— enterprise, one for that reason often taken up late in life (though the potential, within the high-tech and financial industries, to make massive fortunes so rapidly has allowed such "retirements" to happen earlier in an individual's life).[23]

Yet the "Giving While Living" tradition offers little guidance as to precisely when the man of wealth should transform himself into a philanthropist. The difficulty of arriving at a satisfying answer with regard to that timing can forestall the commitment to active philanthropy and can leave it vulnerable to critique once it has been made. Andrew Carnegie, for instance, vowed on several occasions to retire from business, but repeatedly backed away, finding the prospect of making more millions irresistible. Indeed, he believed the responsible man of wealth had an obligation to "increase his revenues." Once he has committed himself to the Gospel of Wealth, "the struggle for more is completely freed from selfish or ambitious taint and becomes a noble pursuit. . . . The more he makes, the more the public gets." The tobacco magnate James Buchanan Duke followed similar logic in establishing the Duke Endowment less than a year before he died. "I am going to give a good part of what I make to the Lord," he explained, "but I can make better interest for Him by keeping it while I live."[24]

More recently, before he had decided to turn over his fortune to the Bill and Melinda Gates Foundation and a handful of other foundations, investor Warren Buffett had planned to give his money to philanthropy only after his death. As he explained in an interview with *Fortune* magazine shortly after announcing the pledge, "I always had the idea that philanthropy was important today, but would be equally important in one year, ten years, 20 years, and the future generally. And someone who was compounding money at a high rate, I thought, was the better party to be taking care of the philanthropy that was to be done 20 years out, while the people compounding at a lower rate should logically take care of the current philanthropy."[25]

There is another response to the challenge of timing the transition from wealth accumulator to philanthropist, which is to deny its necessity entirely and thereby to deny the salience of the issue of timeliness more generally. At nearly every moment of great wealth creation in the United States, including the present one, those who accumulated the bulk of it have argued that entrepreneurship is itself a form of philanthropy, providing employment, goods and services to the public. In his autobiography, for instance, Standard Oil founder John D. Rockefeller declared the highest form of philanthropy to be "the investment of effort or time or money, carefully considered with relation to the power of employing people at a remunerative wage, to expand and develop the resources at hand, and to give opportunity for progress and healthful labor where it did not exist before." In fact, he praised businessmen who refused to retire even when they had "acquired a competency" for this reason. More recently, this argument has been bolstered by a techno-utopian strain that promotes the creation and dissemination of technological advances as a form of philanthropy. Such a line of reasoning was invoked to celebrate Apple cofounder Steve Jobs when he died in 2011; Jobs had shown little interest in charitable giving, but his defenders insisted that he understood his stewardship of Apple as his philanthropic contribution. He was giving while living with every new iPhone rollout.[26]

The model embodied by Steve Jobs represents the greatest contemporary challenge to "Giving While Living"—besides, of course, pure avarice. But the Giving While Living ethic offers another alternative approach as a response, one increasingly embraced by a younger cohort of tech philanthropists. By emphasizing the active engagement of the wealthy in the practice of philanthropy, the ethic has underscored the ways in which the same personality traits that have led to wealth accumulation can and should be directed toward giving that wealth away. It thus holds out the possibility of their *simultaneous* application: giving while living *while* accumulating.

That possibility is still largely unfulfilled; philanthropy is still, for most large-scale donors, a post-entrepreneurial activity, consummated in the final decades of a donor's life. A 2015 report from Wealth-X and Arton Capital states, "UHNW [ultra-high net worth] philanthropists are, on average, over six years older than the typical UHNW individual. This suggests that traditional philanthropy is particularly relevant for UHNW individuals who have passed the wealth accumulation stage, regardless of how their wealth was made. Only 1.1 percent of all UHNW philanthropists are under 40 years old . . . while 12.6 percent are over 80." Similarly, the median age of living donors in the *Chronicle of Philanthropy*'s 2020 list of the fifty largest donors was sixty-six.[27]

Yet there are signs that a shift in the time frames that dictate large-scale giving may be on the horizon. In part, this is due to the speed with which colossal private fortunes have been accumulated in the last decades; self-making has become temporally compressed. The gestation period of the billionaire can now often be measured in years, not decades, especially in the technology and finance sectors. IPOs, scheduled relatively shortly after a company's establishment, can provide founders with greater (and potentially more liquid) wealth to direct to philanthropy. Bill Gates became a billionaire in his thirties; Mark Zuckerberg achieved that distinction in his twenties, an age at which the major philanthropists of an earlier era were still completing their entrepreneurial apprenticeships. There were fifteen billionaires under the age of forty on the 2021 *Forbes* list of the richest four hundred Americans. Such early and astronomical financial success allows these men and women, if they so choose, to assume the identity of the active philanthropist much earlier in life. Furthermore, as a 2015 report from UBS/PricewaterhouseCoopers states, even if most self-made billionaires do not reach that milestone until well after their fortieth birthdays, the entrepreneurial and business breakthroughs that are responsible for their fortunes are now occurring when they are considerably younger. So these entrepreneurs are anticipating bearing considerable philanthropic responsibilities, and at times making significant philanthropic pledges of prospective activity, at an earlier age as well.[28]

Not surprisingly, then, a small but significant cohort of younger wealthy entrepreneurs, clustered in the technology sector, has explicitly embraced a strict commitment to "Giving While Living." It's possible they represent a vanguard that augurs a more sweeping transformation of attitudes toward "giving in time."[29] In 2014, for instance, the *Chronicle of Philanthropy* highlighted a "stunning rise in the number of tech entrepreneurs under 40" on their list of the nation's top fifty philanthropists. There were, it should be noted, only three (less than half the number of nonagenarians) but they made their giving count—they each donated more than $500 million (only three other donors gave more). The year before, the *Chronicle* noted, Mark Zuckerberg and Priscilla Chan became the first donors under thirty to head up their list.

In a December 2015 interview with *Inside Philanthropy*, Nick Tedesco, then the director of the west-coast office of J.P. Morgan Private Bank's Philanthropy Center, also remarked upon this trend among young tech entrepreneurs. They are "thinking about philanthropy as a complement to their existing careers," Tedesco explained, and not as a capstone to them.

Significantly, he added that the developing culture of "Giving While Living" within the tech community had become a mark of status, sparking a dynamic competition. "These tech entrepreneurs are challenging each other to engage in philanthropy," suggesting that many had embraced the third, public and performative strand of "Giving While Living," as well.[30]

Such developments suggest an important shift within the contemporary instantiation of the "Giving While Living" ethic. Previously, it had not been associated with youthfulness; "Giving While Living" had been set in opposition to the bequest (or to not giving at all) and all that was really necessary for an individual to claim its mantle was not to be dead—or at least, to give at an age at which active engagement in philanthropy was possible. But increasingly, a significant cohort of philanthropists interprets "Giving While Living" to mean Giving While Young. In doing so, they have transformed youthfulness itself, as opposed to experience or longevity, into a valuable philanthropic asset.

In his influential 2015 *Wall Street Journal* op-ed, Sean Parker makes this case explicitly. "Youth and philanthropy haven't historically mixed," he concedes. Yet a new global hacker elite was emerging, many of who made fortunes before their fortieth birthday, and who see no need to postpone their engagement with philanthropy into some indefinite future. (Parker himself has vowed to spend down his $600 million foundation during his lifetime.) Parker articulates an updated version of a stewardship ethic in which the qualities that define the "hacker" and that led to his or her entrepreneurial success and wealth—idealism, "an antiestablishment bias, a belief in radical transparency, a nose for sniffing out vulnerabilities in systems . . . and an almost religious belief in the power of data to aid in solving those problems"—are applied *concurrently* to his or her philanthropic enterprises.[31]

The Giving While Living ethic, as refracted through the culture of Silicon Valley, gained particular prominence with the announcement in December 2015 by Facebook CEO Mark Zuckerberg and his wife Priscilla Chan that they planned to turn over 99 percent of their shares of Facebook stock—worth approximately $45 billion—to a limited liability company that would direct the funds toward charitable causes. The couple pledged to do so "during our lives," a vow which (if fulfilled) represented, at the time, the largest single commitment to "Giving While Living."

"We're not at the end of our lives giving away capital," Chan later explained. We've made an investment to decide to run [the Initiative] ourselves. That's a proactive choice, a deliberate choice." Indeed, much of the public discussion surrounding the announcement interpreted it as an exemplary demonstration of "Giving While Living," paying particular attention to the couple's youth. Former New York mayor Michael Bloomberg, for instance, remarked that the couple's pledge had signaled that "30 is the new

70" for philanthropists. "The traditional approach to giving—leaving it to old age or death—is falling by the wayside, as it should," he announced."[32]

Responding to a query from a *New York Times* reporter on Facebook, Zuckerberg explained his commitment to "Giving While Living" (though he did not use that term, instead speaking of the importance of "start[ing] early") with reference to two main motivations. The impact of current spending compounds over time, he pointed out, in a common argument made by donors who favor giving now over giving later. "If we can help children get a better education now then they can grow up and help others too in the time we might have otherwise waited to get started," he wrote. He also insisted that philanthropy, like any other activity, requires practice, and so "if we want to be good at it in 10-15 years, we should start now."[33]

Starting philanthropy early, at least relative to a tradition of post-retirement engagement, provides a much longer time span over which to hone one's craft. "You're going to have a lot more decades of very successful people deeply engaged in these issues," Bill Gates told interviewer Charlie Rose. "That really wasn't typical if you look back at the history of philanthropy." Paradoxically, however, tech philanthropy has participated in a general sector-wide trend toward "venture philanthropy," focusing on quantifiable short-term impact over a narrower time span. Young tech philanthropists have joined more seasoned donors from the world of finance in cultivating a strategic impatience, if not impulsiveness, regarding their gifts. As Eric Kessler, the founder of the philanthropy advisory firm Arabella Advisers remarked, these young philanthropists "move fast, and they are looking for a return in their philanthropy. They earn money on Monday, and start giving it away on Tuesday." In fact, Sean Parker has linked the speed at which fortunes are accumulated to the speed at which they are diffused back through society via philanthropy. He has suggested that those who acquired their wealth gradually, over decades, tend to deploy philanthropy in a relatively cautious manner, whereas those who have made money quickly tend to favor risk-taking and a faster payout. He defined "hacker" philanthropy against what he terms "incrementalism," in both accumulation and redistribution.[34]

Of course, the broader temporal vista ahead of young philanthropists committed to "Giving While Living" can also encourage longer time horizons. Zuckerberg and Chan, for instance, have warned of the dangers of "short term thinking" and have insisted that the greatest challenges require "investments over 25, 50, or even 100 years." What unites these short- and long-term perspectives is an understanding of the iterative dimension of philanthropy; the decades stretching out in front of young mega-donors provide space for detours and corrections. Those who promote "hacker philanthropy" tend to emphasize their willingness to make mistakes; they advance a celebration of failure, as in the hothouse laboratories of the tech sector, as a necessary condition of the risk-taking that breeds entrepreneurial success. "I think it's better to be known for failing than for failing to try," Parker has insisted. The philanthropic gift becomes a learning exercise, undertaken in order to develop into a more effective philanthropist with benefits to the public accruing sometime in the indefinite future—though the learning process itself can be understood as a public good. Such an approach represents one way that the philanthropist can balance a temporal focus between the near- and far-term.[35]

In the assumption that their learning should be broadcast across a wide social network of peers, through a Facebook post or a *Wall Street Journal* op-ed, Zuckerberg, Chan, and Parker signal adherence to the third strand of the Giving While Living ethic. (It is also the case that the leading tech entrepreneurs command a disproportionate amount of media attention and so their philanthropic endeavors can more easily take on an educative function.) This focus reflects one of the more fundamental transformations in attitudes toward philanthropy over the last century, from an understanding of it as a private endeavor to a recognition of it as a public vocation.

At the turn of the last century, the shift was fueled in part by a recognition from the nation's leading philanthropists that the size of their fortunes and the scale of their ambitions would necessarily invite public scrutiny. John D. Rockefeller, who prefaced the section of his autobiography on the topic of his giving with the apology that it is "beyond the pale of good taste to speak at all of such a personal subject," grudgingly came to this realization, largely due to the need to parry the insinuations about the ulterior motives that were assumed to fuel his benefactions.[36]

The inducements to publicity for Andrew Carnegie, however, were less defensive and directly shaped the Giving While Living ethic. Carnegie came to regard philanthropy as a public vocation not only so that the wealthy could be held accountable (and could therefore legitimize capitalism) but so that they could serve as models for emulation. Indeed, the distinctiveness of his "Gospel of Wealth" lies not so much in its content, which was shared by other devotees of an ethic of stewardship, but in its unabashed public articulation. As Henry Potter, the bishop of the Episcopal Church in the United States, explained in an 1891 review of Carnegie's essay, "At this moment, I cannot recall, in our generation, any other instance of one possessed of exceptional wealth who has undertaken to discuss, publicly and at any length, the question of its disposition." Carnegie added an additional responsibility to those associated with great wealth: not only directing one's own fortune toward beneficent ends during one's lifetime but exhorting others to do the same.[37]

In the next generation, this charge was taken up by Julius Rosenwald, the long-serving head of Sears, Roebuck, who masterminded the company's transformation into a mail-order behemoth. Rosenwald, more so than Carnegie or Rockefeller, turned to philanthropy at the peak of his business career, and so could be said to exemplify the Giving While Living imperative even more strongly, to the extent it is staked on the temporal proximity between accumulation and philanthropic redistribution. In fact, he considered an ethic of "timeliness" to make up the "warp and woof" of his foundation (whose assets he insisted should be spent down twenty-five years after his death) and to be "one of the basic prerequisites of worthwhile philanthropy." As he explained in the *Saturday Evening Post*, "The generation which has contributed to the making of a millionaire should also be the one to profit by his generosity. Contemporary needs are the only needs of which we can be certain, and it is those needs that we must seek to serve."[38]

Like Rockefeller, Rosenwald too overcame an aversion to publicity in giving. It stemmed less from his preference for privacy or his humility—although he was, according to his biographer, a "generally self-effacing man"—than from basic apprehensions regarding the philanthropic project itself. He worried that too much attention directed toward his role as a philanthropist would detract from the focus on the responsibilities of communities to contribute to their own social good. He insisted, for instance, that the name of the Chicago museum he founded be changed from the Rosenwald Museum to the Museum of Science and Industry, to ensure that the public would not assume itself absolved from supporting it with their own contributions in the years to come. "If no name is used," he wrote, the building would "belong to the people."[39]

Indeed, Rosenwald was keenly aware of the power of a philanthropist to promote broader voluntaristic engagement through his own reputational leverage. He put this theory into practice for a publicly orchestrated giving campaign in honor of his fiftieth birthday. He gave eight large donations to a number of key institutions with which he was associated—including Associated Jewish Charities of Chicago, the University of Chicago, and the Tuskegee Institute. His desire to promote his theories of responsible giving was not a secondary consideration of this campaign but its primary aim. He chose the beneficiary organizations carefully, not just in terms of the good they could do, but the message about philanthropy they would communicate.[40]

Rosenwald hired the editor of the *Chicago Record-Herald*, H. H. Kohlsaat, to manage the publicity surrounding the gifts, which were announced to the public by his friend, the noted social reformer Jane Addams. Kohlsaat coined a slogan for the campaign: "Give While You Live," which was affixed to materials sent out to newspapers around the nation to announce the gifts. In a cartoon that ran in the *Record-Herald* in August 1912, the slogan is shown on an embroidered sign hanging on a wall, while Rosenwald hands out money to various representatives of his chosen causes. The cartoon is captioned: "Other millionaires please take note—this form of birthday party is not copyrighted."

The campaign seems to have been a success from a public relations perspective; newspapers around the nation picked up the story of his donations, and several Chicago papers ran interviews with the benefactor. He was able to communicate to a local and national audience the two key tenets behind his "Give While You Live" push: the satisfaction that could be derived from giving and the need to do so wisely and expeditiously—when in one's prime. Yet beyond that message, the campaign itself suggested the third strand: the need to publicly promote those ideals to one's contemporaries. The philanthropist's responsibility to "the generation which has contributed to the making of a millionaire" was also educative.[41]

The incorporation of educative duties within an understanding of philanthropic responsibility raises several important questions about how to account for and assess giving in time as well as about the relationship between the ethic's three strands. To what extent does the announcement of a philanthropic pledge, offered to spur greater giving, satisfy the conditions of Giving While Living, even if there is no indication when an actual transfer of significant funds will occur? This issue has been raised most recently by the Giving Pledge, the campaign led by Bill and Melinda Gates and Warren Buffett to convince fellow billionaires to commit more than half their wealth to philanthropy. The Pledge, by design, has captured the attention of the press. It must be made publicly—each signatory offering a testimonial that is posted on the campaign's official website—in order to spread the gospel of large-scale giving into the high-net-worth ranks.[42]

Its organizers have claimed sympathy with the "Giving While Living" movement, yet the pledge makes no distinctions between bequests and *inter vivos* gifts (at its conception, Bill and Melinda Gates had suggested "Give Now" as one of the Pledge's four principles, along with "Give Big," "Give Smart," and "Give to Inequities." But Warren Buffett argued against any prescriptive focus and his view won out).[43] To the extent it makes temporal demands on givers for greater urgency, it only compels billionaires to engage in a public discourse on philanthropy—but not actually to give resources—sooner rather than later. As Melinda Gates explained during an interview with Charlie Rose shortly after the Pledge was unveiled, its founders considered the metric of success for the Pledge to be "getting people earlier in life to *think* about how they are going to give their money back, whether it is during their lifetimes or whether it's at their death." And when Buffett explained to Rose what he hoped the Pledge might achieve in a decade, he pointed to an increase in charitable bequests, as revealed on estate tax forms.[44]

Although Chuck Feeney served as an inspiration to Gates and Buffett, he initially refused to sign the Giving Pledge, in part because it did not satisfy the full tenets of "Giving While Living." And when he finally did sign, he made sure his own testimonial made clear these differences. As he wrote:

> I cannot think of a more personally rewarding and appropriate use of wealth than to give while one is living—to personally devote oneself to meaningful efforts to improve the human condition. More importantly, today's needs are so great and varied that intelligent philanthropic support and positive interventions can have greater value and impact today than if they are delayed when the needs are greater. I urge those who are taking up the Giving Pledge example to invest substantially in philanthropic causes soon and not postpone their giving or personal engagement.[45]

Sean Parker, for his part, has continued to decline to sign the Pledge. In explaining his reasoning, he pointed to an even broader ambiguity within the Giving While Living ethic: the Giving Pledge could be satisfied through intergenerational transfers to foundations, without philanthropic resources directly reaching beneficiaries. In other words, Parker insisted on a direct link between "Giving While Living" and limited-life philanthropy, between individual and institutional giving, that had been forged by Julius Rosenwald and Chuck Feeney but that other disciples of the ethic do not fully endorse.[46]

The rise of donor-advised funds, which, unlike private foundations, do not have any mandated payout rate, makes the question of the timing of when funds actually reach beneficiaries even more pressing in considerations of the Giving While Living ethic. In fact, these considerations can lead to a redefinition of what actually *counts* as giving. In its most recent tally of the philanthropy of the world's billionaires, for instance, *Forbes* decided only to include "out the door" gifts. In an effort to "shine a light on the billionaires who are putting their philanthropic dollars to work," it did not include gifts to foundations or donor-advised funds, or philanthropic pledges, as it has in the past.[47]

This change point to some possible tensions between the various strands of the Giving While Living ethic, as well as some emerging challenges in appraising the extent to which givers have honored them. A philanthropist might be commended for fulfilling the educative imperative of the ethic through a public commitment—say, for instance, by telegraphing via Twitter an intent to make a major donation by asking for advice on how best to disburse philanthropic funds, as Amazon founder Jeff Bezos did in June 2017. Yet that attention might divert attention away from his fulfillment of the other strands, relieving pressure on the philanthropist to give away a greater proportion of his wealth, sooner and with more active engagement.[48]

In fact, many of the philanthropists who have most publicly championed "Giving While Living" have made only modest inroads into directing substantial portions of their wealth to philanthropy. In many cases, because of investment gains, their fortunes have grown *larger* since they began cultivating status as public philanthropists. Bill Gates, for instance, was worth $54 billion when he unveiled the Giving Pledge in 2010; by the end of 2019, his wealth had more than doubled to $110 billion. Warren Buffett's net worth has also nearly doubled during those years, even as he continues to transfer Berkshire Hathaway stock to the Gates Foundation. Mark Zuckerberg's wealth increased by $27.3 billion in 2019. Making good on his pledge to devote 99 percent of his Facebook stock to philanthropic ends will require a massive disbursement of funds, unlike any we've seen in the past, sometime in the indefinite future. Can we say a mega-donor is practicing "Giving While Living" as his or her net worth continues to swell? Does Giving While Living requires some active diminution of personal wealth?[49]

The blurring lines between nonprofit and for-profit enterprise also adds a complication to assessments of "Giving While Living." To what extent can socially conscious investments be considered to honor the Giving While Living mandate? This question joins a host of others that this chapter has shown surrounding the ethic: When within a lifetime must significant philanthropic activity begin in order to satisfy the Giving While Living mandate? What proportion of personal wealth must be committed? Can the process of learning about philanthropy which might prepare the way for disbursement of philanthropic funds at some point in the future be said to initiate the Giving While Living process? To what extent does the cultivation of a public identity as a philanthropist fulfill the ethic? Does it require funds to reach an operating charity, or does transferal to an intermediary institution—a foundation or donor-advised-fund—suffice?

To answer these questions requires weighing the various intertwined strands within the Giving While Living ethic. Yet it is unlikely that a full resolution will arrive for any of them in the coming years. To some extent, that open-endedness might make it more difficult to hold donors accountable to the ethic. Yet indeterminateness could also serve as a fuel, one that propels continued engagement with issues of temporality in the practice of philanthropy. "Giving While Living," in other words, would then continue to serve as a prime guarantor of the salience of "giving in time."

NOTES

1. Sean Parker, "Philanthropy for Hackers," *Wall Street Journal*, June 26, 2015.

2. I received funding from Atlantic Philanthropies to conduct a history of 'Giving While Living,' from which parts of this chapter are taken. See Benjamin Soskis, *The History of the Giving While Living Ethic* (Atlantic Philanthropies, 2017), https://

www.atlanticphilanthropies.org/wp-content/uploads/2017/05/History_of_the_Giving
_While_Living_Ethic.pdf. Charles F. Feeney to Bill Gates, February 3, 2011, http://
givingpledge.org/#charles+f._feeney.

3. Tony Proscio, *Harvest Time for Atlantic Philanthropies 2011–2012: Focus, Exit, and Legacy* (Duke Sanford School of Public Policy, 2012), 1; Charles F. Feeney to Bill Gates, February 3, 2011.

4. Peter Brown, *Through the Eye of a Needle: Wealth, the Fall of Rome, and the Making of Christianity, 350-550 AD* (Princeton, NJ: Princeton University Press, 2012), 62–64; Rob Reich, *Just Giving: Why Philanthropy is Failing Democracy and How it Can Do Better* (Princeton, NJ: Princeton University Press, 2018), 29–35.

5. Brown, *Through the Eye of a Needle*, 439–40.

6. Le Goff quoted in Jenny Kermode, *Medieval Merchants: York, Beverley and Hull in the Later Middle Ages* (Cambridge: Cambridge University Press, 1998), 124.

7. Suzanne Roberts, "Contexts of Charity in the Middle Ages: Religious, Social, and Civic," in *Giving: Western Ideas of Philanthropy*, ed. J. B. Schneewind (Bloomington: Indiana University Press, 1996), 37, 38; Philippa Maddern, "A Market for Charitable Performances?: Bequests to the Poor and the Recipients in Fifteenth-Century Norwich Wills," in *Experiences of Charity, 1250–1650*, ed. Anne Scott (Farnham, England: Ashgate, 2015), 81; Brown, *Through the Eye of a Needle*, 440 (Salvian quote).

8. Donna Andrew, *Philanthropy and Police: London Charity in the Eighteenth Century* (Princeton, NJ: Princeton University Press, 1989), 40, note 80 (quote from Henry Waring); Rhodri Davies, *Public Good by Public Means: How Philanthropy Shapes Britain* (London: Alliance Publishing Trust, 2015), 139, 141; Maddern, "A Market for Charitable Performances," 80.

9. My thanks to Prof. Adam Davis for supplying me with de Vitry's quote. de Vitry's quoted in "Edition of Jacques de Vitry's Sermons to Hospitallers," in *Religion and Medicine in the Middle Ages*, eds. Joseph Ziegler and Peter Biller (Woodbridge, Suffolk, Medieval Press, 2001), 129; Stow quoted in Claire S. Schen, *Charity and Lay Piety in Reformation London, 1500–1620* (Aldershot, England: Ashgate, 2002), 63.

10. Ilana Krausman Ben-Amos, *The Culture of Giving: Informal Support and Gift Exchange in Early Modern England* (Cambridge, UK: Cambridge University Press, 2008), 114.

11. Andrew, *Philanthropy and Police*, 19 (quote), 40, 48, 49.

12. Andrew, *Philanthropy and Police*, 47; Ray D. Madoff, *Immortality and the Law: The Rising Power of the American Dead* (New Haven, CT: Yale University Press, 2010), 91; Evelyn Brody, "Charitable Endowments and the Democratization of Dynasty," *Arizona Law Review* 39 (Fall 1997), 903–5.

13. Christine Leigh Heyrman, "A Model of Christian Charity: The Rich and Poor in New England, 1630–1730" (PhD diss., Yale University, 1977), 42; Boston *Traveller* cited in Sigmund Diamond, *The Reputation of the American Businessman* (Cambridge: Harvard University Press, 1955), 39.

14. Robert Gross, "Giving in America: From Charity to Philanthropy," in *Charity, Philanthropy, and Civility in American History*, eds. Lawrence J. Friedman, L. and Mark D. McGarvie (New York: Cambridge University Press, 2003); Brody,

"Charitable Endowments and the Democratization of Dynasty," 907; Madoff, *Immortality and the Law*, 91.

15. Stanley Katz, Barry Sullivan, and C. Paul Beach, "Legal Change and Legal Autonomy: Charitable Trusts in New York, 1777–1893," *Law and History Review* 3, no. 1 (Spring 1985), 52; S.F.D. Jr., "Enforcement of Charitable Trusts in America," 456–58; Benjamin Soskis, "The Problem of Charity in Industrial America," (PhD diss., Columbia University, 2010), 274–75.

16. Joseph Frazier Wall, *Andrew Carnegie* (New York: Oxford University Press, 1970), 730, 790, 812 (quote), Andrew Carnegie, "The Gospel of Wealth," in Andrew Carnegie, *The "Gospel of Wealth" Essays and Other Writings*, ed. David Nasaw (New York: Penguin, 2006), 1, 12.

17. Carnegie, "Gospel of Wealth," 12; Diamond, *Reputation of the American Businessman*, 10–12.

18. Conor O'Clery, *The Billionaire Who Wasn't: How Chuck Feeney Secretly Made and Gave Away a Fortune* (New York: Public Affairs, 2013), 99, 104, 122, 170.

19. Matthew Bishop and Michael Green, *Philanthrocapitalism: How the Rich Can Save the World* (New York: Bloomsbury Press, 2008), 13; Darren Walker, *From Generosity to Justice: A New Gospel of Wealth* (New York: Ford Foundation, 2019).

20. Wall, *Andrew Carnegie*, 1042–43; David Nasaw, *Andrew Carnegie* (New York: Penguin Press, 2006), 801.

21. Carnegie quoted in Robert Sidney Martin, "Introduction," in *Carnegie Denied: Communities Rejecting Carnegie Library Construction Grants, 1898–1925*, ed. Robert Sidney Martin (Westport, CT: Greenwood Press, 1993), vii.

22. As late as 1999, the philanthropy scholar Peter Frumkin, writing on a recent $1 billion gift from the Gates Foundation to support science scholarships for minority college students, noted, "Philanthropy has become a controversial matter these days, particularly when donors make their own decisions about how and when to spend their money rather than leaving those details to professionals in the foundations they have set up." Peter Frumkin, "He Who's Got it Gets to Give it," *Washington Post*, October 3, 1999. Waldemar A. Nielsen, *The Golden Donors: A New Anatomy of the Great Foundations* (New York: E.P, Dutton, 1985), 18, 19; Peter Elkind, "The Man Who Sold Silicon Valley on Giving," *Fortune*, November 27, 2000, https://fortune.com/2016/08/24/peter-hero-silicon-valley-giving/.

23. The energy trader John Arnold, for instance, retired from finance at age thirty-eight to devote himself to philanthropy. As *Wired* reported, "Arnold has said that the first phase of his life was '100 percent trying to make money' and that it's now '100 percent trying to do good.'" Sam Apple, "John Arnold Made a Fortune at Enron. Now He's Declared War on Bad Science," *Wired*, January 22, 2017, https://www.wired.com/2017/01/john-arnold-waging-war-on-bad-science/. For more on Arnold's advocacy of the Giving While Living ethic, see Arnold, "Put a Stake in 'Zombie Charity.' Philanthropy is for the Living," *Chronicle of Philanthropy*, September 4, 2019, https://www.philanthropy.com/article/Put-a-Stake-in-Zombie/247026?cid=cpfd_home. Soskis, "The Problem of Charity in Industrial America," 202; Jonathan Levy, "Altruism and the Origins of Nonprofit Philanthropy," in *Philanthropy in*

Democratic Societies, eds. Rob Reich, Chiara Cordelli and Lucy Bernholtz (Chicago: University of Chicago Press, 2016), 36.

24. Andrew Carnegie, "The Advantages of Poverty," in *"Gospel of Wealth" Essays*, 50; Duke quoted in Waldemar A. Nielsen, *The Big Foundations* (New York: Columbia University Press, 1972), 183.

25. See William MacAskill's chapter in this volume for a further elaboration of this argument. Carol Loomis, "Warren Buffett Gives It Away," *Fortune*, July 13, 2006, http://archive.fortune.com/magazines/fortune/fortune_archive/2006/07/10 /8380864/index.htm.

26. For this attitude toward Jobs, see, for instance, Dan Pallotta, "Steve Jobs, World's Greatest Philanthropist," *Harvard Business Review*, September 2, 2011, https://hbr.org/2011/09/steve-jobs-worlds-greatest-phi.html. John D. Rockefeller, *Random Reminiscences of Men and Events* (New York: Doubleday, Page & Co., 1909), 75, 142; Diamond, *Reputation of the American Businessman*, 61.

27. Wealth-X and Arton Capital, *Philanthropy Report 2015*, http://www.wealthx .com/wp-content/uploads/2015/12/Wealth-X-Arton-Capital-Philanthropy-Report -2015.pdf; email from Maria Di Mento, January 9, 2022.

28. "Giving While Living" while still at the helm of a public company does present some challenges for donors who hope to contribute a large number of shares to philanthropy without relinquishing a controlling stake in the company. See, for instance, Erin Griffith, "Mark Zuckerberg Controls Facebook and He Intends to Keep It That Way," *Fortune*, April 27, 2016, http://fortune.com/2016/04/27/zuckerberg-facebook -control; Theodore Schleifer, "The Big Decision before Elon Musk, Now the Richest Person in the World," *Vox*, January 22, 2021, https://www.vox.com/recode/22221173 /elon-musk-tesla-foundation-philanthropy-wealthiest-person. Hank Tucker, "15 Under 40: The Youngest Billionaires on the 2021 Forbes 400," Forbes.com, October 5, 2021, https://www.forbes.com/sites/hanktucker/2021/10/05/15-under-40 -the-youngest-billionaires-on-the-2021-forbes-400; Bishop and Green, *Philanthrocapitalism*, 16, 269; UBS/PWC 2015 Billionaires Report, "Billionaires: Master Architects of Great Wealth and Lasting Legacies," 6.

29. For a statement that such a change, along with the spreading popularity of limited-life philanthropy, is part of "a seismic shift in philanthropic practice," see Joel L. Fleishman, *Putting Wealth to Work: Philanthropy for Today or Investing for Tomorrow* (New York: PublicAffairs, 2017), xix.

30. Some of the material in this section first appeared in the blog post, Benjamin Soskis, "To be Young, Rich, and Philanthropic," *HistPhil*, January 11, 2016. David Callahan, "How Does an Emerging 'Army' of Tech Donors Think? Ask This Guy," *Inside Philanthropy*, December 14, 2015, http://www.insidephilanthropy.com/home /2015/12/14/how-does-an-emerging-army-of-tech-donors-think-ask-this-guy.html.

31. Parker, "Philanthropy for Hackers." *Wall Street Journal*, June 26, 2015; Maria Di Mento, "Sean Parker Outlines Big Plans for His $600-million Foundation," *Chronicle of Philanthropy*, June 23, 2015; Soskis, "To Be Young, Rich, and Philanthropic."

32. Robert Safian, "The Amazing Ascent of Priscilla Chan," *Quartz*, October 1, 2018, https://qz.com/1402697/the-amazing-ascent-of-priscilla-chan/; Vindu Goel and

Nick Wingfield, "Mark Zuckerberg Vows to Donate 99% of His Facebook Shares for Charity," *New York Times*, December 1, 2015.

33. Mark Zuckerberg, "A Letter to Our Daughter," Facebook post, December 1, 2015, accessed at https://www.facebook.com/notes/mark-zuckerberg/a-letter-to -our-daughter/10153375081581634/; Megan O'Neil, "Chan Responds to Questions About Plans for Facebook Fortune," *Chronicle of Philanthropy*, December 22, 2015.

34. Gates on *Charlie Rose*, June 5, 2010; Kessler quoted in *Turning Passion into Action: Giving While Living* (Atlantic Philanthropies, 2010), 5, https://www.atlanti cphilanthropies.org/wp-content/uploads/2010/06/GWL_050510_1723.pdf; Michael J. de la Merced, "Sean Parker Seeks a New Approach to Charity," *New York Times*, June 23, 2015; Parker, "Philanthropy for Hackers."

35. Mark Zuckerberg, "A Letter to Our Daughter"; Merced, "Sean Parker Seeks a New Approach to Charity"; Dale Russakoff, "Mark Zuckerberg Tried Philanthropy Before—and Stumbled. Here's What He Learned," *Post Everything*, December 7, 2015, https://www.washingtonpost.com/posteverything/wp/2015/12/07/mark-zuck-erberg-tried-philanthropy-before-and-stumbled-heres-what-he-learned.

36. Rockefeller, *Random Reminiscences*, 156; Frederick Taylor Gates, *Chapters in My Life* (New York: The Free Press, 1977), 209; Soskis, "Problem of Charity in Industrial America," 278–79, 323–24, 333.

37. Bishop Henry Potter, "The Gospel for Wealth," *North American Review* 152, no. 414 (May 1891), 514.

38. Peter M. Ascoli, *Julius Rosenwald: The Man Who Built Sears, Roebuck and Advanced the Cause of Black Education in the American South* (Bloomington: Indiana University Press, 2006), 57, 134, 142, 299, 376; Julius Rosenwald, "The Burden of Wealth," *Saturday Evening Post* (January 5, 1929), 12.

39. Ascoli, *Julius Rosenwald*, 131, 139, 270 (quote), 328.

40. Ascoli, *Julius Rosenwald*, 123, 213.

41. Ascoli, *Julius Rosenwald*, 131, 132 (copy of cartoon).

42. See https://givingpledge.org/.

43. Marc Gunter and Drew Lindsay, "Has the Giving Pledge Changed Giving?" *The Chronicle of Philanthropy*, June 4, 2019.

44. *Charlie Rose*, June 5, 2010 (italics my own).

45. Charles F. Feeney to Bill Gates, February 3, 2011.

46. Bill and Melinda Gates have announced that their foundation will close its doors twenty years after their deaths. Bill and Melinda Gates Foundation, "Who We Are: Foundation Trust." https://www.gatesfoundation.org/who-we-are/general-infor-mation/financials/foundation-trust. Di Mento, "Sean Parker Outlines Big Plans."

47. Jennifer Wang, "The New Forbes Philanthropy Score: How We Ranked Each Forbes 400 Billionaire Based on Their Giving," *Forbes*, September 8, 2020.

48. *New York Times*, June 15, 2017; Benjamin Soskis, "The Way Jeff Bezos Unveiled His $10 Billion Announcement Maximized Publicity and Avoided Scrutiny. And That's a Problem," *Chronicle of Philanthropy*, February 26, 2020.

49. David Callahan, "The Richest Americans are Sitting on $4 Trillion. How can they be Spurred to Give More of It Away?" *Inside Philanthropy*, December 4, 2018, https://www.insidephilanthropy.com/home/2018/12/4/the-richest-americans-are

-sitting-on-4-trillion-how-can-they-be-spurred-to-give-more-of-it-away; Tom Metcalf, "Bill Gates Is Once Again the Richest Person in the World," *Forbes.com*, November 16, 2019, https://fortune.com/2019/11/16/bill-gates-net-worth-richest-person-in-the -world-jeff-bezos/; Adam K. Raymond, "The World's 500 Richest People Increased Their Wealth by $1.2 Trillion in 2019," (New York Magazine) *Intelligencer*, December 27, 2019, http://nymag.com/intelligencer/2019/12/worlds-500-richest-upped -wealth-by-usd1-2-trillion-in-2019.html.

Chapter 3

Against Perpetuity

Rob Reich

There is no fact in history which posterity will find it more difficult to understand, than that the idea of perpetuity, and that of any of the contrivances of man, should have been coupled together in any sane mind.

—John Stuart Mill

For most people, the time horizon of an individual act of philanthropy is short. We donate money to an organization of our choosing, and the transfer of funds immediately fulfills our philanthropic purpose. Rather than directing funds to an existing organization, however, some people—in practice, almost always the wealthy—choose to create a new entity of their own. They create a charitable trust or a philanthropic foundation. The typical mechanism is to endow the new entity with funds and to confer upon it a charitable purpose.

The creation of charitable trusts and philanthropic foundations is facilitated by laws across many societies that do not merely permit but actively encourage the creation of such entities through tax concessions and a set of special permissions that do not typically attach to other corporate forms. These special permissions include setting the charitable purpose of the new philanthropic entity, which a board of trustees is legally bound to uphold, harnessing the assets to only those charitable purposes set by the donor. And most importantly, and peculiarly, setting a perpetual time horizon for the new entity. Charitable trusts and philanthropic foundations are legal creatures that are typically designed to last forever.

This is a description of charity law as it has long existed. Over the past generation, however, the rise of wealth and income inequality has produced many more millionaires and billionaires, and this in turn has stimulated a boom in the creation of foundations. We now see growing scrutiny of both philanthropists and the laws that undergird their activity. In this chapter, I focus attention on a series of questions that cut to the heart of institutional philanthropy. Should a government be permitted to interfere with a philanthropic organization's purpose? Should it be allowed to appropriate a foundations' assets and redirect them to causes not intended by the original donor? And should a charitable trust or philanthropic entity be designed to last in perpetuity?

The questions may strike contemporary readers as settled, yet they weren't always. When John D. Rockefeller asked the US Congress in the 1910s to charter the creation of the Rockefeller Foundation, for example, he encountered strident criticism at the notion that a wealthy person's philanthropic foundation should be welcomed and celebrated as a useful contribution to a democratic society. Rockefeller offered in response a series of concessions that would give the public a governance role in the foundation and that would require it to spend down its assets no later than a century after its creation, or within five generations. These concessions were meant to allay anxiety about the democracy-corrupting influence of a large, unaccountable, and everlasting private foundation. But they still were not enough for the US Congress, which refused to pass a law that would incorporate the Rockefeller Foundation. Rockefeller returned to his home state, where the New York legislature granted approval without any of his proposed concessions to the public interest. Counterfactual history is always an effort at speculation, but I think it is reasonable to suggest that the people's representatives in Washington, DC lost a chance to control the world's largest philanthropy. Instead, Rockefeller's success at chartering his foundation in New York without any of the public governance and time limitations that he had been willing to accept in discussion with the US Congress set in motion the legal framework for the unaccountable and perpetual private family foundation that is still the standard a century later.[1]

The default legal time horizon for the establishment of a philanthropic foundation is perpetuity—for the entity and the charitable purpose of the founder to extend indefinitely without oversight. True, donors can opt to spend down the principal or specify a spend-out date if they wish, but the vast majority of foundations are created with a legal direction not merely to outlive the donor but to exist forever. A recent report pegs the figure at roughly 70 percent of all foundations.[2] "In perpetuity" is often seen as a beneficial aspect, as if the founder's good intentions deserve to be honored forever and as if perpetuity redounds to society's benefit as well. And some also believe that an invitation to see one's charitable desires last forever constitutes an invitation to immortality, coaxing out of wealthy people more money for philanthropy than they might otherwise give.

John Stuart Mill would beg to differ on all counts, and his nineteenth-century arguments against perpetuity deserve renewed appreciation. Mill sees the important political dimensions of philanthropy, and in understanding Mill, we can build a strong argument in our current era for rejecting perpetual time horizons.

Finding it "so obvious" that he could scarcely conceive how any "earnest inquirer" could think otherwise, Mill wrote that the intentions of the endowment's founder should be legally protected for his lifetime and perhaps a short duration thereafter. But no foundation should have its purpose fixed forever.

Mill was not unique. There is no shortage of arguments about why perpetual existence of a charitable entity and conferring power upon the dead hand of donors is a problem.[3] The French Enlightenment thinker Anne-Robert Turgot wrote a well-known essay in 1756 for the famous *Encyclopaedie* of Diderot, arguing that perpetual foundations were massively inefficient and, over time, grossly ineffective and vainglorious vehicles for social improvement. And Enlightenment thinker *par excellence*, Immanuel Kant, echoed Turgot's conclusions in 1797: "Even perpetual foundations for the poor, and educational institutions, cannot be founded in perpetuity and be a perpetual encumbrance upon the land because they have a certain character specified by the founder in accordance with his ideas; instead the state must be free to adapt them to the needs of the time."[4] No foundation, even those dedicated to admirable ends and constituted by well-intentioned donors, should live forever.

In giving particular attention to John Stuart Mill's arguments, we gain special insight into the connection between the laws that govern philanthropic entities and social well-being. Mill, the great utilitarian and defender of individual liberty, affords us reason to see why perpetuity is contrary to both social improvement and a proper understanding of individual liberty.

Moreover, in understanding what's wrong with perpetuity, we can understand better how public policy can structure philanthropy to support rather than subvert democratic governance. In previous work, I argue that the legal form of the foundation is defensible only when philanthropic assets are directed for long-term social experimentation.[5] Rockefeller's proposal to Congress that the life span of his foundation be capped at five generations is a sufficiently long horizon in which to engage in the important, democracy-supporting work of discovery. But perpetuity is too long a time horizon—indeed, it is injurious to the social utility of a foundation. The arguments of Mill help to show why.

Mill wrote three essays about foundations over the course of thirty years in the mid-nineteenth century. His most significant statement on the subject, "Corporation and Church Property," was published in 1833 in a periodical called *The Jurist*.[6] It was also issued as an anonymous pamphlet in the same year under the more telling title "Corporation and Church Property Resumable by the State."

His framework helps us understand how a liberal democratic state should treat philanthropic endowments established by the wealthy or corporate entities. Mill was deeply critical of the actual operation of foundations around him, especially the church, writing that foundations were among the "grossest and most conspicuous of the familiar abuses of the time." Yet, in his writing, he also left room for a principled defense of their existence. His general argument was that endowments should be permitted, in some cases even celebrated, but that they should never be perpetual and that the state must always retain the right to intervene in a philanthropic endowment. His baseline conclusion: "All endowments are national property, which the government may and ought to control."[7]

Mill rejects the eternal rights of founders and funders, as well as claims that the state, by interfering with a foundation, is violating property rights. The dead have no property rights, Mill claims.

It is worth examining Mill's arguments in some detail, not merely for the clarity with which he sets out his case but for the refreshing lack of reverence or sentiment he has for philanthropy. Mill sings no hymns of praise to the wisdom of wealthy men or to the public spirit of philanthropic entities. What, Mill asks, are the rights and duties of a legislature with respect to endowments and foundations? His answer is unambiguous. There is "no moral hindrance" to a legislature in interfering with endowments, even if such interference amounts to "a total change in their purposes."[8] His exposition is philosophical, by which I mean he is chiefly concerned with the moral principles at stake that make the inquiry general. But he admits to a practical motivation, too: a "most pressing" need for the public and the British Parliament to decide what may and should be done with the property of the church and other public corporations.

There is therefore a question of political ethics: Would state control over foundations amount to a violation of liberty, property, and first principles of justice? There is also a practical question, since permanent endowments already exist, and therefore Mill asks under what circumstances, and to what end, a government might assert control over a foundation. The practical question is only worth addressing if the answer to the philosophical question is to defend state control over foundations. So Mill focuses the lion's share of his attention on the general and philosophical question.

In so doing, Mill sets aside consideration of the projects and motives of individual philanthropists. If foundations as a class are to be found objectionable, it should not be on the grounds that one dislikes or disapproves of the particular interests of a donor. Let any person have an opinion on any foundation, and yet separate from the mind, says Mill, all impression or evaluation of the character of the donor or the purposes of the endowment. "We have our opinion, like other people, on the merits or demerits of the clergy, and other holders of endowments. We shall endeavor to forget that we have any."[9]

Having established the clear ground of principle on which to proceed, Mill begins his inquiry by taking note of the "exceedingly multifarious" purposes for which foundations have in many different countries been created. Schools, hospitals, orphanages, and almshouses, monasteries and universities, corporations local and national in scope, funded by money or real estate—all have been part of the tradition of foundations that direct what had once been the private assets of an individual to a public purpose in perpetuity. Should it ever be permitted, Mill asks, for the government to interfere with this purpose or to appropriate the foundations' assets?

His answer is immediate and blunt. Finding it "so obvious" that he can scarcely conceive how any "earnest inquirer" could think otherwise,[10] Mill asserts that the founder's intentions in establishing an endowment should be legally protected only for his lifetime and perhaps a very short duration thereafter. No foundation should have its purpose fixed forever.

Mill argues that circumstances change, societies evolve, old needs dissipate and new needs arise, and no founder could ever be so wise as to infallibly predict the future. To permit foundations to exist in perpetuity amounts to making "the dead judges of the exigencies of the living." "Under the guise of fulfilling a bequest" a foundation transforms a "dead man's intentions for a single day" into a "rule for subsequent centuries."[11] Summoning all his rhetorical powers to signal the strength of his conviction, Mill concludes:

> There is no fact in history which posterity will find it more difficult to understand, than that the idea of perpetuity, and that of any of the contrivances of man, should have been coupled together in any sane mind: that it has been believed, nay, clung to as sacred truth, and has formed part of the creed of whole nations, that a signification of the will of a man, ages ago, could impose upon all mankind now and for ever an obligation of obeying him:—that, in the beginning of the nineteenth century, it was not permitted to question this doctrine without opprobrium.[12]

Mill rejects the eternal rights of founders and funders and sweeps aside any claim that by interfering with a foundation, the state is engaging in a violation of property rights. The dead have no property rights, Mill claims. Neither do the trustees of a foundation, who serve as successors to the initial founder and are obliged to carry out the founder's purposes. To the extent there is any property interest, Mill says the property belongs to the intended beneficiaries of the endowment, the people for whom the foundation had been created. It is therefore no crime "to disobey a man's injunctions who has been dead five hundred years."[13]

Take, as an example, the state reclaiming church land or assets. To the objection that Mill's argument amounts to a defense of robbing the church, he replies that it is not the clergy but the congregants who own the church's endowments, and that it is permissible for the state to act on behalf of these congregants to redirect the purposes of the endowment, if need be, to their own benefit. Mill is scoring some easy points here, and only later does he confront the real legal obstacle and objection to his position. That objection is that the church is a corporation, and foundations of many kinds have been incorporated by the state. Corporations are legal personifications, they can possess property, and therefore it is the church as a corporate body that would be robbed were the state to expropriate any church endowment and redirect it to some ostensibly more socially useful purpose. This line of reasoning would apply as much today as it did in Mill's time. Mill concedes the point, namely that the church is a corporate body with legal claims of personhood and ownership. His reply is straightforward, a paradigmatic expression of Mill's Socratic impulse: "Because the law is so, does it follow that it ought to be? Or that it must remain protected against amendment?" Mill's response, in effect, is that the law is morally bad and should be changed. Neither the dead nor corporate entities should be entitled to any rights, or at least rights of the same kind of significance that attach to the living. Mill announces here a striking claim: "The only moral duties which we are conscious of, are towards living beings, either present or to come; who can be in some way better for what we do or forbear." Indeed, Mill says he would not be troubled at all should a government push aside the alleged rights of founders, of trustees, or of corporate bodies. To the contrary, he would "sleep with an untroubled conscience the sleep of the just; a sleep which the groans of no plundered abstractions are loud enough to disturb."[14]

Mill concludes by explaining under what circumstances and for what purposes the government ought to intervene in a perpetual endowment. He offers two criteria, first, that intervention is warranted only for purposes of social utility; and second, that when a government intervenes, it should do so by hewing as closely as possible to the intentions of the founder. Mill is concerned not to authorize state action that would permit confiscation of endowments for any purpose at all, especially for purposes that might tempt legislators looking for means to pay off state debts or diminish burdens of taxation more generally. These criteria, and Mill's discussion of them, are less significant for my purposes than is his reasoning against perpetual foundations and his endorsement of time-limited foundations that serve to support and enhance democratic government. This latter aspect of Mill's argument is especially important, for it provides an example of how the rules and norms that structure philanthropy can render its activities supportive of democratic ideals.

So Mill provides us with a clear argument against perpetuity as the time horizon for philanthropic entities. What policy implication does this have for foundations and trusts today? One answer is obvious: no foundation should be permitted to exist in perpetuity when tethered by law to the donor's mission or purpose. The broader the philanthropic purpose, the broader the ability of successive foundation trustees to interpret the mission for current social conditions. The narrower the philanthropic purpose, the more constrained the ability of such trustees to adapt. So the law should move in two directions: it should abolish perpetuity for philanthropic foundations, and it should permit longer time horizons for philanthropic entities that have a general rather than narrow purpose. We should not be overly prescriptive, however. No argument on principle can specify the optimal life span of a foundation; the relevant consideration here is that foundations have an incentive structure that encourages work on a time horizon longer than that of other social institutions such as the marketplace or public agencies in a democratic government.

This last remark about evaluating the role philanthropic assets play in comparison to capital assets in the marketplace and public assets in government agencies is important. It opens the path to seeing how Mill's argument results not just in a negative conclusion about perpetuity. It allows us to see the positive case for foundations, the important role they can play—when not perpetual and with appropriate democratic oversight—in the healthy functioning of democratic society and social betterment for all people.

In other words, a society that fosters philanthropic endowments in a particular manner can improve upon ordinary democratic governance. Mill, in fact, offers three distinct reasons why foundations, especially educational and cultural endowments, directed solely by the preferred projects of donors, *so long as their preferences are not guaranteed in perpetuity*, can play a salutary social role.

First, governments are fallible, and though it is important for the state to undertake its own projects and to express its preferences about the provision of various goods, it should not block or deter others from attempting to provide the same goods in different ways or different goods altogether. "A government," Mill says, "when properly constituted, should be allowed the greatest possible facilities for what itself deems good; but the smallest for preventing the good which may chance to come from elsewhere."[15]

Second, Mill points out that under a democratic government, "the opinion of the majority gives the law." Therefore, permitting the creation of time-limited foundations affords minority opinions a voice and a public hearing.

It permits minorities a mechanism to produce the kinds of public goods that they cannot manage to convince a majority to authorize through elected representatives. In so doing, minorities can attempt to persuade the majority and shift the provision of their preferred goods to the public purse. Even if they fail in persuading others, Mill says they are still a "convenient mode of providing for the support of establishments which are interesting only to a peculiar class, and for which, therefore, it might be improper to tax all the members of the community."[16]

Mill provides here a forerunner of a familiar economic argument that considers philanthropic foundations as an important vehicle for partially decentralizing the process of producing public goods and diminishing government orthodoxy in the definition of public goods. In a diverse democracy, there will be heterogenous preferences about what kinds of goods to supply through the direct expenditure of tax dollars. Foundations, powered by the idiosyncratic preferences of their donors and free from the accountability logic of the market and democratic state, can help to provide, in the aggregate, a welcome pluralism that helps to create an ever-evolving, contestatory, and diverse arena of civil society. Such decentralization tempers government orthodoxy in a democracy.

This should strike the reader as a familiar case. It represents, in many respects, the actual law in the United States today. In a 1983 US Supreme Court opinion, Justice Lewis Powell rejected the idea that the primary function of a tax-exempt organization is to enact only government-approved policies. For Powell, the provision of tax subsidies for nonprofits, including presumably foundations, "is one indispensable means of limiting the influence of government orthodoxy on important areas of community life."[17]

Third, democratic states that permit the creation of foundations undertake what we could call Millian "experiments in living." It might be the case that particular foundations are genuinely eccentric and contribute little, if anything, to the greater part of the public. With a multi-generational, but not perpetual, life span, it is the activities of foundations in the aggregate, however, that command democratic attention. When private individuals can publicly express their individual, even idiosyncratic views about the public interest not merely through their voices but through their wallets, it not only makes space for minority views, but can also be an important mechanism of social progress. Private foundations in the aggregate can supply variety, diversity, and experimentation in a never-ending conversation and contestation about what counts as a public good or a worthy social service. Mill issues a ringing defense of such endowments: "What is called tampering by private persons with great public interests . . . means trying to do with money of their own something that shall promote the same objects better. . . . It is healthy rivalry."[18]

But, one might ask, wouldn't a perpetual life span guarantee even more philanthropic experiments, more diversity in philanthropic purpose? In certain respects, this is true, if the only metric of consequence was diverse experimentation. But Mill did not see experimentation as the ultimate good to promote. Ever the utilitarian, experimentation is just an instrument for social improvement. So the task is to balance donor-directed diversity in philanthropic experiments alongside the authority of the government to intervene in donor-directed endowments that have outlasted their utility.

Are foundations in the United States today fulfilling their role in a democratic society? A rigorous assessment is beyond the scope of my argument, but skepticism is certainly warranted. For starters, the vast majority of philanthropic endowments are set up in perpetuity. True, some prominent large foundations have declared a commitment to spending out, such as the Bill and Melinda Gates Foundation, the Raikes Family Foundation, and Chuck Feeney's Atlantic Philanthropies, the latter of which has already spent out. Time-limited endowments are growing in popularity, perhaps stimulated by Feeney's encouragement of "giving while living." (See chapter 11). However popular such sentiment may be, the better path would be to avoid reliance on donor inclination to spend out and simply to change the law to make spending-out the default legal arrangement. Following Mill's arguments, the rules that structure philanthropy should militate against perpetuity and diminish the power of the dead over the living, not merely because the dead should have no right to control the living but also because the dead hand of the donor is less likely to be intelligently responsive to social problem-solving.

What's more, the time horizon of philanthropy is connected to the legitimacy of philanthropic activity in a democratic society. Do the endowments that fuel foundation grant-making need to be perpetual? Does democracy need the founder's intent to be honored in perpetuity? On these matters, I side with John Stuart Mill in believing that perpetuity and legally guaranteed donor control are injurious to democracy and erect foundations as unaccountable plutocratic forms of power.

No argument on principle can specify the optimal life span of a foundation; the relevant consideration here is that it has an incentive structure that encourages work on a time horizon longer than that of other social institutions. What Rockefeller's advisers proposed to Congress in 1911, that the life span of a foundation be capped at one hundred years, or five generations, seems to me a more-than-adequate horizon in which to engage in the important, democracy-supporting work of social experimentation.

Beyond the issue of perpetuity, the sad reality, according to many prominent foundation observers, including those who are friends of foundations, is that foundations are underperforming when measured on almost any yardstick of success. They are certainly underperforming if measured by the standard of funding risk-taking social experimentation. In 1949, Edwin Embree, who had served as the head of the Rosenwald Fund, which was the first foundation to spend down on the wishes of its founder, wrote an article for *Harper's Magazine* called "Timid Billions," concluding that, despite obvious social problems and ample philanthropic assets, there was "an ominous absence of that social pioneering that is the essential business of foundations." More recently, Gara LaMarche, who spent more than fifteen years at two of the world's largest foundations (the Atlantic Philanthropies and the Open Society Institute), concluded that foundations tend to be risk-averse, rather than risk-taking. "Courageous risk taking is not what most people associate with foundations," he writes in *Boston Review*, "whose boards and senior leadership are often dominated by establishment types. If tax preference is meant primarily to encourage boldness, it doesn't seem to be working." Joel Fleishman, the former director of the Atlantic Philanthropies and author of *The Foundation: A Great American Secret*, thinks that foundations would do their work better if they were more transparent and risk-taking. Others, such as Waldemar Nielsen, a prominent author on the subject of philanthropy in the 1970s and 1980s, have challenged foundations' support for innovation, arguing that they are more frequently on the "trailing edge, not the cutting edge, of change."

If these critics are correct, then so much the worse for the foundations, and so much the worse for the distinctive institutional privileges that currently attach to them, including the permission to live forever. Rather than exhorting philanthropists to do better, to give while living, my aim here is to show why changes in the law are essential, and nowhere more essential than in setting the time horizons for philanthropy. The distinctive advantage of philanthropic assets in a foundation is their capacity to go long, to work beyond the short time horizons of the marketplace and public institutions of democratic government. But a long time horizon should not be a perpetual time horizon, for all the reasons offered more than a century ago by John Stuart Mill.[19]

NOTES

1. For more details, see Reich, *Just Giving*; and Eric John Abrahamson, Sam Hurst, and Barbara Shubinski, *Democracy and Philanthropy: The Rockefeller Foundation and the American Experiment* (New York: Rockefeller Foundation, 2013).

2. Ruth McCambridge, "More Foundations Are Opting Out of Perpetuity—So What?" *Nonprofit Quarterly*, January 21, 2020, https://nonprofitquarterly.org/more -foundations-are-opting-out-of-perpetuity-so-what/.

3. See Ray Madoff, *Immortality and the Law: The Rising Power of the American Dead* (New Haven, CT: Yale University Press, 2010).

4. Immanuel Kant, "The Metaphysics of Morals," in *Practical Philosophy: The Cambridge Edition of the Works of Immanuel Kant*, trans. and ed. Mary Gregor (New York: Cambridge University Press, 1996), 503.

5. Reich, *Just Giving*.

6. J.S. Mill, "Corporate and Church Property," in *The Collected Works of John Stuart Mill, Vol. IV—Essays on Economics and Society Part IV*, ed. J. M. Robson (Toronto: University of Toronto Press, 1963–1991); J.S. Mill, "Educational Endowments," in "Report on Commissions on Education in Schools in England, Not Comprised within Her Majesty's Two Recent Commissions on Popular Education and Public Schools," *Parliamentary Papers* 28, p. 2 (1867–1868), 67–72; J.S. Mill, "Endowments," *Fortnightly Review* (April 1869), 377–90.

7. J.S. Mill, *Autobiography* (London: Longmans, Greer, Reader and Dyer, 1873), 128.

8. Mill, "Corporate and Church Property," 189–89.

9. Mill, "Corporate and Church Property," 189.

10. Mill, "Corporate and Church Property," 190.

11. Mill, "Corporate and Church Property," 191.

12. Mill, "Corporate and Church Property," 191. It is an argument that echoes that of Thomas Jefferson: *"That our creator made earth for use of the living, and not of the dead; that those who exist not can have no use nor rights in it, no authority or power over it."* Thomas Jefferson, "Letter to James Madison," September 6, 1789, in *The Works of Thomas Jefferson*, vol. 6., Federal Edition (New York and London: G.P. Putnam's Sons, 1904–1905).

13. Mill, "Corporate and Church Property," 191.

14. Mill, "Corporate and Church Property," 198.

15. Mill, "Corporate and Church Property," 203.

16. Mill, "Corporate and Church Property," 204.

17. 461 US 574 *Bob Jones University v. United States* (1983). A version of the argument can also be seen in remarks made by an early president of the Carnegie Corporation, Frederick Keppel, who wrote in 1930, "Clearly, there is the greatest variety alike in the size, the purpose, the organization, the program, and the geographical range of American foundations; we are far from agreement as to the most useful form or organization or as to the most fruitful type of program. But all this is, of course, as it should be, since the ultimate basis of the utility of the foundation as an instrument of progress will probably rest upon this very diversity." Frederick Keppel, *The Foundation: Its Place in American Life* (New York: MacMillan, 1930), 12.

18. J. S. Mill, "Endowments," *The Collected Works of John Stuart Mill, Vol. IV—Essays on Economics and Society Part V*; 1869, 177.

19. Portions of this chapter are adapted from Rob Reich, *Just Giving: Why Philanthropy is Failing Democracy and How It Can Do Better* (Princeton, NJ: Princeton University Press, 2018).

Chapter 4

Endowed for Eternity

*American Jewish Philanthropy in Time**

Lila Corwin Berman

With few exceptions, the American nonprofit sector views endowment -building as an unmitigated good. Endowments balance puritanical virtue with capitalist drive, solicitude for the needs of the present with a regard for those of the future. They stand for security, stability, and foresight, and with every gain in their investments, they serve as proof that the bounties of market capitalism can be harnessed to serve the public good, in due time. Yet beyond their ability to interlace restraint with high growth potential, endowments, most importantly, dangle the promise of immortality.[1]

In each quest to find an elixir for eternal life, we find a record of how individuals, communities, and societies imagine their futures. In the case of charitable endowments, which grew in frequency and valuation in the decades after World War II, Americans envisioned their futures through the ownership and deployment of capital. As a vehicle that combines private interests with public governance, through the subsidies and regulations enacted upon philanthropy by the state, charitable endowments represent a balance between democracy and capitalism enacted not only at any given moment but also with respect to time itself. Today's private gains could be directed toward tomorrow's public good.

* My gratitude to the *American Historical Review* and Oxford University Press for granting me permission to reprint sections from my article "How Americans Give: The Financialization of American Jewish Philanthropy," *American Historical Review* 122, no. 5 (Dec 2017): 1459–89. Also, I owe thanks to Benjamin Soskis for helping to wrestle this chapter into shape, and ongoing appreciation to Ray Madoff for crafting and convening crucial conversations about American philanthropy. For an extended analysis of many of the themes and topics discussed in this chapter, see Lila Corwin Berman, *The American Jewish Philanthropic Complex: The History of a Multibillion-Dollar Institution* (Princeton, NJ: Princeton University, 2020).

This chapter traces the transformations that led to the expansion of charitable endowments after World War II through an exploration of when, why, and how American Jewish institutions embraced endowment as the crux of their philanthropic activism. It argues that only in the decades following World War II did Jewish leaders start to accept endowment—premised upon the goals of charitable wealth accumulation and perpetuity—as a valuable philanthropic strategy. The confluence of developments in the American political economy, rendered through tax policy and shifting conceptions of the state, and the Jewish political economy, tied to historically shaped concerns about Jewish survival, made endowment attractive to American Jews. In drawing attention to the twentieth-century formation of Jewish endowment strategies, we can apprehend the historical roots of contests between philanthropic accumulation and philanthropic distribution and understand how endowment practices addressed questions about power, capital, and the public good through a changed understanding of the nature of time itself.

In order to understand the striking growth in endowment-building that occurred within American Jewish philanthropy and that echoed across other philanthropic entities in the post–World War II years, we first must map out broad shifts in the American state. Historians describe the rise of the interventionist state, slowly appearing in Progressive era reform efforts and, then, flourishing with the passage of New Deal legislation, followed by wartime measures, and postwar recovery efforts. Across the first half of the twentieth century, the American state intruded into average people's lives in unprecedented ways, provisioning for their well-being while also extracting the costs of its growth from them. So visible was this form of state growth and centralization, that historians for many years seemed to miss its counternarrative: the rise of private modes of public governance.

Critics and boosters of the interventionist state helped carve out new ways for private capital to exercise public power. Not only did New Deal programs rely on a rising number of partnerships between private industry and the government, but especially by the Cold War era, economic ideals of free enterprise, unfettered by government constraints, merged with patriotic discourse about "the American Way"—in contrast to the Communist way. Beginning in the 1960s, an increased number of social welfare programs involved state efforts to parcel out its power to private purveyors and mirrored the trend toward using the force of the American state, through subsidies and tax relief, to "free" or deregulate private markets or entities. Across partisan divides, a rather contradictory philosophy of government—what one scholar usefully depicts as the "submerged state"—arose that called for governmental restraint when it came to public health and social welfare programs yet justified massive government spending to support capitalism through private enterprise.[2]

In the decades following World War II, these transformations in American state power reshaped American Jewish philanthropy and its approach to capital generation, distribution, and accumulation. While the core technology of American Jewish philanthropy had been a rapid system of capital intake and output, primarily mediated through mass fundraising appeals, by the 1950s, Jewish philanthropic leaders began to approach philanthropic capital with a different attitude about time, driven in part by the American state's embrace of policies to encourage the growth of private capital and to outsource governing responsibilities to private entities. A new technology, premised upon capital accumulation and growth and oriented toward conserving power for the future, became increasingly attractive to Jewish philanthropic organizations. In the form of endowments, Jewish leaders could draw the fullest benefits from new state policies and could offer a capital solution to the era's anxiety about post-Holocaust long-term Jewish survival.

PHILANTHROPY FOR THE PRESENT

At the end of the nineteenth and beginning of the twentieth century, global forces of urbanization, industrialization, and economic depression reconfigured world demographics and brought millions of Jews to American shores. The burden of providing for the basic needs of this tide of new immigrants hastened Jewish organizations to reconfigure their missions and led to the creation of new institutions, most notably the Jewish federation system, which began in 1895 in Boston and expanded over the coming decades. Local federations centralized the collection and distribution of philanthropic dollars to Jewish agencies that did the work of serving the Jewish community and, especially, its new immigrant population. In theory, these agencies would be relieved of their individual fundraising responsibilities, and, with annual disbursements from federations, could focus instead on meeting Jews' immediate needs. Often, the disbursements were a matter of controversy, as agencies felt slighted in the calculations of needs against resources or worried that the leaders who made allocation decisions brought biases to the process. Nonetheless, by World War I, twenty-three cities in the United States had Jewish federations, and, by World War II, almost every city or town with an established Jewish population sought to organize its own federation.[3]

As the federation system expanded, its financial mechanism became the standard of philanthropic practice in Jewish life. Much like a revolving door, federations worked to distribute funds at the same rate that they collected them; they harbored a strong temporal focus on the demands of the present. In fact, most federations, from their inceptions, constrained their own ability to hold assets as part of their corpus because they perceived endowment practices to be antithetical to their mission of redistributing dollars to meet pressing needs in Jewish communities. New York City's federation, founded in 1917 to coordinate domestic philanthropic efforts (international efforts were coordinated by the United Jewish Appeal) for the largest and most concentrated Jewish population in the United States, offers a window into the distributive logic that governed Jewish philanthropy from World War I until the post–World War II decades when Jewish philanthropy started to embrace a new future-oriented logic of capital accumulation.

In its bylaws, the federation of New York City explicitly eschewed endowment: "The Federation shall discourage the making of legacies and devises [bequests of real estate]. . . . The Federation shall not accept legacies and devises by which the principal is to be held in trust by Federation and only the income is to be available for distribution." Any legacies it happened to receive were to be distributed within three years, and its "Emergency Fund," that is money held and not distributed, was capped at $1 million.[4] Federation conceived of its authority as rooted in its consistent ability to raise money annually and to spend those funds expeditiously. Its leaders believed that their ability to circulate philanthropic capital in a timely fashion was the best method for ensuring future gifts; donors would see that their dollars fulfilled immediate needs, so they would give the next year and beyond.

Even so, some members of the New York board worried about the limitations of revolving-door philanthropy on two counts: its constraints on individual freedom, and its lack of sustainability. In 1921, Felix Warburg, a scion of a wealthy German banking family and the founding president of the federation's board, argued that individuals who had substantial resources would expect a measure of freedom to give away those resources when and how they wished. He convinced the board to loosen its bylaws by adopting more neutral language—that federation "shall neither solicit nor encourage" the collection of endowments—in place of simple discouragement. At the same time, the board maintained its commitment to spending all of the funds within three years and decided to lower the cap on the Emergency Fund from $1 million to $500,000 "to allay any fears, however unwarranted they may be, that the [modification of the bylaw] might result in enabling Federation to amass funds without limit, thereby creating for itself a position of power that might make for evil in the community" or create the perception of federation as a "menacing, all-powerful 'charity-trust' so called."[5]

Clearly responding to the rise of huge private foundations, especially Carnegie and Rockefeller, federations sought to differentiate themselves from these "charity-trusts" that consolidated power through stores of philanthropic capital.[6] In 1925, a New York board member reaffirmed that one of the "greatest boons of Federation is the education of the public to an understanding of and sympathy for the charitable and philanthropic requirements of the community as a whole," and, thus, any policy that controverted the ultimate aim of investing capital in the community must be quashed.[7] Even as the board steadily raised the cap on its reserve funds, until by 1927 it reached $3 million, it did so in the context of buttressing the annual campaign and its ability to prove through rapid expenditure its ongoing need for broad support.[8]

Inexorably, as the New York federation held more assets, its financial instruments became more complicated. Assets held in non-distributive funds had to be invested and gifts that came as securities had to be valued for tax purposes and were generally sold and reinvested.[9] The Great Depression, of course, interrupted the pace of asset amassment, and by 1932, New York's federation had depleted its reserve funds to meet its allocation commitments.[10] After World War II, the Board of Trustees returned to the task Warburg had quietly set out in 1921, when he suggested that for the sake of individual freedom and Jewish sustainability, federation's self-discipline against endowment should be re-assessed. In 1947, a committee charged with revisiting these bylaws recommended the creation of a new financial logic for endowment: a rule determining that capital funds sequestered from the allocation process only had to be spent down when their aggregate total exceeded the sum of the past two year's distributions (approximately $20 million at the time). Even with the passage of the new bylaw, the New York federation had just $5 million in its endowment fund by the late 1940s, a far cry from the $20 million that would necessitate a spend-down.[11]

In observing the wider philanthropic world—especially universities and foundations—Jewish leaders saw that not all philanthropic funds moved so seamlessly from intake to circulation as theirs did. Jewish federations throughout the United States shared New York's resistance to implementing an endowment model. Yet these leaders also shared a new interest in exploring the temporal logic of endowment, not only because it might appeal to wealthy individuals and insure philanthropic sustainability but also because of the multiple forces that seemed to recommend it. From Jews' rising socio-economic position alongside their post-Holocaust existential fears to new state-based policies that offered immediate encouragement for private entities to hold capital designated as a future investment in the public good, endowment held new appeal in the post–World War II years.[12]

PHILANTHROPY FOR THE FUTURE

The rising professionalization and growth of American Jewish philanthropy were indicative of the postwar transformation that Jews, alongside many other white Americans, experienced from scarcity to abundance. In its distinctly Jewish manifestations, this shift could be viewed through the establishment of the State of Israel; the defeat of Nazism; and the striking material gains that American Jews achieved after the war. These factors stood together in undermining the general sense of shortage and urgency that had animated American Jewish philanthropy in its earlier incarnations.[13] In the international sphere, American Jews were able to extend the logic of immediate, need-based philanthropy by channeling their own abundance to help the fledgling Jewish state build its infrastructure.[14]

In the domestic realm, however, Jewish abundance stimulated a crisis, sometimes expressed through the shorthand of assimilation or Jewish survival. When Jewish needs were no longer immediate and material in nature, how could leaders still convince average Jews to connect themselves to a Jewish community through philanthropic behavior? Appreciated for its ability to bring unity to a politically, religiously, and nationally diverse Jewish population, philanthropy might retain its centrality in Jewish life if repurposed as a purveyor of culture or identity, enabling individuals to gain access to Jewishness through the acts of both funding and consuming it.

Professional leadership could help with this new mandate. In 1932, Jewish leaders had created a national body, the Council of Jewish Federations, to help manage federation growth and to "develop inter-city cooperation on common problems."[15] In its efforts to standardize federation practices, the national council fostered the same sort of professionalization that was occurring across American philanthropy. By 1940, roughly sixty cities had at least one full-time staff member working at its federation, and by the late 1950s, that number had more than doubled, with 125 cities boasting at least one—and often more— full-time staff member, the majority of whom were trained in social work.[16]

The new resources to support the professionalization and growth of American Jewish philanthropic institutions bore the imprint of the expansion of the American welfare state. Writing in 1949, the executive director of the newly reorganized Jewish federation of Chicago suggested to his colleagues that far from the "death knell of private philanthropy as a whole, and Jewish private philanthropy in particular," New Deal social welfare programs could usher in a new era of Jewish philanthropic vitality. He speculated (rightly so, as it turned out) that the federal government would become increasingly reliant on private channels to distribute its resources and services. Well-organized Jewish philanthropic agencies could assume this role, and, at the same time, develop their own internal identity-based Jewish agenda now that the social service agencies which they had once borne the main responsibility for funding would be subsidized through government grants. The Chicago executive director underscored the intimate relationship between finance and philanthropic purpose, noting that as federations stepped into new roles, "Even our great central funds will change, and new ways of providing funds may have to be created."[17]

Postwar transformations in Jewish philanthropy, including its professionalization, its shift away from providing for immediate time-sensitive needs wrought from scarcity, and its position within an expanded social welfare state, fostered a new financial logic predicated upon a very different time scale. The practice of endowment, for many decades, avoided by federation leaders, came to hold appeal since it staked its value not in the immediate distribution of resources, but rather in the valuation of capital through its future potential. By accumulating and growing capital and not distributing it immediately, American Jews could will a future into existence. Endowment offered a salve for people who were increasingly resource-rich but anxious about its future. The aftershocks of the Holocaust and the heights of possibility for Jews to assimilate in the United States wove together with American Jews' growing expertise in finance and law, to create a strategy to buy time or, at least, capitalize a Jewish future.

Starting in the 1950s, as federation leaders in New York ploddingly revised their bylaws and started to raise endowment revenue, leaders in other cities, with smaller Jewish populations, worked with more agility and moved into the business of endowment faster and with greater verve. More than any other city, Cleveland was on the cutting edge of endowment innovation, extending its reputation as a philanthropic trendsetter. It was home to one of the earliest Jewish federations, established in 1904; the first community chest organization in the nation, founded in 1913 and modeled upon the federation; and the first community foundation, created in 1914.[18]

Until 1955, the Jewish federation of Cleveland had only about $1 million in endowment assets, but from that point forward, its leaders became devotees of endowment growth as an existential strategy as much as a financial one. In the following six years, Cleveland's endowment increased sixfold, with a million dollars added each year. The annual campaign simply could not generate the necessary capital to offset emergency expenses, especially as Israel faced new pressures, and, also, to reserve money for "constructive work in research . . . and for intensified activities in the cultural and educational fields" that were increasingly vital to a new generation of American-born Jews.[19] According to the executive vice president of the Cleveland federation, speaking in 1968, "It may safely be predicted that Federations which properly mine the endowment fund will reap rich rewards. . . . Because of the nature of endowment fund money, we may confidently expect that the Federation of the future will be able to engage much more imaginatively in programs which go beyond bread-and-butter support of basic community programs."[20] A decade later, the director of Cleveland's federation speculated that if only other cities would follow its embrace of endowment, then "the national total [of Jewish endowment dollars] would already be about $1 billion."[21]

THE AMERICAN STATE AND THE JEWISH FUTURE

After two decades of hearings on foundations' practices and the passage of piecemeal and incremental reforms to their tax-exempt status, Congress enacted the Tax Reform Act of 1969.[22] The new law, although anticipated by trends already in motion, shifted American Jewish philanthropy more strikingly than ever toward the practices of future-oriented capital accumulation and growth. In the months leading up to its passage, Jewish federations worked with lawyers to understand how proposed elements of the law would affect their work. Alongside other philanthropic professionals, they provided testimony in front of congressional committees enumerating their case against reducing tax incentives for charitable giving. At a meeting of the Board of Trustees of New York's federation in the early fall of 1969, George Heyman, president of the board and of a Wall Street banking firm, raised an alarm that "it will be a very critical day, not only for Federation, but for all organized voluntary philanthropy in this country" if the proposed legislation, which included new limits on personal deductions for charitable giving, especially of appreciated securities, were passed. Federation, he continued, would have to "reconsider how to meet its obligations to this community."[23]

In its final form, the 1969 Tax Reform Act did not reduce charitable deductions in the ways that Jewish and other philanthropic leaders had feared. But their deliberations about the law served to stimulate more interest than ever among Jewish philanthropic professionals about the tax climate and its relationship to new philanthropic models. As Norman Sugarman, a tax attorney from Cleveland who provided consultation for Cleveland's federation and the national Council of Jewish Federations, explained to a group of Jewish leaders in 1970, the law offered an opening for the Jewish community to lead the way in philanthropic innovation. By investing in tax lawyers and other experts who could navigate the complex legal terrain of tax and finance, "Jewish community federations can provide leadership in such efforts in the interest of protecting valuable community resources and making them more effective under the new law."[24]

As it turned out, the most consequential element of the 1969 tax law was its imperfect attempt to distinguish between what it termed public and private charity. Although the distinction had been drawn as early as 1943, it only gained substance in 1969, when private foundations, as opposed to public charities, became subject to specific regulations aimed to thwart their excessive accumulation of capital through annual spend-out requirements and a considered, though not ultimately legislated, measure to limit their life span. According to the new law, private foundations were defined as controlled by donors or their designees and, as a result, were subject to greater regulations than public charities, distinguished by their broad-based support or their clearly public missions. Congress maintained that private foundations deserved state benefits in the form of reduced tax burden for donors and the foundation, but in return, the state would demand greater regulatory control over both, through reporting and spend-out requirements, and would put more restraints on the public subsidies foundations could receive, by levying certain taxes on them.[25]

In its effort to define what separated a private foundation from a public charity, however, the law left a lacuna when it came to specifying the types of philanthropic capital that public charities could hold while still preserving their special status. Tax attorneys and advisers to Jewish federations helped lead the way in crafting interpretations of the legislative silence that stretched the new law to accommodate so broad a definition of public charities as to allow them to hold privately-designated funds without ceding their tax privileges. In interpretations approved by the Internal Revenue Service, tax attorneys argued that Congress intended to put as much capital as possible under the auspices of public charities. Thus, even if it meant relinquishing its oversight of spending behavior, it would still prefer to see public charities as opposed to private foundations grow.[26]

In the summer of 1972, Cleveland attorney Sugarman testified in front of Congress about regulations that the IRS was considering in its effort to implement the 1969 Tax Reform Act. Sugarman, who had worked for the IRS in the 1940s and early 1950s before going into private practice, understood that these regulations, related to the termination of private foundations and the transfer of their assets into public charities, could help his clients, including Cleveland's federation and the national Council for Jewish Federations, change their financial model toward an endowment-based future-oriented one. Later, he recounted to the director of Cleveland's federation, "The fact that others did not testify in these areas is some indication of the complexity of the statute and regulations and that apparently very few other people have bothered to keep up with these developments. . . . However, I believe these are very important areas and, as you will detect, there are a number of regulation provisions which may be important to you."[27]

Sugarman's interpretation of tax law, accepted by IRS rulings, enabled Jewish federations to establish an array of in-house financial vehicles with similar ends: to facilitate the movement of private philanthropic dollars, some previously held in private foundations, into funds designated as public charities. For example, in the early 1970s, New York's federation leaders met with Sugarman and the director of Cleveland's federation to learn how they could follow Cleveland's example and expand their charitable holdings. With Sugarman's guidance, the New York leaders resolved to establish a "Jewish Communal Foundation which will be maintained by Federation and subject to the control of the Federation, in which donors can place existing private Foundations, or future funds which they may wish to create."[28]

As the plan developed, the New York leaders determined to create a Jewish community foundation, with the status of a public charity, as an independent institution managed by a board comprised of representatives from the federation and the United Jewish Appeal, a fundraising campaign that raised dollars for Israel and other foreign Jewish causes. Even in the earliest stages of planning, the architects of what was established in 1972 as the Jewish Communal Fund recognized the legal tension that existed within their model: "It should be pointed out that one of the essential ingredients of this plan is that the Board of Trustees retains ultimate control over the allocation of such funds, but it is the operating practice to insure that the reasonable recommendations of donors be respected."[29]

By the 1970s, leaving behind their "money-in-money-out" imperative, Jewish leaders came to believe that their philanthropic power derived as much from the funds they held as from the money they distributed, suggesting a reconceptualization of "giving in time." This is why they invested resources in creating vehicles to hold philanthropic dollars that continued, by most measures, to operate as private foundations. To be certain, as they persuaded private foundations to dissolve and transfer their assets into federation-controlled funds and, also, persuaded donors of the tax benefits of donating appreciated securities to these same funds, they gained convening power and, often, the ability to determine how at least some of these irrevocably charitable dollars were spent. But in tracing how Jewish leaders managed these funds, it becomes clear that they were at least as interested in holding them as they were in having power over their disbursement. With the provisions of the new tax law and Sugarman's meticulous efforts to gain approval for his interpretations, these leaders understood they had a strong product to sell, regardless of where and *when* the philanthropic money eventually flowed.

ON BALANCE: CAPITAL AND TIME

New York's Jewish Communal Fund, similar to other Jewish and non-Jewish community foundations, should be regarded as an artifact of state policies that inexorably empowered private dollars to do public good after World War II.[30] Even more than this, these philanthropic vehicles must be understood as imprinted with the rationality of a financial model that calculates value as a function of future potential: How might the capital grow for an imagined future, regardless of whatever apparent needs exist in the present? Philanthropic leaders sold new charitable funds, held in public charities but dictated by private actors, to donors as valuable investments, which could endlessly appreciate and be reinvested—and they sold themselves as expert investors, capable of managing complicated portfolios and answering to donors as if they were stockholders. The more that federations could position themselves as financial institutions, the more they could prove their capacity to manage, if not spend, their donors' capital.

The temporal logic of endowment and the proliferation of donor-designated and de-facto donor-controlled funds ran in opposition to earlier imperatives of philanthropic distribution. To be certain, these charitable funds made allocations, but the public charities stood to gain, whether real assets through management fees or the intangible power of controlling a large sum of capital for an unknown future, from their accretion.[31] By 1986, the entire Jewish federation system held $1 billion in endowment funds, and by 2013, it valued its endowment at $16 billion, a number that included over $5 billion held in donor-advised funds, a direct legacy of Sugarman's tax acumen.[32] In recent calculations, the Jewish Communal Fund claims to hold 4,100 philanthropic funds, valued at $2 billion.[33] Whether held in federation endowments or in the Jewish Communal Fund; whether allocated or not; and whether overseen by an individual donor or not, the law treats all of these dollars as public charitable assets. And each dollar that does not flow into philanthropic circulation is constantly reinvested, growing the heft of these accumulated funds and their enmeshment with other forms of private capital.

The public, in turn, has augmented the power of charitable endowments through sizable tax expenditures, and in the process, has underwritten a particular approach to "giving in time." Or, to put a finer point on it, the public has endorsed giving, but not in any particular time. In law and practice, money held in endowment or in donor-designated funds in public charities is vested with the power of proxy for the public good and the public will. The responsibility to act in the name of the public is a grave one, yet the structural realities of philanthropy have stripped the public of its ability to monitor capital ostensibly raised on its behalf. In the form of massive endowments, with carve-outs for individually designated funds, the public is told to trust the process and believe that a rich future is in store.

Faith in charitable endowments is not necessarily misplaced. Survey the landscape of higher education or the arts and culture in the United States, and one will find plenty of reasons to feel confident that charitable endowments will pay dividends. However, approached from a different direction, that same faith may appear vestigial, reflective of a different economy and a different set of state policies that more effectively used tax policy and other mechanisms to smooth out the imbalances of capitalism. As economists explain, since the 1970s, the inequality gap between the wealthiest and the rest has taken a steep upward turn, with massive amounts of capital held in the hands of a few.[34] Charitable organizations may exist for times like these, to help direct the flow of capital to the neediest who are underserved by other social and economic instruments. And, yet, in this moment, charitable organizations with significant and growing endowments seem bound to the logic of the future, no matter its costs for today.

NOTES

1. Evelyn Brody, "Charitable Endowments and the Democratization of Dynasty," *Arizona Law Review* 39 (Fall 1997): 873–948; and Henry Hansmann, "Why Do Universities Have Endowments?" *The Journal of Legal Studies* 19:1 (January 1990): 3–42.

2. Suzanne Mettler, *The Submerged State: How Invisible Government Policies Undermine American Democracy* (Chicago: University of Chicago Press, 2011). See also, Angus Burgin, *The Great Persuasion: Reinventing Free Markets since the Depression* (Cambridge, MA: Harvard University Press, 2012); Alfred Chandler, *The Visible Hand: The Managerial Revolution in American Business* (Cambridge, MA: Harvard University Press, 1977); Jefferson Cowie, *The Great Exception: The New Deal and the Limits of American Politics* (Princeton, NJ: Princeton University Press, 2017); Gerald Davis, *Managed by the Markets: How Finance Reshaped America* (New York: Oxford University Press, 2009); Greta Krippner, *Capitalizing on Crisis: The Political Origins of the Rise of Finance* (Cambridge, MA: Harvard University Press, 2011); William Novak, "The Myth of the 'Weak' American State," *American Historical Review* 113, no. 3 (June 2008): 752–72; Kim Phillips-Fein, *Invisible Hands: The Businessmen's Crusade Against the New Deal* (New York: Norton, 2010); and Judith Stein, *Pivotal Decade: How the United States Traded Factories for Finance in the Seventies* (New Haven, CT: Yale University Press, 2010).

3. For histories of the Federation system, see Daniel Elazar, *Community and Polity: The Organizational Dynamics of American Jewry* (Philadelphia, PA: Jewish Publication Society, 1995), 211 for a catalogue of each Federation and when it was established; Marc Lee Raphael, *A History of the United Jewish Appeal* (Chico, CA: Scholars Press, 1982); and Jonathan Woocher, *Sacred Survival: The Civil Religion of American Jews* (Bloomington: Indiana University Press, 1986), chapter 2. On the influx of Jewish immigrants at the end of the nineteenth century and tensions caused among settled American Jews, see Naomi Cohen, *Encounter with Emancipation: The German Jews in the United States, 1830-1914* (Philadelphia, PA: Jewish Publication Society, 1984); and Hasia Diner, *A Time for Gathering: The Second Migration, 1820-1880* (Baltimore, MD: Johns Hopkins University Press, 1992). For two studies that chart the gender dynamics connected to these shifts and philanthropic responses, see Idana Goldberg, "'Sacrifices upon the Altar of Charity': The Masculinization of Jewish Philanthropy in Mid-Nineteenth Century America," *Nashim* 20 (Fall 2010): 34–56; and Beth Wenger, "Masculinizing American Jewish Philanthropy," copy in author's possession.

4. Board of Trustees Meeting, December 12, 1921, 4–5; all board meetings can be found in Subgroup I, Series 1, Subseries a, Subsubseries i, United Jewish Appeal-Federation of New York Collection, 1909–2004, Center for Jewish History, New York City (online access), hereafter UJAFed-NY.

5. Board of Trustees, December 12, 1921, 6, UJAFed-NY.

6. See Inderjeet Parmar, *Foundations of the American Century: The Ford, Carnegie, and Rockefeller Foundations in the Rise of American Power* (New York: Columbia University Press, 2012).

7. Board of Trustees, May 11, 1925, 21, UJAFed-NY.

8. Board of Trustees, May 23, 1927, 11, UJAFed-NY; Parmar, *Foundations of the American Century*.

9. Board of Trustees, January 13, 1930, 7-10, UJAFed-NY.

10. Board of Trustees, April 18, 1932, UJAFed-NY. On the effects of the Great Depression on Jewish organizational life in New York City, see Beth Wenger, *New York Jews and the Great Depression: Uncertain Promise* (New Haven, CT: Yale University Press, 1996).

11. Board of Trustees, January 13, 1947, 19, 26; and Board of Trustees, February 10, 1947, 3, UJAFed-NY.

12. Universities, especially the most elite, and some of the largest foundations in the postwar period, including Carnegie, Rockefeller, and Ford, had substantial endowments. See Hansmann, "Why Do Universities Have Endowments?"; and Parmar, *Foundations of the American Century*.

13. On the politics and culture of Jewish abundance in the United States, see Lila Corwin Berman, "American Jews and the Ambivalence of Middle Classness," *American Jewish History* 93:4 (December 2007): 409–34; and Rachel Kranson, *Ambivalent Embrace: Jewish Upward Mobility in Postwar America* (Chapel Hill, NC: University of North Carolina Press, 2017).

14. See J.J. Goldberg, *Jewish Power: Inside the American Jewish Establishment* (New York: Addison-Wesley, 1996), especially part 2; Theodore Sasson, *The New American Zionism* (New York: New York University Press, 2014); Melvin Urofksy, *We Are One! American Jewry and Israel* (Garden City, NY: Anchor Press, 1978); and Jack Wertheimer, "American Jews and Israel: A 60-Year Retrospective," *American Jewish Year Book* 108 (2008): 3–79.

15. Report from the General Assembly of the National Council of Jewish Federations and Welfare Funds, Jan 3–6, 1935, appended to Board of Trustees Meeting, Jan 21, 1935, UJAFed-NY; also, see discussion at Board of Trustees Meeting, Oct 11, 1932, UJAFed-NY.

16. Philip Bernstein, *To Dwell in Unity: The Jewish Federation Movement in America since 1960* (Philadelphia, PA: Jewish Publication Society of America, 1983), 8. On the professionalization of American philanthropy in the interwar years, see Peter Dobkin Hall, *Inventing the Nonprofit Sector and Other Essays on Philanthropy, Voluntarism, and Nonprofit Organization* (Baltimore, MD: Johns Hopkins University Press, 1992), 91–94; and Olivia Zunz, *Philanthropy in America, A History* (Princeton, NJ: Princeton University Press, 2012, chapter 2. On the rise of social work and especially its prevalence among American Jews in the early- to mid-twentieth century, see Daniel Walkowitz, *Working with Class: Social Workers and the Politics of Middle-Class Identity* (Chapel Hill, NC: University of North Carolina Press, 1999).

17. Samuel Goldsmith, "Trends for the Future," *Journal of Jewish Communal Service* 26:1 (Sept 1949): 45. On the expansion of New Deal social service programs

and practices of outsourcing services, see Elisabeth Clemens, "In the Shadow of the New Deal: Reconfiguring the Roles of Government and Charity, 1928-1940," in *Politics and Partnerships: The Role of Voluntary Associations in America's Political Past and Present*, eds. Elisabeth Clemens and Dough Guthrie (Chicago, IL: University of Chicago Press, 2010); Jacob Hacker, *The Divided Welfare State: The Battle over Public and Private Social Benefits in the United States* (New York: Cambridge University Press, 2002); and Jennifer Klein, *For All These Rights: Business, Labor, and the Shaping of America's Public-Private Welfare State* (Princeton, NJ: Princeton University Press, 2006). The literature on the rise of Jewish "identity" as a discourse and politics is vast. For an important historical framing of it, see Michael Staub, *Torn at the Roots: The Crisis of Liberalism in Postwar America* (New York: Columbia University Press, 2002). And for a broader contextualization of identity discourse in American politics, see Matthew Frye Jacobson *Roots Too: White Ethnic Revival in Post-Civil Rights America* (Cambridge, MA: Harvard University Press, 2008).

18. On Goff and the Cleveland Foundation, see Zunz *Philanthropy in America*, 54–55; and http://www.clevelandfoundation100.org/foundation-of-change/invention/goffs-vision/, accessed July 22, 2015. For historical perspectives on Cleveland, see W. Dennis Keating and David Perry, eds., *Cleveland: A Metropolitan Reader* (Kent, OH: Kent State University Press, 1995), especially Part 5, "Governance: Public and Private"; Carol Poh Miller and Robert Wheeler, *A Concise History of Cleveland* (Bloomington: Indiana University Press, 1997); and Jon Teaford, *Cities of the Heartland: The Rise and Fall of the Industrial Midwest* (Bloomington: Indiana University Press, 1993). For the classic history of Jewish life in Cleveland, see Lloyd Gartner, *History of the Jews of Cleveland* (Cleveland, OH: Western Reserve Historical Society, 1978).

19. David Myers, "A Federation Endowment Program with Special Reference to Trust Fund," November 19, 1961, Folder 1159, Box 49, Cleveland Federation Papers, MS 4835, Western Reserve Historical Society, Cleveland, Ohio, Fed-Cleveland.

20. Henry Zucker, "What Every Jewish Social Worker Should Know about Federated Jewish Fund-Raising," *Journal of Jewish Communal Service* 45, no. 1 (Fall 1968): 64.

21. Letter from Henry Zucker to Norman Sugarman, June 28, 1977, Folder 1033, Box 43, Fed-Cleveland.

22. See Eleanor Brilliant, *Private Charity and Public Inquiry: A History of the Filer and Peterson Commissions* (Bloomington: Indiana University Press, 2000).

23. Board of Trustees Meeting, September 15, 1969, UJAFed-NY; and "George Heyman, Jr., Philanthropist, 86," *New York Times*, June 4, 2003, accessed on August 16, 2016 at http://www.nytimes.com/2003/06/04/nyregion/george-heyman-jr-philanthropist-86.html.

24. Norman Sugarman, "New Opportunities in Endowment Funds," Address before the 39th Annual General Assembly of the Council of Jewish Federation and Welfare Funds, Kansas City, Missouri, November 1970, Articles and Addresses, vol. 5, 1966-1970, Box 2, Norman Sugarman Papers, O-633, American Jewish Historical Society at the Center for Jewish History, NewYork, New York, NS.

25. Brilliant, *Private Charity and Public Inquiry*; and Thomas Troyer, "The 1969 Private Foundation Law: Historical Perspective on Its Origins and Underpinnings," *The Exempt Organization Tax Review* 27, no. 1 (January 2000): 52–65.

26. See Lila Corwin Berman, "Donor Advised Funds in Historical Perspective," *Boston College Law Forum on Philanthropy and the Public Good*, vol. 1 (Oct 2015): 17–21.

27. Letter from Sugarman to Zucker (Cleveland Federation), August 10, 1972, Folder 1060, Box 44, Fed-Cleveland. He is discussing §507 regulations, passed into law in December 1969. They can be found in full at https://www.irs.gov/irm/part7/irm_07-026-007.html#d0e215. On Sugarman, see Lila Corwin Berman, "How Americans Give: The Financialization of American Jewish Philanthropy," *American Historical Review* 122, no. 5 (Dec 2017): 1459–89.

28. Board of Trustees Meeting, Dec 14, 1970, UJAFed-NYC.

29. Ibid.

30. My formulation of these public charitable vehicles as an artifact—and not an invention—of the state is drawn directly from Rob Reich's similar contention and language about private foundations. See Reich, Just Giving: Why Philanthropy Is Failing Democracy and How It Can Do Better (Princeton, NJ: Princeton University Press, 2018), ch. 1.

31. For a provocative argument that managing entities, and not donors, gain from the tax benefits extended to DAFs, see John Brooks, "The Missing Tax Benefit of Donor-Advised Funds," *Tax Notes*, February 29, 2016: 1013–24.

32. For a recent valuation of Federation endowment dollars, see 2013 Annual Survey of Planned Giving and Endowment Programs, Jewish Federations of North America, copy in author's possession. For comparative data from the 1980s and 1990s, see Jack Wertheimer, "Current Trends in American Jewish Philanthropy," *American Jewish Year Book* (Philadelphia, PA: Jewish Publication Society, 1997): 3–92.

33. See Jewish Communal Fund Giving Report, 2020, available by request at https://jcfny.org/2020givingreport/.

34. Thomas Piketty, *Capital in the Twenty-First Century* (Cambridge, MA: Belknap Press, 2014).

Part II

THEORY

Chapter 5

"That the Earth Belongs in Usufruct to the Living"

Intergenerational Philanthropy and the Problem of Dead-Hand Control[*]

Theodore M. Lechterman

A century has now passed since the death of Andrew Carnegie. The form of elite philanthropy that he helped pioneer, the private charitable foundation, has received no shortage of critical appraisal. Citizens and scholars of various stripes have questioned the compatibility of elite philanthropy with the principles that undergird a well-ordered liberal democracy. While some regard elite philanthropy as an unexceptional exercise of economic liberty,[1] others charge that it depends upon, and serves to reinforce, objectionable disparities in wealth.[2] Some look to foundations to solve entrenched social problems;[3] others challenge the asymmetries in power that come along with foundation-driven experiments in social policy.[4] But whatever verdict awaits an overall assessment of philanthropy, one distinctive dimension of this practice hasn't generated significant scrutiny. This is the temporal dimension. A striking, albeit little noticed, fact is that although Carnegie and his peers are no longer living citizens, they are nonetheless still empowered to restrict the use of property and project influence over social conditions.[5]

[*] Parts of this chapter originally appeared in Theodore M. Lechterman, *The Tyranny of Generosity: Why Philanthropy Corrupts Our Politics and How We Can Fix It* (New York: Oxford University Press, 2021) and is used with permission from Oxford University Press. I thank Chuck Beitz, Paul Brest, Des Jagmohan, Melissa Lane, Ray Madoff, Maribel Morey, Shmulik Nili, Philip Pettit, Rob Reich, Benjamin Soskis, Marty Sulek, Leif Wenar, and John Young for helping to clarify my thoughts about this material. The chapter has also benefited significantly from feedback I received at presentations at the International Society for Third-Sector Research biennial conference, the IUPUI Lilly Family School of Philanthropy, Stanford University, and the "Giving in Time" conference at Boston College Law School. I am grateful to the Society for Applied Philosophy for financially supporting preliminary research on this project.

Dead donors enjoy these powers because contemporary societies recognize "intergencrational charitable transfers" ("ICTs"), legal devices that allow members of one generation to mark off property for charitable purposes in future generations.[6] The most prominent form of ICT is the *private charitable foundation*, typically designed as a perpetual endowment that makes grants for enumerated charitable purposes—a form that Carnegie himself helped to popularize. Other forms include the ordinary *charitable bequest*, which allows a person to dedicate his or her estate to a charitable cause upon her death, and the *restricted charitable gift*, a donation made to a charity for the sake of perpetually endowing a specific activity.

Other chapters in this collection consider how a society should regulate ICTs, or how individual philanthropists should make the best use of these tools. The present chapter begins with a question that is in a sense more fundamental, even if its practical relevance may at first seem obscure. That is, do ICTs have a legitimate place in a liberal democracy? Is there a convincing justification for permitting such transfers at all? If ICTs are ultimately impermissible, then questions about how to regulate them or how to make the best use of them take on a much different character. The chapter reaches the conclusion that ICTs do indeed have a place in a well-ordered liberal democracy, but it's a role that comes with noteworthy limitations. In turn, I show how this exploration of the justification of ICTs helps us to answer pertinent questions of public policy.

The argument unfolds in six parts. To ground the philosophical discussion that follows, I proceed in the next section by describing the key features and prevalence of intergenerational charitable giving, particularly as it manifests in the contemporary United States. Drawing on the poignant remarks of Thomas Jefferson, Part III develops a skeptical challenge to the justification of ICTs. Jefferson prompts us to see that ICTs are a form of "dead-hand control," a way by which the past restricts the liberty of the living and unborn. But, in Jefferson's view, the dead have no right to control the living. This casts the case for ICTs into doubt. Part IV examines recent attempts by political theorists to justify ICTs. Although these views contribute essential foundations to a response to the Jeffersonian challenge, I show that the arguments behind them fall short of justifying dead-hand control. Section V fills in the gap. It contends, *pace* Jefferson, that in the case of philanthropy, dead-hand control isn't categorically objectionable. Rather, dead-hand control is objectionable to the extent that past persons lack the capacity to make sound judgments about temporally distant conditions. Part VI concludes that the resulting policy challenge becomes how to prevent the past from curtailing actions in the future on the basis of demonstrably false beliefs. Recent policy trends toward *cy-près* reform appear to be a step in the right direction, but they are not sufficient.

THE PRACTICAL CONTEXT

Instead of automatically relinquishing property to named heirs or remitting it to the state, testation empowers a decedent to decide what shall happen with her property after she is no longer around to manage it. Donating property to a charitable purpose is a popular use of this power. A substantial portion of the resources committed to charitable causes comes from gifts at death (bequests) and gifts that continue to pay out after death (trusts).

Bequests on their own provide only a small portion of the funding for organized charitable endeavors today. The proportion of charitable dollars from living individuals (69 percent) now dwarfs that of bequests (9 percent) by nearly eightfold.[7] But the declining status of bequests has been offset by the rising significance of perpetual charitable trusts. A charitable trust—whether established during one's life or through a bequest—allows a property owner to create a perpetual endowment by appointing agents (trustees) to invest and spend the entrusted property in a way that preserves its principal. Although the settlor of a charitable trust can opt to limit the trust's lifetime, perpetuity is the default. Barring gross mismanagement by trustees, national economic crisis, or changes in the law, a charitable trust can be expected to persist indefinitely.

Charitable trusts that are funded by a small number of people are called private foundations. Private foundations typically make grants to other charitable organizations rather than engaging directly in charitable work.[8] Despite some prominent exceptions, most private foundations are structured to exist in perpetuity.[9] The number and size of these entities have grown astronomically over the past few decades. According to estimates of the Internal Revenue Service, between 1985 and 2011 the number of foundations tripled (from 31,171 to 92,990), and the value of assets held by foundations grew by sixfold (from $95 billion to $641 billion, in inflation-adjusted dollars).[10] In turn, the nonprofit sector has come to depend more heavily on foundations over time, with the proportion of funding that charitable endeavors draw from foundations rising from 5 percent in the 1980s to 19 percent in recent years.[11]

Restricted charitable gifts provide another possible example of perpetual philanthropy. Restricted charitable gifts are donations to charities for the purpose of supporting particular programs, typically on a perpetual basis. The receiving entity is bound to administer the gift according to the terms set out by the donor, which can be more or less specific. Restricted gifts, in other words, are charitable trusts under the trusteeship of individual charities. No statistical agency currently tracks the prevalence or extent of restricted gifts. However, some evidence suggests that the vast majority of "major gifts"— typically exceeding $1 million—possesses this quality.[12]

To be sure, bequests, foundations, and restricted gifts raise many interesting issues apart from their relationship to time. However, as will become clear in what follows, philanthropy's temporal aspects are rarely examined, poorly understood, and tremendously important. Finding a legitimate place for ICTs runs into a host of challenges.

THE JEFFERSONIAN CHALLENGE

Though it hasn't exercised many contemporary theorists, the power of dead persons to restrict how property can be used in the future was particularly disturbing to many commentators in the past.[13] Thomas Jefferson was one of the most caustic critics. In his 1789 letter to James Madison, he considers it "self evident 'that the earth belongs in usufruct to the living'; that the dead have neither powers nor rights over it."[14] (To own something "in usufruct" is to enjoy rights to its use and fruits without rights to diminish or destroy it.)[15] Invoking the authority of nature, Jefferson points out that no "law of nature" entitles persons to control property after death. Although positive laws often recognize rights of bequest and inheritance, these legal rights shouldn't be conflated with moral rights. A legal right of testation is merely a social convention designed to solve the problem of property's succession: What should happen to the property after its owner dies? Jefferson isn't entirely clear on what he wants his reader to draw from this observation. One strong possibility is that since dead persons have no natural right to control property beyond their lifetimes, succeeding generations shouldn't be in any way constrained by their wishes. In turn, a society ought to organize its laws of succession to prioritize the interests of the living and unborn.

Jefferson's remarks thus suggest one reason for preliminary discomfort with the idea of intergenerational philanthropy: the fact that it restricts the way in which future persons may use the property. A society has multiple alternatives at its disposal for organizing the succession of property and the finance of charitable enterprises. Some of these options would afford a greater say to future generations. For instance, the property could transfer to future generations without any restrictions on its use, leaving future generations entirely free to choose how much to devote to charitable purposes, as well as which purposes to pursue. Alternatively, a society could permit persons to dedicate property for future charitable purposes while leaving the choice of those purposes entirely up to future persons. Or, a society could license ICTs, but restrict their duration or subject them to the possibility of amendment. Given that the succession of charitable resources could be organized in different ways that afford greater control to future generations, we have reason to question whether the status quo is defensible.

Jefferson's remarks also furnish us with an additional source of skepticism about ICTs. He appears to believe that coexisting members of a political community stand in a much different relationship with each other than they do with past or future members of the same community. The letter continues, "We seem not to have perceived that, by the law of nature, one generation is to another as one independant nation to another [*sic*]." Jefferson appears to believe that coexisting in time and space is a necessary condition of membership in a political community. Only through membership in such a community do we acquire claims against other members of that community, including a say in community affairs. Just as each nation is entitled to sovereignty, to exclude other nations from control over its own internal affairs, so too is a generation entitled to sovereignty, to exclude past generations from control over the affairs of living persons.[16] If we follow this analogy to its end, we reach the implication that instances of dead-hand control are tantamount to colonialism, an implication that should be even more unsettling to us today than it would have been to Jefferson's contemporaries.

Even if we could overcome the obstacle that dead persons have no natural right to testation, these remarks indicate that justifying ICTs faces an additional challenge. The challenge emerges in light of a crucial difference between charitable and non-charitable gift-giving. The practice of interpersonal gift-giving is primarily a private affair. Its immediate effects are limited to the giver and the receiver. By contrast, charitable giving aims to affect wider civic conditions. Its point isn't to benefit a friend or family member, but to promote one's particular conception of the public good. In a liberal democracy, however, what constitutes the public good and how to promote it are inherently contested questions. Opinions differ considerably about the proper size of the charitable sector within a society's broader political economy, and about the relative merits of different potential charitable causes.

This distinction between interpersonal and charitable giving interacts with the passage of time in a normatively significant way. Arguably, part of the justification for respecting the charitable choices of our contemporaneous fellow citizens, even when we find them misguided, is the fact that our contemporaries are equally susceptible to our own such choices. We have reason to tolerate their philanthropic choices insofar as they respect ours. This isn't to say that the reciprocal liberty to make philanthropic gifts is all that matters in the justification of philanthropy within a single generation. For instance, vast inequalities in wealth that make philanthropy the province of a tiny elite might pose a serious challenge to this justification. Nonetheless, the very possibility of this kind of mutual toleration is absent in the case of intergenerational philanthropy. ICTs unilaterally impose past persons' conceptions of the public benefit upon future generations. Because time moves in one direction, future generations enjoy no reciprocal opportunity to influence civic conditions in the past.[17] From the future's perspective, the expectation to honor the philanthropic directives of the past may seem like an unwarranted invasion. Why ought we allow former citizens a say in our common affairs?

Thus, Jefferson's letter gives rise to two related but distinct worries about intergenerational philanthropy. The first concern is that intergenerational philanthropy depends upon recognizing a right of testation as a solution to the succession of property. This solution appears to be prejudicial to future persons, who have an interest in receiving property unrestricted. The second concern is that intergenerational philanthropy allows past persons to influence civic conditions in future generations, encroaching on the sovereignty of future generations to determine social conditions for themselves.

RECENT JUSTIFICATIONS OF
INTERGENERATIONAL PHILANTHROPY

A Right of Testation?

As discussed earlier, part of the Jeffersonian challenge to intergenerational philanthropy is the absence of a natural right to testation. Jefferson makes plain that he regards this as a "self-evident" proposition needing no elaboration or defense. But we should try to flesh out this idea in some greater detail. Theories of natural rights typically hold that rights derive from a fundamental entitlement to individual self-ownership, an entitlement that preexists and constrains political institutions. According to Steiner and Vallentyne, such theories diverge on the question of which sorts of agents have these rights.[18] On one view, agents are eligible for natural rights if they are capable of making *choices*. If some class of agents possesses the capacity for choosing among alternative options, that class of agents is a bearer of natural rights. On another view, agents are eligible for rights if they are the sorts of being that have *interests*—regardless of whether they are able to make choices of their own. Important for our purposes is that both views tend to converge on the conclusion that the dead have no rights. Clearly enough, dead persons are incapable of making *choices*, because choice-making is a mental process that requires a living brain. So, the dead can't be rights-bearers on the choice-making conception of natural rights. To have an *interest* in something, meanwhile, is precisely to be in a position to derive benefits from its success and harm from its failure. But, a person is incapable of suffering setbacks or enjoying achievements once she has died.[19] The interest-holding conception of natural rights thus has little to offer to the dead either. If recognizing a right to testation depends upon ascribing rights to dead persons, the case for testation is in peril.

Testation would be ruled out from the start if the government can't act legitimately except for the sake of protecting natural rights—as many libertarians believe. But Jefferson wasn't a thoroughgoing libertarian, and his letter leaves open the possibility that positive laws can derive legitimacy from sources other than natural law.[20] Might testation be justified on alternative grounds? Indeed, numerous scholars have recently observed that, even if persons have no natural right to testation, testation can nonetheless be valuable as a social practice.[21] A social practice of testation can be valuable, according to this view, not because it respects our posthumous rights as such, but because it increases the options available to us while alive and incentivizes greater social productivity.

One reason that testation is desirable is that it allows us to extend our plans and projects beyond our mortal existence, thereby affording us opportunities to pursue more or better options *during life*.[22] Suppose you are a person of advancing age with a deep commitment to your local community theater. However, you also face declining health, and a concern about having sufficient funds to cover your medical expenses prevents you from making more than token donations to the theater company during annual fundraising drives. Without the power of testation, each donation to the theater company would be money not saved for medical expenses, increasing your risk of facing greater suffering. Things look different with the power of testation, however. With that power, you can forgo the annual contributions and instead arrange things so that whatever property remains in your possession at death goes to the theater group. This removes the trade-off between promoting your conception of the public good and protecting your own basic interests. By extending the range of available options in this way, testation facilitates the formulation and execution of a rational life plan.

A secondary benefit of a practice of testation is that it provides incentives for productivity and social savings that are generally advantageous to a society.[23] Lacking the option to pass on the property after death might make it harder for us to undertake difficult or long-term projects.[24] If I'm not permitted to pass on my furniture store to my children, why should I put myself through the thankless travail of starting and running a business? But, clearly enough, the health of a market economy significantly depends on individuals' willingness to take such long-term risks. Part of what makes such risks worthwhile lies in the ability to pass on the successes of our endeavors to successors.

Besides these potential effects on productivity, a right of testation might also induce greater savings. If we couldn't pass on property beyond our lifetimes, we would face pressure to consume as much as possible before death. The opportunity to control property beyond our lifetimes thus provides an incentive to preserve resources for future persons, rather than consume it all ourselves.[25]

These considerations indicate that attempts to justify intergenerational transfers need not ascribe natural rights to the dead. Rather, they indicate that recognizing a practice of testation can be a way of facilitating the interests of a society's members in living richer lives. Other things equal, a society that refused to honor the wishes of the dead would be impoverished in many respects. But the fact that testation can be valuable as a social practice doesn't prove that it's justified in any and every possible form. For instance, an unlimited right of testation may very well lead to objectionable social conditions in the succeeding generation. It could also deprive members of a previous generation of their fair share of resources, if testators chose to save too much for the future. As the next subsection details, two notable strands of thought in contemporary political theory have explored in some detail what forms of testation are ultimately consistent with justice. They converge on the conclusion that while justifying interpersonal transfers faces certain challenges, the case for recognizing charitable transfers remains fairly strong.

ICTs and Equality of Opportunity

Several recent scholars have challenged the traditional practice of testation on the grounds that it leads to objectionable inequalities in resources among members of the succeeding generations.[26] An unfettered right of individuals to make unilateral transfers can conflict with a society's attempts to secure or maintain conditions of background fairness, namely equality of opportunity. As it happens, those who make intergenerational transfers often tend to transfer their estates to kin. This promotes the accumulation of wealth within families and serves as a catalyst for socioeconomic stratification. Heirs of great fortunes receive opportunities unavailable to those who inherit less or nothing at all. Under regimes that recognize a right of testation, the success of one's life plans may depend more on the accident of being born into a particular family than on one's merit or one's status as an equal citizen. Furthermore, unless a society takes special measures to insulate public affairs from accumulations of wealth, inheritance also threatens the integrity of democratic processes. The beneficiaries of accumulated family wealth can come to serve as gatekeepers for political office, as recent empirical research on campaign finance suggests.[27] This undermines a sacred constituent of the ideal of democracy, that citizens are entitled to equal opportunities for political influence.

However, the same liberal-egalitarian theorists who rail against the effects of inheritance on equality of opportunity tend to acknowledge that intergenerational transfers of wealth aren't inherently unjust. In particular, these scholars typically treat charitable gifts as unmitigated exceptions to the problem of justice in property succession. Several explicitly encourage ICTs and seek to protect them from the restrictions that they would impose on non-charitable transfers.[28] This is so for two main reasons. First, because ICTs are gifts for purposes, rather than gifts to persons, their benefits tend to be widely distributed and, in turn, less prejudicial to distributive fairness. A bequest to a nature preserve, for example, benefits all who choose to visit the preserve, rather than any one heir. Encouraging charitable bequests and trusts helps to divert wealth from inequality-generating ends to ends that are inequality-neutral. A second reason for the liberal-egalitarian support of ICTs is that ICTs can work to combat the same objectionable inequalities that inherited wealth helps to create. This position reflects the thought that many charitable causes have as their aim the mitigation of poverty and inequality. For this reason, a practice of testation focused on charitable transfers might ultimately serve to reduce conditions of background injustice among members of succeeding generations.

These claims deserve some critical qualification. While it's true that ICTs don't pass on wealth to family members, they may in fact work against equality of opportunity in other ways. For instance, a testator might erect a family foundation and install her children as its trustees, allowing them to inherit the associated power and social status. Or, an ICT might be used to provide collective goods that predominantly benefit wealthy persons, either by concentrating its work in a wealthy suburb, or by funding goods that predominantly appeal to richer people.[29] The liberal-egalitarian position can nonetheless respond that, odious as they are, the inequality-generating features of ICTs are only contingent possibilities, which we might manage through regulation or simply accept as lesser evils. This marks an important distinction between ICTs and intergenerational non-charitable transfers. For, whereas ICTs can contingently serve to perpetuate certain kinds of inequality, the transmission of dynastic privilege is a more inherent and inexorable function of non-charitable transfers of wealth.

Another challenge for this position is that the extent to which ICTs serve as instruments of poverty or inequality reduction depends on which purposes a society designates as charitable and how it structures the choice among different purposes.[30] In the contemporary United States, according to one recent estimate, less than 31 percent of donated dollars end up benefiting the disadvantaged.[31] Some believe that a society ought to provide greater incentives for charitable gifts aimed at reducing poverty and inequality.[32] Though I harbor some considerable doubts about the desirability of trying to combat poverty through charitable donation, for the sake of argument here I am willing to concede that the justification for ICTs would be strengthened if such transfers did indeed serve a genuinely redistributive function.

ICTs and Justice in Savings

Other scholars have made a more direct case for an affirmative policy toward ICTs, holding that ICTs are valuable not, or not only, because of their salutary effects on inequality *among* members of succeeding generations, but because of these salutary effects on inequality *between* generations. A significant aspect of the problem of justice between generations reflects the fact that each generation has a conflicting interest in consuming as much property as its members desire. Solving this problem requires determining what a present generation is obliged to save for the future, and what future persons can reasonably demand from their predecessors. John Rawls is often credited with helping to introduce this problem, as well as with offering a compelling general solution to it.[33] The "just savings principle," in Rawls's terms, directs generations to share the burden of developing and maintaining just institutions over time. Though rather vague in its particulars, the principle is distinct for holding that generations are neither to discount the interests of future persons (as economists often suggest), nor to engage in self-effacing sacrifice in the hope of delivering a future utopia. It's also distinct in holding that the aim of saving isn't to expand the economic pie continuously, but rather to establish stable just institutions.

Cordelli and Reich argue that ICTs can serve as part of a strategy for satisfying Rawls's conception of justice in savings between generations.[34] In so doing, they draw attention to Rawls's overlooked remark that the savings required for this project may take various forms, including the conservation of natural resources, investment in buildings and technology, and the development of education and culture.[35] Building upon this idea, Cordelli and Reich posit three elements—social capital, disaster preparedness, and social innovation—that are at once critical for securing just institutions over time and unavailable through public administration alone. Maintaining just institutions over time requires continuous investment in social capital, which provides indispensable support for the virtues of democratic citizenship. The reproduction of social capital requires a diverse, vibrant, and independent civil society, supported by voluntary donation. The stability of just institutions also requires research into, and instruments to mitigate, low-probability, high-magnitude catastrophes. Though the state might take certain steps to address general disaster scenarios, Cordelli and Reich believe that private supplementation of state efforts is necessary to hedge against obscure cataclysmic events. Finally, Cordelli and Reich contend that ICTs serve as a corrective to democratic "short-termism," the tendency of democratic processes to disregard the interests of future generations. Because of their insulation from electoral pressure and their extended time horizons, ICTs are especially suited to financing long-term projects whose discoveries contribute to just conditions in the future.

For these authors, a society can't develop and maintain a just basic structure without ongoing, affirmative measures to finance social capital, disaster preparedness, and technological innovation. Though they acknowledge that there might be other ways of investing in such goods, Cordelli and Reich hold that charitable bequests and trusts have much to recommend themselves in this respect.

REASSESSING THE JEFFERSONIAN CHALLENGE

The forgoing section concluded that testation needn't presuppose that the dead have natural rights and can instead be justified by reference to its benefits to living and future persons. Testation in all its forms may not necessarily conform to the demands of justice, but there are good reasons to believe that recognizing charitable acts of testation can in fact satisfy certain compelling principles. ICTs may help to promote (or at least not necessarily undermine) equality of opportunity, and ICTs may also help to satisfy a principle of justice in savings between generations. These considerations go some way toward showing that devices of intergenerational philanthropy aren't nearly as prejudicial to the living and unborn as some have thought. But it isn't obvious that these considerations are sufficient to extinguish concerns about dead-hand control.

Recall that a constitutive feature of charitable bequests and trusts is that they impose the judgments of past generations onto future generations. In this way, such devices restrict the liberty of future generations to make their own economic decisions. Resources that might otherwise be theirs entirely, to allocate as they choose, must instead serve the purposes declared and specified by their forebears. In turn, because ICTs are public investments, designed to alter the nature and extent of collective goods within a society, these transfers restrict the degree of control that future generations may exert over the qualitative features of the social world they inhabit. Why ought future generations not enjoy sovereignty over these decisions?

A fixed point of political morality is that moral equals are entitled to a presumption of liberty. By default, each agent is entitled to govern her own affairs by her own lights. Your attempt to exercise practical authority over me—to substitute your judgment for mine over how I am to act—must be justifiable to me. If a convincing justification isn't available, I am in turn justified in denying your authority and taking steps to resist it. One popular way to show how practical authority can be justified is to appeal to instrumental considerations.

Instrumental justifications of practical authority hold that an authority is legitimate if obeying its commands leaves subjects better off, in some relevant sense, than they would otherwise be.[36] To determine that future generations ought to abide by the directives of past generations, therefore, might involve showing that obeying the wills of the past makes future generations better off, in some relevant sense. In turn, a compelling reply to the Jeffersonian challenge could hold that obeying the wills of the past places future generations under conditions that are more beneficial and more just than they would be if future generations were to act independently. And it strikes me that each of the claims from the preceding section supplies an instrumental argument for the authority of the past over the future. That is, without ICTs, future generations would be less able to advance their substantive aims, less able to maintain equality of opportunity, and less able to maintain various pillars of a just basic structure over time. To consider the forgoing justifications for ICTs as instrumentalist arguments for practical authority is also to open them up to pertinent objections, however.

Generational Sovereignty: An Intrinsic View

Obviously enough, some might reject instrumentalist justifications of authority out of hand. One might hold that, just as each nation is entitled to self-determination with respect to other nations, so each generation is entitled to self-determination with respect to other generations. It's generally wrong for one nation to colonize another on grounds that it has superior knowledge or capacity to promote justice, and it's equally wrong for past generations to "colonize" future generations in this way. If we reject colonial rule, must we also reject ICTs?

Answering this question requires that we consider positive arguments for collective self-determination, arguments that purport to show why it's distinctively valuable for a collectivity to control its own affairs. Such arguments hold that even if it were true that a benevolent despot, or a supercomputer, or a sacred text could more reliably track justice's demands, our lacking collective control over our laws and policies would be objectionable.[37] According to Zuehl, it would be objectionable because in some sense it would make our world not fully our own. We wouldn't be able to identify with, or see ourselves in, the decisions that affect our lives. We would feel like guests in a hotel room rather than residents of a home. The social world would confront us as other and alien.

One might think that ICTs undermine collective self-determination precisely in this way. These devices impose the judgments of the past upon the future. They reflect the wills of past persons and not those of current co-citizens. I suspect, however, that ICTs can be made consistent with an appreciation of the value of collective self-determination.

For Zuehl, members of a collectivity can reasonably feel at home in their social world when their institutions are causally responsive to their will, as it's expressed through well-functioning representative democratic institutions. But members of a collectivity don't need to control each individual law and policy in order to be collectively self-determining in the relevant sense. Rather, Zuehl claims that a collectivity is self-determining when, by way of democratic decision-making, its "core institutions" intentionally reflect its "core values."[38] Thus, collective self-determination is undermined when the state isn't governed democratically, or when the state can't reliably regulate the society's core institutions in accordance with citizens' articulated values.[39] From this, I believe we can also infer conditions for preserving collective self-determination in the face of external influences. Namely, a society suffers no objectionable setback to self-determination when such forces respect the collective's sovereignty over its core institutions or the conditions that core institutions are meant to regulate: fundamental rights, duties, and opportunities.[40]

Now we can begin to see how ICTs aren't morally equivalent to directives from a colonial administrator. A distinctive feature of colonial rule, and other forms of undemocratic authority, is that it involves domination of the society's core institutions and thereby deprives citizens of the opportunity to control their own affairs. But it's difficult to see ICTs as dominating in any meaningful sense. This is so for three reasons. First, even if ICTs require a future generation to pursue causes or implement strategies that it disapproves of, ICTs are expected to supply only a portion of the funding for charitable pursuits. Future generations can still make their own charitable investments to counteract or supplement the investments of the past.[41] Second, given the wide range of charitable purposes, most ICTs bear only a tenuous relation to the distribution of fundamental rights, duties, and opportunities. It's difficult to see, for instance, how trusts for the preservation of historic landmarks or bequests for advancing excellence in the performing arts bear on matters of basic justice. The value of collective self-determination might tell against the privatization of basic education and welfare provision, insofar as such measures inhibit citizens from effectively regulating the content and distribution of fundamental rights, duties, and opportunities. But offhand, it seems that at least some degree of private provision can be consistent with living citizens holding the reins that establish basic liberties and entitlements to essential resources. Third, even if these first two conditions somehow failed to hold, ICTs don't prevent a well-functioning democratic state from asserting legislative supremacy over questions of basic justice. Legislation to nationalize health care, for instance, would instantly supersede ICTs designed to finance the provision of medical services.

At the very least, then, ICTs don't categorically prevent a generation from exercising control over its common affairs in the way that colonialism does to a society. I take these observations to show that although ICTs subject a society to control by alien forces, this control is reconcilable with one central reason we have for wanting freedom from that kind of control.[42]

Generational Sovereignty: An Epistemic View

As I have framed it, the challenge for the proponent of ICTs is to show that, although ICTs impose the judgments of the past onto the future, this imposition can be justified. It can be justified if it's true that obeying the wills of the past leaves future generations under conditions that are more beneficial and more just than they would be if future generations were to control property completely independent of the past. The immediately preceding subsection deflected a preliminary objection to this line of reasoning, that rule by the past would be impermissible even if it led to perfectly just outcomes. The present subsection considers a more direct challenge: that complying with the directives of past generations doesn't necessarily satisfy the instrumentalist justification at all. Complying with the directives of the past can often leave future generations in suboptimal conditions.

To see the force of this objection, consider some examples. When the Englishman Thomas Betton died in 1723, he ordered his estate placed into a trust. His will declared that half of the trust's annual income be paid "forever to the redemption of British slaves in Turkey or Barbary."[43] Despite his good intentions, however, Betton failed to foresee that the white slave market would disappear in the 1830s, when France seized Ottoman territories and in short order rooted out the trafficking of human beings. Fidelity to Betton's stated wishes would require that the funds continue to accumulate unused should those markets somehow reappear. Also consider Bryan Mullanphy of St. Louis, Missouri. He died in 1851, but not before establishing a trust "to furnish relief to all poor immigrants and travelers coming to St. Louis on their way, bona fide, to settle the West."[44] Within a few decades, the West was mostly settled, and innovations in transportation made wagon stops in St. Louis obsolete. If Mullanphy had his way, his trust would still be idly accumulating funds, waiting perhaps for the Pacific Garbage Patch to become habitable.

The arguments in favor of ICTs that we considered earlier wouldn't necessarily rule out these kinds of troubling cases. Both cases appear consistent with the liberal-egalitarian perspective on inheritance, which approves of ICTs insofar as they are inequality-neutral or inequality-reducing. The succoring of weary immigrants and travelers, for instance, reduces a pertinent form of inequality. Each case also appears consistent with the justice-in-savings perspective on ICTs, which holds that ICTs are valuable as fonts of social capital, disaster preparedness, and technological innovation. Preserving Betton's slave-rescue fund would be a hedge against a kind of rare disaster. The slave-rescue and repatriation organizations that it would fund could eventually contribute to the stock of social capital. The innovative methods that these organizations might develop could be adapted or scaled up by other organizations or by the state.

What we notice when we reflect on these cases is that although the donors in question appear to have been attempting to benefit future generations, the passage of time has called their judgment on this score into question. Clearly enough, Betton and Mullanphy respectively assumed that British slavery and waggoneer weariness would remain serious problems into the indefinite future. These judgments turned out to be false. Armed with new information, future generations charged with preserving these trusts might well believe that the risks of British slavery and weariness among St. Louis waggoneers are now too remote to warrant saving so much resources for them. They might think other causes more urgent or more cost-effective investments.

The challenge for ICTs is that although their putative justification depends upon their resulting in significant benefits for future persons, past generations are entirely unreliable judges of what will be specifically useful to succeeding generations. Living persons are generally much better at gauging and satisfying the interests of their contemporaries. Partly this is because living donors have access to more intimate knowledge of the preferences of their potential beneficiaries. Being alive also enables them to update their judgments in response to new information. If I discover that no one is attending the museum that I have been supporting, I can change the direction of my donation (by funding some other cause) or change the strategy of my gift (say, by funding the museum's marketing efforts rather than its collection development). These features disappear with intergenerational philanthropy. For once I die, there is no guarantee that the judgments I formed while alive will satisfy the interests or preferences of any potential beneficiaries who survive me. The greater the separation of time, the worse the likely discrepancy between past judgments and future interests. Generally speaking, future generations may also be more reliable judges because of their privileged position in the historical sequence. Living later in time gives them access to improvements in technology and accumulations of historical data to draw more reliable causal inferences.

These initial considerations would appear to undercut the case for ICTs. If past generations are generally less wise about the interests of future persons and how to promote them, respecting directives from the past will not make future generations better off. In turn, future generations would then have no reason to regard these directives as binding. But this isn't the end of the story, as another example will help clarify.

Marie Robertson made a restricted gift to Princeton University in 1961.[45] The terms of the trust stated its purposes as "the education of men and women for government service." Particularly in the years after Robertson's death in 1981, Princeton started to interpret "government service" more loosely, using the gift to train students for careers in public service outside of formal government employment. The university believed a changing labor market for public service had rendered Robertson's intentions obsolete. The size of the federal bureaucracy had been shrinking while opportunities for jobs with private contractors and nonprofit agencies had become more numerous.

Princeton's actions set off a rancorous dispute with Robertson's surviving family members, who believed that her gift was meant explicitly to train officials for the federal government.

For the sake of illustration, let us suppose that Robertson did intend her gift to express a specific commitment to government work as such. She might have believed, for instance, that official state agencies are more democratically accountable than private firms and nonprofits and thus more legitimate ways of administering public policy. Had she lived to observe them, Robertson might well have opposed recent trends toward outsourcing state functions and Princeton's willingness to follow suit. In this respect, the dispute didn't arise because Robertson failed to predict future circumstances accurately, but because of a principled disagreement between Robertson and her trustees. It would certainly not be unreasonable for someone to hold that a liberal democracy ought to rely more heavily on a well-trained official bureaucracy than on outsourcing, and that training students for official roles is an essential mission of schools of public administration.

I take this case to indicate something distinctive about the epistemic virtues of ICTs. Namely, not all disputes with dead donors come about as a result of the donors' lack of foresight. At least some disputes turn on matters of principle, where the past's judgment may ultimately be as wise as, or wiser than, the future's. Clearly, in cases where the judgments of the past are superior to the judgments of the future, deferring to the judgments of the dead would help the future better advance its own interests. With this in mind, suppose that Robertson's view about public service ultimately is the most reasonable position. If we were to think about the matter carefully and abstract further from the status quo, we would come to accept this position as uniquely correct. The case would then show that prohibiting ICTs risks depriving future persons of the superior wisdom of the past.

One might also think that a certain amount of deference to past judgments can be valuable even when their apparent wisdom is more controversial. Suppose we find, after due reflection, that Robertson's position provides a reasonable alternative to the status quo, but not an obviously superior alternative. Even so, we might agree that ICTs that are merely controversial, as opposed to those that depend upon patently false beliefs, can still be useful to present and future persons, though in an indirect way. Obeying the reasonably controversial wills of the past can be useful because it forces the present and future to engage with conceptions of the public good that challenge the conventional wisdom of the moment. We don't need to endorse a thoroughgoing Burkean conservatism to appreciate that in some cases encountering judgments of the past exposes us to certain valuable advice that we wouldn't have otherwise considered.[46] At the very least, confronting the different practical judgments of past persons, as they manifest in the organizations of civil society, requires us to test the robustness of the propositions to which we are initially inclined. Thus, the fact that ICTs require the present generation to share the task of directing civil society with past persons can have certain educative effects on the present generation. Even when ICTs aren't altogether epistemically privileged, they can work in indirect ways to improve the present generation's ability to advance its aims consistent with the demands of justice.

Taken together, the observations of this section indicate that an instrumentalist justification for ICTs reaches mixed conclusions. Obeying the terms of ICTs that depend on patently false assessments would deeply undermine the ability of future generations to advance their interests. However, obeying the terms of ICTs that depend on assessments that are merely reasonably controversial might in fact leave future generations better off in relevantly valuable respects. Where does this leave us? If I am right, the resulting policy challenge that a society faces isn't the binary one of allowing ICTs or prohibiting them; it's one of fine-tuning the regulation of intergenerational transfers so as to screen out ICTs that become obsolete while protecting those that reflect merely controversial judgments. The final section offers some general thoughts on how different regulatory strategies might meet this challenge.

POLICY IMPLICATIONS

One might think that a way of avoiding the possibility of obsolete ICTs is to restrict them to very general purposes. Restricting ICTs to general purposes would allow future trustees significant discretion over how to interpret and administer them. Future trustees would be able to make these decisions with reference to current understandings of empirical conditions. An immediate problem with this proposed solution, however, is that it squelches one of the main incentives for making ICTs in the first place. Arguably, a prime incentive for donors in making such transfers is the opportunity to give effect to their specific judgments about the public benefit. The pleasure in legacy giving is as much an expression of the donor's thoughtfulness and taste as it is an expression of her generosity. A scheme that significantly limits the degree of choice among potential objects of philanthropy would make ICTs much less attractive to most potential donors.[47] This would be an unfortunate implication in light of the hypothesis that ICTs are important instruments of justice.

Perhaps a more serious problem with confining ICTs to general purposes is that it would deprive ICTs of one of their chief virtues. As we have seen, one of the chief virtues of ICTs lies in their ability to preserve unique ideas from the past and counteract biases of the present. Confining trusts to general purposes would allow future generations to inherit the generosity of the past, but not its wisdom.[48] And, as discussed earlier, the promise of epistemic benefits is an integral component of a successful defense against the Jeffersonian challenge. If the past has no knowledge to offer the future, the future has fewer reasons to respect the past's attempts to meddle in future social conditions.

A second policy option is to prevent donors from making perpetual trusts. A one-time bequest, or a trust that spends down its assets after a limited number of years, stands a good chance of avoiding the tendency toward obsolescence. I think this strategy would also prove over-inclusive, however. Certain types of initiatives take many years to get off the ground. Their benefits might not become apparent for many decades, if not centuries. Term limitations on ICTs would discourage the kinds of long-term thinking that some claim as one of their chief strengths.[49]

A third and more promising possibility is to take a permissive attitude to the terms of the ICT, allowing donors to select the narrowness of their aims and the duration of their purposes. This permission would be qualified, however, by periodic review. A proposal along these lines has enjoyed the support of some prominent figures. One is John Stuart Mill.[50] (See Rob Reich's contribution to this collection for a deeper investigation of Mill's views on this matter.) Mill argues that perpetual trusts pose a particular dilemma. On the one hand is the fact that even a "prudent man" lacks the foresight to predict what will be useful twenty or thirty years after his death. On the other hand is a danger in inviting the state to step in to revise the terms of a trust once that foresight proves faulty. Mill worries that public officials would be tempted to abuse this power, such as by reallocating trust funds to compensate for temporary budget shortfalls in other areas of public spending. He thus proposes to expose perpetual trusts to review after a fixed period of time (no longer than "the foresight of a prudent man may be presumed to reach") but to limit the revisions that public officials may make. Public officials, he contends, may only resolve to amend a trust's terms if they have in fact become obsolete. And in revising obsolete terms, officials must seek, first, to deploy them toward efficient uses and, second, to select uses that are as close as possible to the trust's original purposes.[51]

Vestiges of Mill's proposal appear in ongoing efforts to reform the judicial doctrine of *cy-près*. In the United States and elsewhere, *cy-près* (from the archaic French *cy près comme possible*) permits public officials (typically judges) to revise a trust that has become obsolete. As it's traditionally practiced, officials are only allowed to revise the terms of the trust when those terms have become illegal by current standards or literally impossible to carry out. By protecting the intentions of the donor to the extent possible, the doctrine preserves the incentives that encourage making ICTs and devoting them to unique purposes. However, the doctrine has also been the object of considerable criticism, particularly since terms can prove objectionably impractical or wasteful despite remaining possible to implement.[52] It's *possible* to accumulate funds for the repatriation of British slaves or the relief of settlers passing through St. Louis. But is it worth saving millions or even billions of dollars for such rare causes?

In recent years, approximately half of American states have attempted to account for this kind of concern in their adoption of reformed guidelines for *cy-près*.[53] The Uniform Trust Code (UTC), a model law proposed by an independent commission of experts and adopted by numerous states, now contains a broadened understanding of *cy-près*.[54] The UTC allows a court to alter the terms of a trust when it judges that such terms have become impractical or wasteful, even if complying with the terms remains technically possible. From the perspective of the account I have offered in this chapter, this is an encouraging development.

A noteworthy limitation of the UTC, however, is that it doesn't automatically subject perpetual trusts to periodic review. For a court to consider applying a *cy-près* remedy, an "interested person" must bring a challenge to the trust in question.[55] A predictable consequence of such a policy is that it exposes to scrutiny only a fraction of potentially obsolete trusts. But in view of Mill and Simes, *all* charitable trusts should come under review automatically after a fixed period of time. Only by subjecting all trusts to review can we be sure to address the problem thoroughly and fairly. (Lest this proposal appears to impose an unreasonably weighty administrative burden, imagine a process that reviews a pseudo-random sample of trusts—much like the Internal Revenue Service's current auditing procedures—with extra attention paid to trusts that control the largest endowments or operate within the most judgment-sensitive areas.)[56]

Altogether, these observations point toward a particular regulative strategy. That is, a society ought to broadly recognize one-time bequests and limited-life trusts. Meanwhile, the price of adopting a longer time horizon is to expose one's endeavors to substantive audit and adjustment at successive intervals. Recent developments in American trust law go some way toward capturing the spirit of this regulatory ideal, but they also leave one significant aspect of the problem—the need for periodic review—unaddressed.

Intergenerational philanthropy involves a conflict over the desire of the past to benefit the future, and the desire of the future to govern itself by its own lights. This conflict is present in some form in any relationship between gift-giving and gift-receiving. But the public-facing nature of philanthropy and the passage of time conspire to make this conflict especially thorny. Attempts to find a place for intergenerational philanthropy in a liberal democracy have pointed to its potentially beneficial effects. I have argued that these attempts are incomplete.

To show that ICTs are justifiable requires showing that such transfers are consistent with the value of generational sovereignty. Part of what makes generational sovereignty valuable, I contended, is the interest a generation has in control over matters of basic justice in its society. We have seen that ICTs don't ultimately pose a threat to the ability of living persons to exercise control over these fundamental questions. Another part of what makes generational sovereignty valuable is the superior knowledge that a generation is likely to have regarding its own interests. Living persons appear best positioned to understand their own interests and to take prudent steps to realize them. Dead-hand control appears to saddle a living generation with the well-meaning but obsolescent conjectures of the departed. I argued, however, that binding the living and unborn to obsolete notions is a dispensable feature of intergenerational philanthropy. Prudent regulation can cabin the tendency of ICTs to reflect obsolete ideas while also leveraging the unique wisdom of the past. The possibility of such regulation, and some encouraging steps currently being taken in its direction, supplies one strong response to the Jeffersonian challenge.

A striking upshot of the forgoing analysis is that it vindicates the enduring influence of persons like Carnegie, whose general-purpose foundation shows no obvious signs of becoming obsolete. Those troubled by this implication may suspect that the analysis is mistaken. My own hunch, however, is that the sources of sound objections to Carnegie's enduring influence lie elsewhere: not in its perpetuity per se, but in its tainted origins and plutocratic proportions.

NOTES

1. E.g., Joanne Florino, "The Case for Philanthropic Freedom," *Alliance* 21, no. 3 (2016).

2. E.g., Anand Giridharadas, *Winners Take All: The Elite Charade of Changing the World* (New York: Knopf, 2018).

3. E.g., Judith Sealander, "Curing Evils at Their Source: The Arrival of Scientific Giving," in *Charity, Philanthropy, and Civility in American History*, eds. Lawrence J. Friedman and Mark D. McGarvie (Cambridge: Cambridge University Press, 200), 217–39; Matthew Bishop and Michael Green, *Philanthrocapitalism: How Giving Can Save the World* (New York: Bloomsbury, 2010).

4. E.g., Emma Saunders-Hastings, "Plutocratic Philanthropy," *Journal of Politics* 80, no. 1 (2018): 149–61.

5. One exception is Ray D. Madoff, *Immortality and the Law: The Rising Power of the American Dead* (New Haven, CT: Yale University Press, 2010).

6. In this terminological choice, I follow Chiara Cordelli and Rob Reich, "Philanthropy and Intergenerational Justice: How Philanthropic Institutions Can Serve

Future Generations," in *Institutions for Future Generations*, eds. Axel Gosseries and Iñigo González (Oxford: Oxford University Press, 2016), 229–44.

7. My calculations, based on data from *Giving USA 2020* (Indianapolis: IUPUI Lilly Family School of Philanthropy, 2021), 22.

8. Private foundations that engage directly in charitable work are called private operating foundations.

9. One notable exception is the Bill and Melinda Gates Foundation, which is set to terminate twenty years after the death of the last to die of Bill and Melinda Gates and Warren Buffet.

10. Internal Revenue Service, Statistics of Income Division, "Historical Table 16: Nonprofit Charitable Organization and Domestic Private Foundation Information Returns, and Exempt Organization Business Income Tax Returns: Selected Financial Data, 1985–2011," October 2014.

11. My calculations, based on data from *Giving USA 1986* (Purdue: Indiana University Center on Philanthropy, 1986) and *Giving USA 2020* (Indianapolis: IUPUI Lilly School of Philanthropy, 2021).

12. Iris J. Goodwin, "Ask Not What Your Charity Can Do for You: *Robertson v. Princeton* Provides Liberal-Democratic Insights onto the Dilemma of *Cy Pres* Reform," *Arizona Law Review* 51 (2009): 75–125, p. 97.

13. E.g., Plato, *Laws*, XI, 923a *et seq.*; William Godwin, *Enquiry Concerning Political Justice, and Its Influence on Morals and Happiness*, vol. 2 (London: G. G. and J. Robinson, 1798), Bk. VIII, Ch. II, pp. 444–48.

14. Thomas Jefferson, "Letter to James Madison," September 6, 1789, in *The Works of Thomas Jefferson*, vol. 6, Federal Edition (New York and London: G.P. Putnam's Sons, 1904–1905).

15. In fact, Jefferson's famous sentence appears to contain a contradiction. If the rights of the living are only usufructory in nature, this doesn't prevent the dead from possessing certain property rights. However, the ordering of the words suggests that Jefferson is using "usufruct" in a more figurative sense to emphasize his view that the property claims of the living deserve more considerable weight.

16. Jefferson was also aware of the challenge of defining the concept of a generation. If we believe that generations of persons are possible subjects of moral claims, we will need some way of distinguishing one generation from the next. But on what basis shall we make this distinction? One could say that "my generation" consists only of the persons born on the same day or within the same year as me. Or my generation might include persons born decades before or after me. Jefferson's letter suggests a complicated mathematical formula for sorting persons into separate generations, a formula that Michael Otsuka has attempted to clarify and operationalize in his *Libertarianism without Inequality* (Oxford: Oxford University Press, 2003), 132–50.

17. A future generation may of course enjoy opportunities to influence social conditions in the generations that follow its own. But this isn't a reciprocal relationship. Nor are the opportunities necessarily equal: given the scarcity of resources, generations that come earlier in the historical sequence may enjoy significantly greater opportunities to shape social affairs in the future.

18. Hillel Steiner and Peter Vallentyne, "Libertarian Theories of Intergenerational Justice," in *Intergenerational Justice*, eds. Axel Gosseries and Lukas H. Meyer (Oxford: Oxford University Press, 2009), 50–75.

19. Although Joel Feinberg once famously tried to argue otherwise—that interests could persist posthumously—he later abandoned this position in his *Harm to Others* (Oxford: Oxford University Press, 1984). Thanks to Ray Madoff for this point.

20. Andrew Holowchak emphasizes the pluralistic origins of Jefferson's philosophical thought in his "Thomas Jefferson," *Stanford Encyclopedia of Philosophy*, ed. Edward N. Zalta, Winter 2019 Edition, https://plato.stanford.edu/archives/win2019/entries/jefferson/.

21. Those who defend views of this type include Janna Thompson, *Intergenerational Justice: Rights and Responsibilities in an Intergenerational Polity* (New York: Routledge, 2009), pp. 60ff., and Rahul Kumar, "Wronging Future People: A Contractualist Proposal," in *Intergenerational Justice*, eds. Axel Gosseries and Lukas H. Meyer (Oxford: Oxford University Press, 2009), 252–71.

22. Reeve holds that the role of bequest in helping to facilitate responsible planning explains the support it enjoys from J. S. Mill, T. H. Green, and John Rawls. See Andrew Reeve, *Property* (Houndsmills: Macmillan, 1986), p. 161.

23. See, e.g., Edward J. McCaffery, "The Political Liberal Case Against the Estate Tax," *Philosophy & Public Affairs* 23, no. 4 (1994): 281–312, pp. 295–6.

24. Samuel Scheffler, *Death and the Afterlife*, ed. Niko Kolodny (Oxford: Oxford University Press, 2013). Scheffler's argument is addressed to the broader importance of posterity to the motivations of present persons.

25. Galle wonders how strong these incentives really are in Brian Galle, "Pay It Forward: Law and the Problem of Restricted-Spending Philanthropy," *Washington University Law Review* 93 (2015): 1143–207, pp. 1168–71.

26. See, e.g., D. W. Haslett, "Is Inheritance Justified?" *Philosophy & Public Affairs* 15, no. 2 (1986): 122–55; McCaffery, "The Political Liberal Case Against the Estate Tax"; Eric Rakowski, "Transferring Wealth Liberally," *Tax Law Review* 51 (1995–1996): 419–72; Liam Murphy and Thomas Nagel, *The Myth of Ownership* (New York: Oxford University Press, 2002), chap. 7.

27. Martin Gilens, *Affluence & Influence* (Princeton: Princeton University Press, 2012).

28. This is true of Haslett, McCaffery, and Rakowski, op. cit.

29. On the first point, see Rob Reich, "A Failure of Philanthropy," *Stanford Social Innovation Review* (Winter 2005): 24–33.

30. This isn't to say that these are the only conditions that govern whether ICTs are effective instruments of redistribution.

31. "Patterns of Household Charitable Giving by Income Group, 2005," Indiana University Center on Philanthropy / Google, Inc. (Summer 2007), available at http://www.philanthropy.iupui.edu/files/research/giving_focused_on_meeting_needs_of_the_poor_july_2007.pdf.

32. See, e.g., Liam Murphy and Thomas Nagel, *The Myth of Ownership*, p. 127; Robert D. Cooter, "The Donation Registry," *Fordham Law Review* 72 (2004): 1981–89; Rob Reich, "A Failure of Philanthropy"; Rob Reich, "Philanthropy and Its Uneasy

Relation to Equality," in *Taking Philanthropy Seriously: Beyond Noble Intentions to Responsible Giving*, eds. William Damon and Susan Verducci (Bloomington: Indiana University Press, 2006), 27–49.

33. John Rawls, *A Theory of Justice*, rev. edn. (Cambridge, MA: Harvard University Press, 1999), pp. 251–62.

34. Cordelli and Reich, "Philanthropy and Intergenerational Justice."

35. Rawls, *A Theory of Justice*, p. 252.

36. Joseph Raz, *The Morality of Freedom* (Oxford: Clarendon Press, 1986), p. 53.

37. Anna Stilz, "The Value of Self-Determination," in *Oxford Studies in Political Philosophy*, vol. 2, ed. David Sobel, Peter Vallentyne, and Steven Wall (Oxford: Oxford University Press, 2016), 98–127; Jake Zuehl, "Collective Self-Determination" (PhD diss., Princeton University, 2016).

38. Zuehl, "Collective Self-Determination," p. 1.

39. Zuehl claims that collective self-determination also fails when citizens lack basic agreement on fundamental assumptions, such as the moral equality of persons (ibid., pp. 68ff).

40. Though Zuehl provides no definition of "core institutions," the common illustrations that he offers (the civil and criminal justice systems, and systems for distributing employment, healthcare, and education) seem to possess a unifying quality (ibid., pp. 42–43). That is, a central unifying feature of such institutions is their role in assigning fundamental rights, duties, and opportunities—what we might otherwise call matters of basic distributive justice. I borrow this definition of "core institutions" from Rawls's comments about the "basic structure," to which Zuehl seems partially indebted. See Rawls, *Theory*, pp. 7, 96.

41. Historically this wasn't always the case. When the primary form of wealth was land, there was a real worry that a society's material basis would someday come to be controlled entirely by dead persons. See Lewis M. Simes, *Public Policy and the Dead Hand* (Ann Arbor, MI: University of Michigan Law School, 1955).

42. An interesting consequence of this view is that it casts doubt on the legitimacy of perpetual constitutions, insofar as they presuppose substantive conceptions of justice. Perpetual constitutions enjoy monopoly or dominating influence over future generations in a way that I've claimed doesn't hold in the case of ICTs.

43. Simes reports this case in *Public Policy and the Dead Hand*, p. 122.

44. Ibid., p. 127.

45. I take these facts from Goodwin, "Ask Not What Your Charity Can Do for You."

46. Edmund Burke, "Reflections on the Revolution in France," in *Select Works of Edmund Burke*, Vol. 2 (Indianapolis: Liberty Fund, 1999).

47. One might object here that the prevalence of general-purpose foundations challenges the idea that the permission to craft narrow terms serves as an important incentive. However, I think it's more accurate to think of general-purpose foundations as exceptions to this rule. Those who possess vast sums of wealth may get as much, or more, satisfaction from endowing a general-purpose institution that bears their name. This alternative incentive isn't available to persons of more ordinary means.

48. I'm grateful to Rob Reich for bringing this point to my attention.

49. Cordelli and Reich, "Philanthropy and Intergenerational Justice."

50. J. S. Mill, "Corporation and Church Property (1833)," in *Collected Works of John Stuart Mill: Essays on Economics and Society Part I*, Vol. IV, ed. John M. Robson (Toronto: University of Toronto Press, 1967), pp. 193–222.

51. The precise details of Mill's position are difficult to pin down. In revisiting the question in 1869, he restates a similar regulatory ideal but appears to suggest a different way of implementing it. Rather than revise the terms of obsolete trusts, he writes in passing that trusts should come under state control, where they can then be redeployed to more lasting public purposes. However, the context of this statement makes it ambiguous as to whether nationalizing trusts is truly what he intends to advocate, and whether this represents his considered position. See J. S. Mill, "Endowments (1869)," in *Collected Works of John Stuart Mill: Essays on Economics and Society Part II*, Vol. V, ed. John M. Robson (Toronto: University of Toronto Press, 1967), pp. 615–29.

52. Simes, *Public Policy and the Dead Hand*, pp. 139–40.

53. Thanks to Paul Brest for bringing this to my attention.

54. *Uniform Trust Code* (National Conference of Commissioners on Uniform State Laws, 2010), sec. 413,

55. Ibid., sec. 201.

56. An audit system can also mitigate the potential for abuse of power by trustees, who can be tempted to spend trust funds for personal advantage (as discussed in Madoff, *Immortality and the Law*, pp. 102–104).

Chapter 6

Intergenerational Justice and Charitable Giving

A Libertarian Perspective

Miranda Perry Fleischer

How should time shape charitable giving policy? This issue permeates the philanthropic world in multiple ways: Should charities have limited lives, or the option to exist in perpetuity? Should we require perpetual structures such as foundations, endowments, and donor-advised funds to spend a certain portion of their income or assets each year? Or, should we limit their spending in order to lengthen their lives? When should donors to such structures receive tax benefits?

Scholarly discussions of these questions generally focus on efficiency or preserving donor intent, largely ignoring a crucial inquiry: Who should benefit from charitable dollars, current or future generations? The few scholars who have addressed the latter issue have emphasized welfarist considerations, arguing that because future generations will likely be better off than current ones, spending charitable dollars now maximizes welfare. Saving for the future, in their view, equals poor-to-rich redistribution.

In contrast, little attention has been paid to what comprehensive rights-based theories of justice say about questions of time and charitable giving.[1] Rights-based discourse is not completely absent; discussions of donor intent address the right of donors to direct charitable dollars after death. The question of donors' rights, however, does not address the full spectrum of intergenerational considerations.

This chapter fills that gap by mining one rights-based theory of justice—libertarianism—for insight into questions of intergenerational justice and charitable giving. Many of libertarianism's principles—such as limited government—are popular with the public, yet tax scholarship focuses overwhelmingly on welfarism and egalitarianism, largely ignoring libertarianism.

This chapter aims to fill that void. Some readers may be surprised by this project, wondering whether libertarianism has anything to say about distributive justice at all, let alone intergenerational justice. Such terms are associated with taxing one group to assist another, and these questions may seem irrelevant from a libertarian point of view. After all, don't libertarians consider all taxation theft? Doesn't libertarianism stand for the proposition that one can do whatever one wants with one's property?

This impression overlooks two key points. First, the libertarian theory is much more nuanced than commonly assumed. Libertarianism is a family of theories sharing various core characteristics: advocating freedom from coercion, extremely strong private property rights, the importance of the free market, and a presumption that market results are just and should not be disturbed.[2] Within this family, theorists rely on a variety of justifications, including natural-rights-based reasoning, contractarianism, and utilitarian considerations. While all such theories impose extremely strong limits on state power, property rights—while of utmost importance—are not quite as inviolable as commonly believed. Several strands of libertarian theory make room for some—albeit limited—redistributive taxation and for some—admittedly minimal—restrictions on what one may do with one's property.[3] Second, charitable tax subsidies mean that charitable institutions do not consist of purely private money. Because of their special tax and legal treatment, philanthropic institutions employ—to a small but non-trivial extent—the coercive power of the state. This coercive power results in redistribution from some taxpayers (non-donors and non-beneficiaries) to others (donors and beneficiaries).[4] To that end, the state subsidization of such organizations must be scrutinized for consistency with the demands of justice.

Exploring the distribution of charitable assets between generations from a libertarian perspective yields four insights. The first two stem from past work arguing that libertarianism justifies subsidizing charitable activity through the tax code only for the narrow purposes of rectification or providing a minimal safety net. One such insight is that *past* injustices impose demands on us today that should be addressed in part through charitable tax subsidies. This point is often overlooked in the debate about charitable giving and time, which overwhelmingly focuses on the relationship between the present and *future*. The second such insight is that whether it is just to use current tax subsidies for a future safety net depends on precisely how one justifies a tax-financed safety net in the first instance.

The final two insights concern unsubsidized charitable activity. The broad latitude accorded property owners under libertarianism means that there is no general justification for precluding current generations from considering the needs of future generations with unsubsidized charitable dollars. The law should therefore not prohibit donors from creating perpetual funds or contributing to permanent endowments for specific purposes. There may be arguments, however, in favor of precluding perpetual family foundations. Such entities bestow power on a donor's remote heirs, and the resulting inequality cannot be justified as an expression of the donor's identity and values.

This chapter proceeds as follows. Section I briefly explains the charitable tax subsidies offered by the government and Section II provides an overview of minimal state libertarianism. Section III explores minimal state libertarianism for insights into the interaction of tax subsidies for charitable activity and time. Section IV addresses unsubsidized charitable activity, and Section V concludes.

I. THE CONCEPT OF TAX SUBSIDIES

The U.S. legal system subsidizes and encourages charitable activity in a variety of ways, ranging from special rules for charitable trusts to state property tax exemptions to federal tax benefits for nonprofit organizations.[5] The latter are perhaps the best known. Section 501(c)(3) of the Internal Revenue Code exempts organizations that further "religious, charitable, scientific . . . literary, or educational purposes" from the income tax; section 170 grants donors to such organizations an income-tax deduction for their contributions.

Most scholars agree that these provisions operate as subsidies from the federal government in support of charitable giving.[6] Consider *Anna*, who is in the 40 percent tax bracket and donates $100 to Duke University, her alma mater. The charitable contributions deduction lowers her tax bill by $40, meaning that the after-tax cost to *Anna* of her gift is only $60. Duke still receives $100; but the government—more specifically, other taxpayers—have made up the $40 difference.[7]

Tax theorists refer to this type of tax provision as a "tax expenditure." Briefly, tax expenditure analysis argues that any deviations from an ideal income-tax base for social policy reasons should be considered the functional equivalent of direct spending by the government.[8] In an ideal income tax as defined by economists and tax policy theorists, personal expenditures are not deductible (and are therefore taxed); business expenditures are deductible (and are therefore not taxed).[9] If *Anna* spends $100 on supplies for her business, the resulting deduction is not a tax expenditure—it simply measures her net income. But if she spends $100 on mortgage interest or solar panels for her house and receives a deduction or credit, those benefits are tax expenditures because such expenses are clearly personal. They are deductible only because Congress has decided to encourage home ownership and solar energy by providing tax benefits.[10] Scholars across the ideological spectrum overwhelmingly (although not unanimously) agree that charitable giving should also be considered a personal expenditure.[11] *Anna* chooses to donate to charity, just as she chooses to spend money on a fine bottle of wine or new clothes. Donors like *Anna* also receive both tangible and intangible benefits from donating: the "warm glow" of giving, the satisfaction of bolstering causes they care about, and prestige and recognition.[12]

Although many libertarians initially resist the notion of characterizing tax benefits as spending, they should embrace tax expenditure analysis. The concept makes clear that tax benefits for social policy reasons employ the coercive power of the state, since they result in redistribution from some tax-payers to others. As a result, the charitable tax subsidies should be scrutinized in the same manner as direct government spending. This chapter adds to prior work scrutinizing the charitable tax subsidies through a libertarian lens[13] by exploring whether the concept of time should play a role in the government's treatment of charitable contributions.

II. MINIMAL STATE LIBERTARIANISM IN BRIEF

This chapter focuses on minimal state libertarianism, which is what most legal scholars associate with the term "libertarianism." Its foundations spring from John Locke's theory of property rights. Locke starts from the dual premises that natural resources are initially unowned, but that each individual has full ownership over her person and her labor. Two conclusions follow. First, because individuals own their labor, they are not required to contribute it to the common good. Second, mixing one's labor with land or other natural resources gives one property rights in that resource.[14]

These rights are not absolute, however. Among other conditions, one may acquire property rights in natural resources for oneself only if "enough, and as good" is left for others;[15] this constraint is known as the "Lockean proviso." (Section III discusses this requirement in further detail.) If an individual complies with the Lockean proviso, then nobody else has a claim on the newly appropriated resource, rendering his or her property rights absolute and redistributive taxation a violation thereof.[16]

Robert Nozick's *Anarchy, State and Utopia*—the most influential modern exposition of libertarian thought—builds upon these principles in elucidating Nozick's "entitlement theory." Like Locke, one building block of Nozick's theory is self-ownership (which Nozick refers to as the separateness of persons). Nozick argues:

> There are only individual people, different individual people, with their own individual lives. Using one of these people for the benefit of others, uses him

and benefits the others. Nothing more. . . . To use a person in this way does not sufficiently respect and take account of the fact that he is a separate person, that his is the only life he has.[17]

In Nozick's view, forcing one person to work for another violates the separateness of persons. And if "forcing each person to work five extra hours each week for the benefit of the needy" violates that principle, so does "a system that takes five hours' wages in taxes."[18] "Taxation of earnings from labor is on par with forced labor" and is therefore, according to Nozick, unjust.[19]

The second building block is that unappropriated resources are unowned and can be appropriated for private use if the Lockean proviso is satisfied. Nozick argues that if an individual justly acquires a resource, then nobody else has a claim on that resource. The acquirer can do whatever she wants with it, including transferring it in a market exchange or by gift or bequest.[20] (Nozick refers to these principles as "justice in acquisition" and "justice in transfer.") If, however, the initial acquisition of property or a later transfer is unjust, the state may engage in redistributive taxation to rectify that past injustice.

Tying these together, minimal state libertarianism means that individuals' freedom to do what they like with their property is almost—but not completely—absolute. The state can intrude upon property rights through taxation (or regulation) only for two purposes. It can tax individuals to fund institutions such as the police and courts that protect private property rights, but it cannot legitimately impose taxes for other public goods. It can also redistribute for purposes of rectification or ensuring that the Lockean Proviso is met, but not to pursue egalitarian or other social goals. As explained below, this imposes severe limits on the extent to which charitable tax subsidies can be justly provided in a libertarian world.

III. MINIMAL STATE LIBERTARIANISM, THE CHARITABLE TAX SUBSIDIES, AND TIME

What minimal state libertarianism demands of charitable giving in reference to time is closely linked to what it demands of the charitable tax subsidies more generally. Because the charitable tax subsidies use the coercive power of the state, they can only be deployed in two specific ways that are compatible with strong private property rights: (1) to pursue rectification or (2) to provide a minimal safety net. As explored below, these justify tax subsidies only for very narrow reasons. Subsidizing charitable activity for other than these two reasons—regardless of whether current or future generations are benefited— is illegitimate. Each justification, however, has differing implications for generational issues. Rectification counsels us to pay more attention to the *past*. Depending on the theory used to justify a minimal safety net, setting aside funds to provide a safety net in the *future* may or may not be justified.

Rectification

Rectification highlights the underexplored question of how the past should influence charitable giving policy. As this section demonstrates, rectification likely demands that the state currently take steps to address past injustices. Recall two principles of Nozick's entitlement theory. Justice in acquisition holds that if an individual justly acquires property, she can do whatever she pleases with it. Justice in transfer holds that any subsequent distribution of justly acquired property that arises from voluntary transfers among consenting participants is also just. "If the world were wholly just," Nozick argues, then "justice in acquisition" and "justice in transfer" would "exhaustively cover the whole subject of justice."[21] No justification for redistributive taxation would exist.

But the principles of justice in acquisition and transfer are not always obeyed. As Nozick recognizes, "Some people steal from others, or defraud them, or enslave them . . . or forcibly exclude others from competing in exchanges. None of these are permissible modes of transition from one situation to another."[22] In such cases, the state may justly engage in "rectification," which is the rearranging of individual holdings so that the resulting distribution approaches the outcome that would have resulted had those principles been obeyed. The state may do so even if rectification requires a more extensive state than would otherwise exist.[23]

Given the conditions that have shaped property distribution in the United States, rectification is almost certainly required. As Jeremy Waldron explains:

> [Nozick] was never prepared to say that the historical-entitlement critique of equality and welfarism in his book amounted to a defense of actually existing market institutions. . . . On the contrary, he thought it undeniable that contemporary holdings would be condemned as unjust by any remotely plausible conception of historical entitlement. (The point of Nozick's argument . . . was that egalitarians were condemning the existing distribution for the wrong reason—that is, simply as unequal—rather than on account of the violence, fraud, expropriation, ethnic cleansing, state corruption, and so on, involved in the history of most holdings of property in America.)[24]

Although Nozick's discussion of how to implement rectification is sparse,[25] it seems to call for redistributing to the victims of past injustices from the beneficiaries of such injustices (and perhaps, to and from the descendants of each respective group). Most (though not all) theorists who study rectification believe that using taxation for this purpose is just;[26] subsidizing private groups as one means of pursuing that goal would therefore also be just. Although using charitable tax subsidies alone to pursue rectification would almost certainly not fulfill that duty, there are strong reasons they should play some role. Namely, they would harness all the benefits associated with the sector—experimentation, pluralism, reducing the scope and size of government, augmenting individual initiative—to enhance state-directed efforts at rectification.

How might they be used? To back up a bit, perfectly implementing the ideal of rectification involves three steps: (1) identifying unjust transfers; (2) determining what distribution would have resulted absent those injustices; and (3) putting the victims in a position comparable to that distribution.[27] Some past injustices are obvious. Slavery, followed by decades of violence, Jim Crow laws, and state-mandated and enforced discrimination, are clear violations of African Americans' rights to their own persons, labor, and property.[28] Native Americans likely acquired much North American land in accordance with the Lockean Proviso before newcomers used theft, fraud, coercion, and force to deprive them of their justly acquired holdings.[29] Past laws that interfered with women's freedom of contract and property rights would likely also trigger rectification. Numerous other past injustices likely exist; this list is meant to be illustrative and not exhaustive.

The second step—identifying with precision who merits rectification because of any given injustice—is complex. We can safely assume that African Americans who are descendants of slaves merit rectification (putting aside the identity problem).[30] But what about other African Americans, who are not direct descendants of slaves or individuals subject to redlining or Jim Crow? One could argue that—even if their ancestors were not *directly* subjected to injustice—their holdings are less than otherwise due to societal conditions arising from such past injustices.[31] Consider poor educational opportunities for many African Americans. Past state-sanctioned redlining contributed to low tax bases, which in turn contributes to underfunded public schools. All students in such schools suffer, not solely those whose ancestors were directly impacted by redlining.

Note that identifying from whom rectification is due is similarly difficult. In theory, only those individuals who benefited from past injustices should bear the burden of rectification. Again, this would clearly include descendants of slaveholders. But what about other individuals whose families hail from Southern states that practiced slavery? Should rectification also be due from Caucasians generally, most (if not all) of whom have likely benefited from the long history of mistreatment of African Americans?[32] Past injustices, for example, reduced competition for and created advantages in jobs, education, and cultural opportunities for white Americans. On the other hand, many Caucasians have ancestors who died fighting for the North in the Civil War; how should rectification account for that?[33]

An even harder task is determining what position members of these groups would find themselves in absent the injustice. As Nozick himself recognized, precisely identifying that distribution would be impossible.[34] Consider the task of identifying the holdings that would have resulted had Native Americans not been defrauded out of their land. We need to know past preferences for consumption versus saving; what past individuals would have done with their holdings at death; and past rates of economic growth.[35] But of course, we do not have that precise information; we only have estimates and assumptions. Estimating the holdings that would have resulted without slavery is even more complicated. How does one account for the fact that we don't know how many Africans (if any at all) would have immigrated here voluntarily?

As Nozick acknowledged, these difficulties mean that the ideal is essentially impossible, and rules of thumb might be necessary to implement it in spirit. One rough solution would be to consider all members of easily identifiable victim groups as meriting rectification.[36] This would justify tax-subsidized charitable efforts to improve the economic position of such groups, including but not limited to private schools, tutoring programs, job training, scholarship programs, and the like serving minority populations. It might also include subsidizing other nonprofits that expand recreational and cultural offerings for such groups (such as museums of African American art). In this manner, the charitable tax subsidies could act as a complement to direct financial resources that would almost certainly be due under rectification.

A second approach is using something like Rawls's difference principle[37] to reflect that the least advantaged are the most likely to be the victims of past injustice. Nozick himself acknowledged this possibility, suggesting that if "those from the least-well off group in the society have the highest probabilities of being (the descendants of) victims of the most serious injustice who are owed compensation by those who benefited from the injustices," and those beneficiaries are "assumed to be better off," then redistribution from the more- to the less-advantaged may be an (admittedly imperfect) way of implementing rectification.[38] Thus, a modestly redistributive tax system could be a "rough rule of thumb" used to "approximate the general results of applying the principle of rectification."[39] Whether this justifies redistributive taxation in a given society depends on its unique history; as previously mentioned, Nozick did not deny that American history contained numerous examples of past injustice in acquisition and transfer of property.

One might argue that using rough rules of thumb ignores individual responsibility, punishes those who never participated in an injustice, and benefits those who were not harmed. Those concerns are admittedly valid, but they are outweighed by the state's inability to make the necessary determinations. The state is ill-equipped to determine precisely who is poor, who is better off, and by how much due to past injustice with precision. Any metric it uses will be imperfect, but this should not dissuade us from attempting to fulfill some small part of our obligation to rectify past injustice, including through tax subsidies for private charity.

What rectification tells us about the future is more complicated. One might assume that because rectification involves correcting past wrongs, setting aside funds to be used in the future is counterproductive. How can benefiting future peoples make up for the worsened position of those alive today due to past injustice? The response is that rectification might take longer than one generation. Consider the fact that on average, the educational opportunities available to African Americans lag those available to others. Waving a magic wand and fully equalizing educational opportunities for this generation may not compensate for past inequalities. Consider the importance of human capital and its replication over generations. It is likely that, all else being equal, children growing up in families with a long history of access to high-quality education have advantages over those who are the first in their family to have such access. Directing some charitable resources toward the next generation might be a necessary component of rectifying past state-sanctioned or state-conducted injustice against African Americans. Rectification probably allows, but does not require, subsidizing future charitable activity geared toward that purpose.

Providing a Minimum Safety Net

Two additional arguments within minimal state libertarianism also justify narrow charitable tax subsidies. These arguments—the first based on the separateness of persons and the second on the Lockean Proviso—both justify charitable tax subsidies only for organizations that provide basic needs to the poor, but they have different implications for generational issues. Although the former does not justify setting aside tax-subsidized funds to provide a future safety net, the latter does.

Vindicating the Separateness of Persons

Philosopher Eric Mack provides the first justification for subsidizing a minimum safety net. He springboards off the classic "Freezing Hiker" example by asking us to imagine a fully prepared hiker on a well-planned excursion. After unpredicted and fatally cold temperatures arise, she comes across a locked but unoccupied cabin. Entering the cabin would violate the owner's property rights, but its shelter, fire, and blankets would save her life. Mack argues that "no plausible moral theory" would require the hiker to honor the cabin owner's property rights at the cost of freezing to death. "No moral theory," Mack writes, "that builds upon the separate value of each person's life and well-being can hold that Freezing Hiker is morally bound to grin and bear it."[40] Insisting that she do so denies the essential premises of Nozick's argument: that each individual is a separate person, her life is the only one she has, and she cannot be forced to sacrifice her one and only life for others—even to honor their property rights. Only extreme need, however, justifies violating the cabin owner's property rights. If she did not face fatal peril, our hiker could not enter simply because she was tired and sore.[41]

What does this have to do with taxation? Next imagine someone who is homeless and destitute through no fault of his own. To survive, perhaps he steals food from our garden, or breaks into our toolshed for shelter. The intuitions supporting the Freezing Hiker example seem applicable here, as well. Any moral theory centered upon the separateness of persons would also allow faultless individuals in life-threateningly dire financial circumstances to engage in self-protection.[42]

As Mack acknowledges, if such intrusions were allowed on an ad hoc basis, "the social world is going to be at least somewhat dangerous, morally risky, and irritatingly messy."[43] An ideal solution, he continues, would be "some system for certifying that individuals are faultlessly (or faultlessly enough) in sufficiently dire straits (e.g., in danger of loss of life, limb, or health), coupled with a system of provision of a minimal income . . . that would undo that distress."[44] Designing such a program, however, would be next to impossible.

The next-best solution is to prevent faultless individuals from finding themselves in the type of dire circumstances that would justify intruding on others' property rights. A minimal safety net does so by removing the conditions under which others can legitimately violate property rights. Counterintuitively, a tax-funded safety net thus absolutizes property rights by insuring property owners against the risk of intrusions by destitute individuals. In order to protect property owners' rights as much as possible without endangering those in the direst of straits, however, there should be two constraints on such a safety net. First, this safety net should be extremely basic—enough for "food, shelter, and basic medical care," but nothing more.[45]

Second, in theory, this safety net would be available only to those willing but unable to work. But—as with determining precisely who is owed rectification—libertarian skepticism of government intrusiveness and competence suggests forgoing such a requirement. It is extremely hard to identify work capability, and the very notion is often subjective (consider those suffering from depression, ADHD, or chronic pain, which are hard to diagnose and observe). Moreover, often the very people with the wherewithal to convince the government that they cannot work are actually among those most capable of it.[46]

Ironically, libertarian skepticism of government therefore weighs in favor of a safety net that does not require a showing of deservingness: the state may justly provide, or subsidize others to provide, basic needs to the poor. As with rectification, charitable services alone would likely not meet the demands of justice. Again, however, there are clear benefits from subsidizing charities to assist in this task.

With that context, we can now tackle the question whether the state can justly subsidize charitable gifts to provide a safety net in the future. If the separateness of persons vindicates that safety net, the answer is no. Recall that the crux of this vindication is that by removing justifications that destitute individuals in life-threatening circumstances may have to violate others' property rights, the state ultimately protects those property rights. Much like the state can tax individuals to fund courts or a police force that protects property rights, the state can also tax individuals to fund a safety net. The small incursion on property owners' rights from the tax is outweighed by the larger protection of their rights that arises from providing that safety net. However, providing a safety net fifty years hence does little to protect private property rights today. Property owners today are still vulnerable to incursions from destitute individuals. Taxing them to subsidize a safety net that may protect future owners' rights is therefore not justified. Of course, nothing would preclude a donor from creating an *unsubsidized* perpetual fund for that purpose.

Satisfying the Lockean Proviso

A final minimal state justification for some amount of state-financed redistribution arises from the Lockean Proviso and Nozick's conception of justice in acquisition. Recall that an individual justly appropriates property only if "enough, and as good" is left for others. The proviso is not literal in the sense that one must leave "enough, and as good" of the exact resource in question for others. If it were, the provision would be impossible to fulfill with respect to any finite resource. Imagine a field of 100 farmable acres and assume that one acre of farmland is enough to feed a family. If *Adam* is the first farmer to find the field, it appears that he can appropriate one acre of it by mixing his labor with it. After all, there is plenty left for *Bonnie*, the next farmer who happens along. It appears she too can appropriate an acre, since more than enough is left to meet the needs of *Charlie* (the third arrival). And so on. The problem becomes clear when *Zach*, the 100th farmer arrives. He cannot claim the last acre, for then nothing is left for the 101st arrival. But under that reasoning, *Yvonne* should not have been able to claim the 99th parcel, since her claiming the 99th parcel prevented *Zach* from claiming the 100th. Likewise, *Xavier*'s appropriation of the 98th parcel prevented *Yvonne* from claiming the 99th. Working backward, it turns out *Adam*'s claiming of the first acre did not leave "enough, and as good" for others.[47]

What, then, does it mean to leave "enough, and as good" for others? Nozick and other right-libertarians interpret the proviso to mean that others are not made worse off *overall* by *Adam*'s appropriation of the farmland, even if they cannot appropriate that particular acre of farmland. *Adam*'s appropriation of the farmland is just if it leaves others in a similar or better position than before his appropriation. This could happen if *Adam* employs *Bonnie* to farm the fields, and *Bonnie*'s wages allow her to live as well or better than if she farmed that acre herself.[48]

Under this view, private appropriation almost always comports with the proviso, since private property encourages value-enhancing cultivation: *Adam* is more likely to plant a field of corn if he knows he can reap its bounty without the risk of those who did not share in the labor harvesting some for themselves. In other situations, private appropriation encourages conservation by solving "tragedy of the commons" problems that can occur from over-grazing, over-fishing or over-cultivation.[49] Assuming that the non-appropriators benefit from the enhanced value (for example, by being able to trade labor or other goods for *Adam*'s corn or fish), then the proviso is generally satisfied. But the fact that private property rights leave non-appropriators better off overall does not mean that nobody is harmed by them. As I've explored elsewhere, redistributing to individuals harmed by a system of strong private property rights ensures that "enough, and as good," is left to such individuals as well.[50]

That said, Locke and Nozick are silent about who constitutes the group to whom enough and as good must be left. Logically, it must include members of the appropriator's generation who happen along after the initial acquisition. Otherwise, nobody would be able to appropriate anything unless contemporaneously surrounded by all her peers. If the proviso includes latecomers of one's own generation, it should logically also include those in later generations. Why should a difference of, say, fifty years affect whether or not one can partake in the benefits of natural resources? If the Lockean Proviso requires leaving "enough, and as good" for others, and those others include latecomers, then subsidizing a safety net for future generations is justified under the Lockean Proviso.

Final Thoughts

This section's exploration of minimal state libertarianism, time, and charitable tax subsidies has admittedly focused on ideal theory. In particular, its starting premise is that charitable tax subsidies for purposes other than rectification or providing a minimal safety net are unjustified, regardless of whether the funds are for current or future use. We do not, however, live in an ideal world. Our current policies subsidize a much broader group of organizations than would be justified under minimal state libertarianism. And in our current, non-ideal world, libertarianism has little to say about whether the tax benefits given to perpetual funds as such are just.

IV. UNSUBSIDIZED CHARITABLE ACTIVITIES AND MINIMAL STATE LIBERTARIANISM

So far, this chapter has focused on the tax benefits given to charitable organizations. But even if there were far fewer or no tax subsidies, charitable organizations would still surely exist. Apart from tax, do any other justice-related considerations rooted in libertarianism preclude a donor from creating a perpetual charitable fund?

The standard answer is no. Per Nozick, most minimal state libertarians believe that the right to dispose of justly acquired property is absolute. One may gift or bequeath it to friends, family, or charity as one chooses. Restrictions—including temporal ones such as the rule against perpetuities and the disfavor of entail—are justifiable only when needed to prevent negative externalities or the depletion of common resources.[51] A high bar thus applies to temporal restrictions on private property. There is no reason to treat charitable trusts (or similar structures such as perpetual foundations) less favorably; they are no more likely to threaten common-pool resources or harm others. Current law reflects this distinction, generally exempting charitable trusts from the rule against perpetuities and other temporal restrictions.[52]

That said, a small minority of minimal state libertarians argue that some limits on gifts and bequests are justified. This more controversial view stems from Locke's emphasis on labor mixing as the key to acquiring private property rights. One such property right is the ability to gift or bequeath property. As Nozick writes, "bequeathing something to others is an expression of caring about them, and it intensifies those bonds. . . . Although to some extent [the recipients] may have earned the continuing affection of the bequeather, it is the donor who has earned the right to mark and serve her relational bonds by bequeathal."[53] Because recipients have not mixed their labor with what they inherit, however, they do not possess the right to pass it along a second time. The objects of their affection do not reflect the intimate bonds of the original transferor, whose labor created the property. Nozick further notes that "resulting inequalities" of "wealth and position" from repeated bequests seem unfair when not accompanied by an expression of the original donor's affection.[54]

This potentially justifies two types of restrictions on the right to bequeath property. First, some have argued that the state can legitimately tax second (and later) transfers of wealth. Consider *Christine*, who earns $700,000 on her own, inherits $300,000 and dies with an estate of $1,000,000. These theorists would allow *Christine* to bequeath her newly earned $700,000 to whomever she chooses but would impose a tax on the $300,000 that she re-bequeaths. Second, some have argued for limiting the ability to make bequests to unborn individuals to prevent "an exceedingly wealthy individual from enriching his complete lineal descent."[55] As *Christine* does not know her unborn great-grandchildren, a bequest to them does not honor her identity the same way bequests to her children or living grandchildren do. The intuition underlying both arguments is that inequality arising from gratuitous receipts is acceptable when it is coupled with a decedent's expression of valued relationships, but unacceptable when divorced from any such expression.

How do these arguments apply to intergenerational charitable gifts? As an initial matter, charitable transfers express one's identity and values just as much as private bequests and in that sense, the two should be treated equally. Focusing on the donor's labor and self-expression thus legitimizes any long-lived charitable gifts that are restricted to specific purposes identified by the donor, such as job training in rural areas. The donor has expressed a connection with this purpose and an intent to further it. Regardless of when the funds are used for that purpose—now or in fifty or in one hundred years—they express that purpose. That future generations may find funds for other purposes more useful is irrelevant; what matters is the donor's intent. Restrictions on perpetual gifts with clearly identified purposes to public charities are thus illegitimate.

Perpetual gifts to charities controlled by the decedent's family—such as perpetual family foundations—present a more complex problem. These structures transfer power to one's heirs in at least two ways. First, family members wield power by being able to choose which grantees to fund; this is true even if the donor identifies a specific purpose for the foundation. Second, family members wield power because they control the investment of assets. Although this power differs in extent from that stemming from private wealth transfers, it contributes to inequality nonetheless.[56] These considerations suggest limiting family control of perpetual charitable funds to one or two generations after the grantor, but no more. Any inequalities in power resulting from the charitable bequest is thus limited to individuals with whom the grantor had some tie, thereby reflecting a donor's expression of value.

V. CONCLUSION

A superficial take on libertarianism and charitable giving policy is that it should have an "anything goes" attitude: Tax subsidies for charitable activity appear to keep money in private hands and out of the government's.

Moreover, any restrictions on what individuals may do with their property would violate libertarianism's commitment to strong property rights. As this chapter has shown, however, the relationship of libertarianism and charitable giving is more complex once one recognizes that private property rights are not absolute, and that the favorable legal treatment accorded charities often employ coercive state power. This recognition yields four insights.

The first two stem from the fact that subsidized charitable activity is justifiable only for the narrow purposes of rectification or providing a minimal safety net. As a result, the first insight is that past injustices impose demands on us today that should be addressed in part through charitable tax subsidies. This point is often overlooked in the debate about charitable giving and time, which overwhelmingly focuses on the relationship between the present and future. Second, whether it is just to use current tax subsidies for a future safety net is unclear and depends on how one justifies a tax-financed safety net in the first instance.

The final two insights concern unsubsidized charitable activity. There is no general justification for precluding current generations from considering the needs of future generations with unsubsidized charitable dollars. The law should therefore not prohibit donors from creating perpetual funds or contributing to permanent endowments for specific purposes. There may be arguments, however, in favor of restricting the extent to which a donor's descendants can staff family foundations or otherwise determine the use of an ancestor's charitable dollars.

NOTES

1. A notable exception is Rob Reich and Chiara Cordelli, "Philanthropy and Intergenerational Justice," in *Institutions for Future Generations*, eds. Axel Gosseries and Inigo Gonzalez-Ricoy (Oxford: Oxford University Press, 2017), 228–44.

2. For overviews of libertarian thought, see Harry Brighouse, *Justice* (Cambridge, United Kingdom: Polity Press, 2004), 84–104; Will Kymlicka, *Contemporary Political Philosophy: An Introduction* (Oxford: Oxford University Press, 2002), 102–65; Eric Mack and Gerald F. Gaus, "Classical Liberalism and Libertarianism: The Liberty Tradition," in *Handbook of Political Theory*, eds. Gerald F. Gaus and Chandran Kukathas (London: SAGE Publications, 2004), 115, 124–29.

3. The most absolute is "anarcho-capitalism," which argues that voluntary associations can adequately protect life and property, thereby negating any justification for the state (and its associated regulatory or taxing power). See, e.g., David D. Friedman, *The Machinery of Freedom: Guide to a Radical Capitalism* (Chicago: Open Court Publishing, 2014); Murray Rothbard, *The Ethics of Liberty* (New York: New York University Press, 1982). Minimal state libertarianism, which tolerates an extremely limited state with very strict limits on its regulatory and taxing power, is next along

the spectrum. Then comes "classical liberalism," which allows a somewhat larger role for the state to provide public goods and address market failures. At the far end of the spectrum—at least with respect to redistribution—is left-libertarianism, which tolerates a considerable amount of redistribution based on the reasoning that initial resources are commonly owned.

4. Eric M. Zolt, "Tax Deductions for Charitable Contributions: Domestic Activities, Foreign Activities, or None of the Above," *Hastings Law Journal* 63, no. 2 (2011–2012): 361, 374.

5. See Miranda Perry Fleischer, "Theorizing the Charitable Tax Subsidies: The Role of Distributive Justice," *Washington University Law Review* 87, no. 3 (2010): 505, 518 for a discussion of the theoretical issues surrounding the tax subsidies.

6. David E. Pozen, "Remapping the Charitable Deduction," *Connecticut Law Review* 39, no. 2 (2006): 552–53.

7. Zolt, "Tax Deductions," 361, 374.

8. Stanley S. Surrey & Paul R. McDaniel, "The Tax Expenditure Concept and the Budget Reform Act of 1974," *Boston College Industrial & Commercial Law Review* 17, no. 5 (1974): 679–81.

9. John R. Brooks, "The Definitions of Income," *Tax Law Review* 71, no. 2 (2018): 262.

10. See Miranda Perry Fleischer, "Libertarianism and the Charitable Tax Subsidies," *Boston College Law Review* 56, no. 4 (2015): 1349–51.

11. Pozen, "Remapping," 552–53. But see William D. Andrews, "Personal Deductions in an Ideal Income Tax," *Harvard Law Review* 86, no. 2 (1972): 346; Boris I. Bittker & George K. Rahdert," "The Exemption of Nonprofit Organizations" from Federal Income Taxation," *Yale Law jounral*, 85 no. 3 (1976): 333.

12. Fleischer, "Libertarianism," 1349–51.

13. Ibid., 1345–46.

14. John Locke, *Second Treatise of Government* (1690), reprint, ed. C.B. Macpherson (Indianapolis: Hackett Publishing Co., 1980), 19.

15. Locke, *Second Treatise*, 21. A second limitation is the spoilage limitation, which requires that one shouldn't appropriate more resources than can be used before they spoil. Ibid.

16. Ibid., 21, 30; Jeremy Waldron, "Nozick and Locke: Filling the Space of Rights," *Social Philosophy & Policy* 22, no. 1 (2005): 81, 89. Not surprisingly, much debate exists as to the meaning of the Lockean proviso. "Right" libertarians interpret the proviso as setting an extremely low bar for the private appropriation of resources, which renders private property rights almost (but not completely) absolute. In contrast, "left" libertarians interpret it more strictly, which imposes additional constraints on the ownership of private property. See, e.g., Peter Vallentyne, "Left-Libertarianism and Liberty," in *Contemporary Debates in Political Philosophy*, eds. Thomas Christiano and John Christman (Oxford: Wiley-Blackwell, 2009), 137, 147–49. Right and left libertarians thus tolerate different levels of redistribution, which bears on the questions of intergenerational justice.

17. Robert Nozick, *Anarchy, State and Utopia* (New York: Basic Books, 1974), 33.

18. Ibid., 169.

19. Ibid.

20. More precisely, the acquirer can do *almost* whatever he wants, for Nozick recognizes limits on one's use in times of catastrophe. Nozick argues that one who owns an island cannot force a shipwrecked castaway to leave. Ibid., 180. Nor could a property owner charge monopolistic prices if he owns the only source of water in a desert. Ibid. This essentially creates a "Lockean proviso" on use, because in neither case may the property owner use his property in a way that makes others worse off.

21. Ibid., 151.

22. Ibid., 152.

23. Ibid., 152–53, 231.

24. Jeremy Waldron, "Nozick and Locke," 81, 103.

25. Nozick, *Anarchy*, 153 (choosing "not [to] attempt [the] task" of specifying the details of the principles of acquisition of holdings, transfer of holdings, and rectification).

26. Many scholars interpret Nozick as implying that rectification is a duty of the state and therefore justifiably financed by taxation. *Cf.* Jan Narveson, "Present Payments, Past Wrongs: Correcting Impressions from Nozick on Restitution," *Libertarian Papers* 1, no. 1 (2009): 1, 3 (noting that many scholars view the just use of taxation for purposes of rectification as an "implication[] widely attributed" to Nozick's theory "including, apparently . . . Nozick himself" but disagreeing with that implication); Adam James Tebble, "The Tables Turned: Wilt Chamberlain Versus Robert Nozick on Rectification," *Economics & Philosophy* 17, no. 1 (2001): 89, 93 (assuming "safely" that the source of rectifying compensation will be taxation).

27. Nozick, *Anarchy*, 152–53; Lawrence Davis, "Nozick's Entitlement Theory," in *Reading Nozick: Essays on Anarchy, State and Utopia*, ed. Jeffrey Paul (New Jersey: Rowman & Littlefield, 1981), 344, 351; Tebble, "Tables Turned," 89, 92–93. Rectification does not involve returning the specific items of property that were the subject of unjust transfers to their proper owners. Davis, "Entitlement Theory," 349. Nor does rectification turn on proving that descendants of individuals previously subject to an injustice have inheritance rights.

28. For an argument that libertarianism requires affirmative action, see Andrew Valls, "The Libertarian Case for Affirmative Action," *Social Theory & Practice* 25, no. 2 (1999): 299–323. Interestingly, Nozick hints at this possibility by citing a "useful" book written by noted tax professor Boris Bittker. Nozick, *Anarchy*, 344 n.2 (citing Boris Bittker, *The Case for Black Reparations* (New York: Random House, 1973)).

29. See David Lyons, "The New Indian Claims and Original Rights to Land," in *Reading Nozick*, 355–79 (arguing that land in the northeastern United States should be returned to Native American tribes).

30. See Roberts, M. A., "The Nonidentity Problem," *The Stanford Encyclopedia of Philosophy* (Fall 2021 Edition), Edward N. Zalta (ed.), https://plato.stanford.edu/archives/fall2021/entries/nonidentity-problem/.

31. Some theorists interpret Nozick as requiring that a given individual establish that he or she would have somehow benefited from a victim's holdings had there been no injustice, whereas others do not require a direct link. See Robert E. Litan,

"On Rectification in Nozick's Minimal State," *Political Theory* 5, no. 2 (1977): 236, 244–45.

32. Ibid., 236.

33. Richard A. Epstein, "The Case Against Black Reparations," *Boston University Law Review* 84, no. 5 (2004): 1177, 1185–87.

34. Nozick acknowledges that estimates and probability distributions will likely be used. Nozick, *Anarchy*, 152–53.

35. Litan, "On Rectification," 234–35; Tebble, "Tables Turned," 103; Valls, "Libertarian Case," 312; Epstein, "Case Against," 1185–87.

36. See Litan, "On Rectification," 242 (positing that one approach might "consist of identifying those characteristics of the present-day population that are most likely to be correlated with past injustices," such that "a very simple rectification procedure would award compensation to the [African Americans] and [Native Americans] for the prior injustices suffered by both groups at the hands of Whites").

37. John Rawls, *A Theory of Justice* (Cambridge, USA: Harvard University Press, 1971), 75–83.

38. Nozick, *Anarchy*, 231.

39. Ibid.

40. Eric Mack, "Non-Absolute Rights and Libertarian Taxation," *Social Philosophy & Policy* 23, no. 2 (2006): 119. Loren Lomasky offers a similar take on the Freezing Hiker that reflects classical liberal reasoning. Lomasky starts by conceptualizing individuals as project-pursuers. Loren E. Lomasky, "Compensation and the Bounds of Rights," in *Compensatory Justice: Nomos XXXIII*, ed. John W. Chapman (New York: New York University Press, 1991), 24. He reasons that individuals have a mutual interest in not interfering with others' project pursuits. Lomasky explains that "basic rights duly emerge as affording . . . those moral constraints that impose minimal demands on the forbearance of others such that individuals can pursue projects amidst a world of similar beings, each with his own life to lead, and each owing the same measure of respect to others that they owe to him." Ibid., 25–26 (internal quotation marks omitted). Lomasky also argues, however, that if "scrupulous regard for another's moral space would directly jeopardize one's own standing as a project pursuer, then all bets are off." Ibid., 29. The Freezing Hiker may enter the cabin. Similarly, Lomasky reasons that extremely indigent individuals without "minimally decent life prospects" lack a mutually beneficial reason to agree to respect the rights of others. Ibid., 38. Providing such individuals with a minimal safety net gives them a reason to agree to mutual non-interference. Ibid. Respecting individuals as project-pursuers both creates property rights in the first instance *and* limits their scope so as to mandate a basic safety net for the extremely indigent.

41. Mack, "Non-Absolute Rights," 129, 133–34.

42. Ibid., 112.

43. Ibid., 140.

44. Ibid.

45. Ibid., 125, 140–41.

46. Miranda Perry Fleischer and Daniel J. Hemel, "Atlas Nods: The Libertarian Case for a Basic Income," *Wisconsin Law Review* 2017, no. 6 (2017): 1210.

47. Nozick, *Anarchy*, 176.

48. Kymlicka, *Political Philosophy*, 115–17; Clark Wolf, "Contemporary Property Rights, Lockean Provisos, and the Interests of Future Generations," *Ethics* 105, no. 4 (1995): 791.

49. Garrett Hardin, "The Tragedy of the Commons," *Science* 162, no. 3859 (1968): 1244; David Schmidtz, "When is Original Appropriation Required?" *The Monist* 73, no. 4 (1990): 504, 513; Wolf, *Property Rights*, 799–800.

50. Fleischer and Hemel, "Atlas Nods," 1211–17.

51. Richard A. Epstein, "The Temporal Dimensions in the Law of Property," *Washington University Law Quarterly* 64, no. 3 (1986): 667, 703–5.

52. Restatement (Second) of Trusts, Section 365 (1959); Adam J. Hirsch, "Bequests for Purposes: A Unified Theory," *Wash. & Lee L. Rev.* 56, no. 1 (1999): 40.

53. Robert Nozick, *The Examined Life* (New York: Simon & Schuster, 1990), 30.

54. Ibid., 30.

55. Ibid., 32.

56. See Miranda Perry Fleischer, "Charitable Contributions in an Ideal Estate Tax," *Tax Law Review* 60, no. 4 (2007): 263–322. Of course, some charitable transfers do exacerbate inequality of opportunity. But that is a problem with what qualifies as charitable, not a problem with the legitimacy of perpetual charitable gifts. See Miranda Perry Fleischer, "Equality of Opportunity and the Charitable Tax Subsidies," *Boston University Law Review* 91, no. 2 (2011): 601–63.

Chapter 7

When Should an Effective Altruist Donate?

William MacAskill

Effective altruism is the use of evidence and careful reasoning to work out how to maximize positive impact on others with a given unit of resources, and the taking of action on that basis. It's a philosophy and a social movement that is gaining considerable steam in the philanthropic world. For example, GiveWell, an organization that recommends charities working in global health and development and generally following effective altruist principles, moves over $240 million per year to its top recommendations. Giving What We Can, which encourages individuals to pledge at least 10 percent of their income to the most cost-effective charities, now has over 7,000 members, together pledging over $2.5 billion of lifetime donations. Good Ventures is a foundation, founded by Dustin Moskovitz and Cari Tuna, that is committed to effective altruist principles; it has potential assets of more than $15 billion, and is distributing over $200 million each year in grants, advised by Open Philanthropy.[1]

Philanthropists in the effective altruism community typically donate to charities that try to improve the well-being of the poorest people in the world, the living conditions of livestock in factory farms, or the long-term survival and flourishing of civilization. Highly regarded charities include the Against Malaria Foundation, which helps distribute insecticide-treated bednets, Mercy for Animals, which runs campaigns to convince large corporations to stop using eggs from caged hens, and the Blue Ribbon Study Panel on Biodefense, which works to ensure that developments in synthetic biology don't lead to catastrophic outcomes, such as a man-made pathogen causing a global pandemic.

However, for the effective altruist, a crucial issue concerns *timing*. Rather than donating as soon as she can, would she have a bigger impact if she saved her money, donating a larger amount of money at a later date? Or, if the opportunities available now are sufficiently good, should she even take out a loan so that she can donate more of her income now, and less in the future? This issue is crucial both for small individual donors in the effective altruism community—most of whom currently donate regularly each year, but some of whom save in order to donate later—and for large donors like Good Ventures, which is attempting to spend down its capital quickly, but is still saving the large majority of its wealth for a later date.[2]

The thought that it might be most effective to invest one's money in order to donate it at a later date often seems to be regarded as a surprising or counterintuitive conclusion; this is the view of both moral philosopher Dan Moller and political philosopher Laura Valentini.[3] Though many individuals might choose to save their money and, for example, donate in their will, this might be at best regarded as a compromise between altruism and self-interest, rather than warranted on the grounds of altruism alone.

However, in other contexts, we seem perfectly happy with the idea that an altruist should delay their impact. For example, it seems obvious that an eighteen-year-old who wishes to use their life to do as much good as possible should, if they can, go to a good university in order to increase their lifetime impact. But, in doing so, they are investing four years of their time in order to have a larger impact over the rest of their life.

Similarly, the idea that foundations should maintain their endowments, spending only close to the legal minimum of 5 percent of their endowments, seems often to be regarded as common sense, while the idea that Stanford or Harvard should spend down their endowment over the next few decades would be regarded as counterintuitive. But, again, this is in effect to take the position that those donations are spent at least as well in the future as they are now.

What's more, though we seem to be intuitively unhappy with the idea that it might be most effective for an individual philanthropist to invest and donate their income at a later date, we *also* seem to find unintuitive the idea that one ought to take out a loan in order to donate even more now. Indeed, such an idea might even be regarded as fanatical. But if there are strong arguments for donating now, then why should we be so surprised if those arguments also motivate taking out a loan, at least when the interest rate is low?[4]

Moreover, when it comes to government spending, it's well accepted that a government ought to borrow in order to be able to spend more earlier on social programs. Yet, to at least some extent, the government doesn't seem so different from a philanthropist: a significant part of the government's aim is to spend its budget in a way that will enhance the living conditions of its citizens.

Perhaps there are real differences between philanthropists, career-seekers, foundations, and governments that explain why the commonly accepted answer to the question "Give now or invest and give later?" is so different for each of them. But it's hard not to suspect that some sort of bias is at play, especially in the discrepancy between how charities spend their money and how foundations spend their money. Perhaps we simply find the status quo acceptable and find any deviations from it counterintuitive. Either way, the fact that we have different attitudes to giving now versus giving later across different domains makes it particularly valuable to investigate the question of when is the socially optimal time to spend money, for it may be that we come to revisionary conclusions for one or more of those domains. Moreover, despite the importance of this question, it has received very little academic attention from either philosophers or economists.

In this chapter, I will canvass what I consider to be all the main considerations that are relevant to whether an effective altruist ought to donate now or later, explaining what each of these considerations do and do not entail. In section I, I discuss what I view as relatively minor considerations, and in section II I move on to what I view as more significant considerations. In section III I will then propose a qualitative framework to help determine, for a given cause, whether you should invest to give at a later date, whether you should give now, or whether you should take out loans in order to donate even more now.

MINOR CONSIDERATIONS

Tax

For individuals, it is generally more tax-efficient to give as you earn. In the UK, for example, the Gift Aid scheme makes it easy for individuals to waive income tax on their donations: simply by ticking a box, the government will add 25 percent onto the donation, paying to the charity the income tax that was paid on the amount donated (if one is in the lowest tax bracket). However, the amount that the government will pay is capped at the income tax one has paid over the last four years. So if one saves until one's retirement and then donates, and the amount to be donated is sufficiently large, one will not be able to add the full 25 percent match from the government onto the donation.

However, this is not a strong consideration in favor of giving now, because one can easily set up a donor-advised fund (DAF) that enables one to donate one's income immediately, gaining the tax benefits, but only spend the money at a later date. For this reason, in my view, individual tax considerations do not provide a strong reason in favor of giving now.

For some people, tax considerations may provide a reason for giving later, if you will predictably enter a higher tax bracket in the future. In this circumstance, one may be able to donate a greater total amount if one waits until one enters that higher tax bracket, because one would get greater tax relief at that time, which could also be donated.

Future Weakness of Will

Another potential argument in favor of giving now is the fact that you might not follow through with your plans to give later; perhaps when you are older, you might choose to spend the money you've saved on yourself instead. If so, then you should discount any potential future returns on investment by the chance that you will keep the money for yourself instead.[5]

However, again you have the option to donate to a DAF. Because DAFs can only pay out to registered charities, you can guarantee that you will not spend the money on yourself at a later date. (The separate issue of whether you'll change *where* you choose to donate is discussed later, in the section on changing values.)

Though weakness of the will doesn't provide an argument in favor of donating now, it might provide an argument in favor of taking out a loan in order to donate even more now. If there is a significant risk that you won't donate more in the future, then taking out a loan is a way of tying yourself to the mast, effectively turning what would be an altruistic decision for your future self (to donate to charity) into a self-interested decision (to repay the loan).

What's More Neglected?

In general, because of diminishing marginal returns, one can do more to address a problem the fewer funds that have already been put toward addressing that problem.

Over time, in the United States, charitable spending has stayed approximately constant at about 2 percent of GDP.[6] However, average income is rising over time as the world gets wealthier, so the amount of total charitable donations is increasing; in the United States it has risen from $75 billion in inflation-adjusted dollars in 1975 to $471 billion in 2020.[7] This suggests that in general, the sorts of problems one would address with charity will receive more money in the future compared to what they receive now. This gives a mild consideration in favor of giving now.

Uncertainty

We don't know for certain what the future will be like. Every year, it's possible that some catastrophe, such as an asteroid strike, a world war or huge depression, will end the human race, destroy civilization, or otherwise make one's current income close to worthless. This ongoing risk gives a mild consideration in favor of giving now. The Stern Review on the Economics of Climate Change, for example, incorporates a 0.1 percent annual discount factor into their cost-benefit analysis as a modelling assumption that represents the possibility of human extinction.[8]

Self-Interest

Saving money provides benefits to the saver, effectively providing insurance in the case of major negative life events (such as unexpected illness or job loss) that require emergency use of money. Insofar as very few people give as much as would maximize their altruistic impact, this gives a mild reason in favor of giving later.

For example, consider someone who faces the following two options:

A. Donate yearly, giving a total of $100,000 (inflation adjusted, i.e., in US 2022 dollars) over their lifetime.
B. Save during their lifetime, and donate $110,000 (inflation adjusted, i.e., in US 2022 dollars) at the end of their life unless a one-in-a-hundred negative life event occurs, in which case they spend the money on themselves.

It may be that the decision-maker prefers B to A on self-interested grounds—because she's happy to donate an extra $10,000, with 99 percent probability, in order to be able to not-donate in the 1 percent likely outcome of a major negative life event—and that B is better than A on altruistic grounds, because B results in an expected $108,900 (i.e., 99 percent × $110,000) going to charity, whereas A results in an expected $100,000 going to charity. So some "give later" options could be better both in terms of self-interest and altruism than "give now" options.

However, donating immediately has benefits, too. By being able to see the impact of your donation, you get a "warm glow" that studies suggest improves happiness.[9] The personal benefits of donating give a reason for spreading out your donation over the course of your life, rather than waiting until the end of your life. For this reason, I think that self-interest provides at most only a mild consideration either way (though the extent of this consideration will necessarily be person-dependent).

MAJOR CONSIDERATIONS

Valuing the Present Generation More Highly

One reason you might have for preferring to donate now is that you value the interests of people alive today over the interests of people in the future.[10]

Moral philosophers typically argue that mere location in time provides no moral reason to discount the interests of future people. If I placed a bomb in some woods and primed it to go off in one hundred years' time, knowing that it will kill a child who is not yet born, that action seems no less wrong than if I were to prime the bomb to explode and kill a child in one week's time.

However, there might be relevant moral considerations that correlate with temporal location, even if they are, morally speaking, independent of it. For example, many people believe that they have a greater duty to their co-nationals than they have to strangers, perhaps because they are in a reciprocal relationship with co-nationals, receiving benefits from the government that are paid from taxes of co-nationals. If this gives a reason for preferring to help one's co-nationals than to help people in other countries, then it would also provide a reason for helping co-nationals that are alive today than co-nationals in the future.

One might think that the idea that some people's interests count for more than others is absurd, and therefore want to reject this consideration out of hand. But that would be too hasty. In other work,[11] I have defended the idea that, given the uncertainty we face about which moral view is correct, rather than simply following the moral view that we think is most likely to be right, we should instead look at all the moral views that we have some degree of confidence in, and take the action that represents the best "hedge" between those views. More precisely, I argue that we should *maximize expected choice-worthiness*, where the expected choice-worthiness of an option is given by the sum, over all possible moral views, of the product of one's credence in each moral view and the choice-worthiness of that option if that moral view were true.

If this is true, then any reasonable person should place *some* extra weight on the interests of those to which one has a special relationship. This is because you should have some degree of confidence that all people's interests should be treated equally, and some degree of confidence that you should weigh the interests of those to whom one has special relationships more heavily; both are popular views. However, you should have almost no credence in the idea that you should weigh the interests of strangers *more* heavily than you weigh the interests of friends, family, or co-nationals. In which case, if you take an expectation over all moral theories in which you have some degree of confidence, then you will give some additional weight to the interests of people to whom you have a special relationship; you should give them a weight in between that given to them by the "special obligations" view and the "impartiality" view. Exactly how much weight depends on the level of credence that one gives to the view that special relationships do matter morally. Personally, I have a fairly high degree of belief that when it comes to philanthropy we should be impartial across all creatures, so this consideration does not affect my decisions too greatly. But others may have different views.

Changing Opportunities

The opportunities that you will have for making an impact will change over time. If the cost-effectiveness of the best opportunities available to you is decreasing over time, then that provides an argument for giving now (or taking out a loan to give more now). If the cost-effectiveness of the best opportunities available to you is increasing over time, then that provides an argument for giving later.

The world is getting richer. Over the last thirty years, PPP-adjusted per-capita GDP has increased from $9,676 to $16,177—a rate of 2.2 percent per year.[12] In that same time, the number of people living in extreme poverty has decreased from 1.9 billion to less than 700 million, even though in that time, the total world population increased by 44 percent.[13]

The fact that the world is getting richer means that in general the best giving opportunities will be drying up, because it means that those who are potential recipients of philanthropy are less badly off. They will have solved the most pressing of their own problems. And, in general, the better off someone is, the more resources it takes to give that person a given amount of benefit.

However, it is not true for every problem that a philanthropist might want to tackle that we're making progress. The real income of the poorest 20 percent of families in the United States has barely increased since 1970;[14] nor has real GDP per capita increased since 1980 in some of the world's poorest countries, such as Central Africa Republic, Liberia or Niger.[15] Moreover, some global problems are a result of our increasing prosperity. The amount of ecological destruction and species loss increases as the population grows and as more greenhouse gases are emitted. The number of animals raised for food increases every year: in the United States, the number has increased from 1.8 billion animals in 1960 to 9.2 billion in 2015.[16] In these cases, we should expect to see less of an effect of the best opportunities decreasing over time.

A second way in which the cost-effectiveness of the best opportunities might change over time is based on the amount of resources going into a particular cause-area. If the amount of resources dedicated to tackling a problem is increasing, then, other things being equal, the cost-effectiveness of the best interventions available will decrease; if the amount of resources dedicated to tackling a problem is decreasing, then, other things being equal, the cost-effectiveness of the best interventions available will increase. This is because, when the amount of money flowing into tackling a problem increases, that spending will use up the room for more funding of the most effective interventions. For example, smallpox was the first disease to be eradicated; it was also significantly easier to eradicate than other diseases, because every infected person shows signs of infection, those signs are very distinctive, the initial appearance of symptoms occurs relatively soon after infection, there is only a human reservoir, and the smallpox vaccine was highly effective and did not require refrigeration. This exceptionality of smallpox is even more glaring when we consider the cost-effectiveness of the eradication effort: it was comparatively easy to eradicate, yet it was the disease that has killed the most people ever. It cost only $1.6 billion in today's money, saving between 60 and 120 million lives—a cost-effectiveness of $27 per life saved. In contrast, efforts to eradicate other diseases such as polio and measles have proven to be more difficult and more expensive.

This consideration is even stronger when we consider increases in resources that are *value-aligned*: that is, where the donors in question do not just support your preferred cause, but also share your values and general worldview. In this case, if you conclude that a particular cause or intervention isn't that promising, or if you discover a new cause or intervention that is particularly promising, then other donors who share your values and worldview are reasonably likely to support that too. When there is other donor money that is value-aligned, you should think of your spending as acting in harmony with the rest of the value-aligned money. If you think that the amount of value-aligned money is going to significantly increase over time, that gives an argument from diminishing marginal returns in favor of giving more now. If you think that the amount of value-aligned money is going to significantly decrease over time, that gives some reason for donating later.

A second line of thought relating to how the cost-effectiveness of the best opportunities might change over time is that entirely new opportunities might arise. For example, gene drive technology has recently been developed, potentially giving us the opportunity to completely eradicate malaria for what in global terms would be a very small amount of money. Of course, whether the use of gene drives to eradicate malaria is feasible and safe is still an open question. But suppose that it was discovered to be safe and feasible. In that case, donors would have an entirely new funding opportunity; if it was the case that the funding opportunity were open, it would be possible that those who are interested in donating to prevent deaths from malaria would have been able to do more good by saving their money to donate to the gene drive-based eradication effort than by donating to a charity like Against Malaria Foundation that distributes bednets.

Similarly, new organizations might come into existence. Perhaps there is some program that is known to be more effective than any other, but no existing charity that implements that program. In which case, it might be best to save in order that, if and when a charity comes into existence that implements that program, one can fund it.

So we have two effects: the world is getting richer, which decreases the cost-effectiveness of the best interventions; but we are making technological and organizational progress, which generates new opportunities for doing good. It's difficult to know which effect is more important, but my guess is that it's the former. When we look at the history of philanthropy's successes, many occurred decades ago, when the lowest-hanging fruit had not been picked: examples include Rockefeller's funding for short-stem disease-resistant wheat that precipitated the Green Revolution; Katherine McCormick's funding of the contraceptive pill; and the funding behind smallpox eradication.

One possible strategy, however, is what I'll call "watch then pounce." In this strategy, you invest your money rather than spend it, watching to see if any new unusually cost-effective opportunities arise. When an unusually cost-effective opportunity does arise, you then completely fill that organization's room for more funding. This is a strategy that could be optimal even if, on average, the best opportunities were decreasing in cost-effectiveness over time.

For example, consider a very simple model where the starting cost-effectiveness of the best donation opportunity is 1. Every year you think it's 10 percent likely that some new opportunity will arise. If the new opportunity does arise, you will be able to fund that opportunity, which has a cost-effectiveness of 2. If the new opportunity doesn't arise, then the cost-effectiveness of the best donation opportunity will decrease by 20 percent.

Now suppose that you choose the "watch then pounce" strategy. You save your money on the possibility that the new opportunity arises, then fund that opportunity when it does. After seven years, there's a cumulative 52 percent probability of a new opportunity arising, so the expected value of waiting for seven years and funding the new opportunity if and when it comes along is $0.52 \times 2 = 1.04$, which is greater than the expected value of simply donating immediately (which equals 1). The expected value of "watch then pounce" increases indefinitely, so if you can wait for seven years or more, the "watch then pounce" strategy does better than donating immediately. This is so even though the *expected* cost-effectiveness of the best donation opportunity is always decreasing.

It can therefore make sense to invest and give later even if cost-effectiveness is decreasing over time, depending on how quickly one thinks that cost-effectiveness over time is decreasing, and how much variance there is in the downward trajectory of cost-effectiveness over time. If cost-effectiveness is only decreasing slowly, or if variance is high, then it can make sense to wait until some new outstanding giving opportunity arises.

Getting Better Knowledge

Another consideration is how one's state of information about different giving opportunities will change over time. While the previous consideration related to how good one's opportunities are, this consideration relates to how good one is at identifying good giving opportunities. All other things being equal, if you have more knowledge of the world, then you'll be able to do better at finding the best giving opportunities.

Our ability to identify the best giving opportunities has certainly increased over time. Over the past two decades, there has been a rise in the use of randomized controlled trials, social science in general has progressed, and new rigorous charity evaluators such as GiveWell have been founded. For almost everyone, this progress happens independently of one's donations; you get the new information almost for free. All other things being equal, therefore, it would make sense to wait as one's ability to pick the most cost-effective interventions improved in light of one's improved epistemic state.

It's unlikely that one's state of information will get worse over time. So, in general, this consideration should only push us in the direction of investing to give later. However, sometimes it might be the case that one can *gain* new information by giving now. You can do this by funding research, or by funding a fledgling nonprofit to give it the capacity to provide you with more information, or as a way of gaining access to organizations that you might not otherwise have access to.

Values Changes

A similar consideration to one's state of knowledge is how one's values might change over time.

It's an interesting philosophical issue to what extent we should trust the values of our future selves. Most of us would agree that you should trust the views of your future self over your own when it comes to empirical beliefs, at least absent brain injuries or any other mitigating conditions, and on the assumption that your future self has had more time to investigate the issue than you have. But when it comes to values, people tend to be more uneasy. It's a common trope that people become more conservative over time, and suppose that you knew that in the future you would be significantly more conservative than you are today. Should this affect your decision about whether to give now or later? On the one hand, you might think that your future self has had more time to reflect and listen to new moral arguments, and therefore is in a better position to come to a set of values than you are today; on this view, the fact that your values might change over time provides a reason for you to invest, so that you can spend the money in a way that's more in line with the correct moral view.

On the other hand, you might see this as "value-drift," providing a reason for you to donate sooner; on this view, it's your *current* values that you should try to optimize for, even if your future self has had more time to reflect. On this view, you should give now, or even take out a loan in order to prevent your future self from spending their money in a poor way.

My own view is that we should defer to our future selves on our values, *if* it's the case that we think that their values are the result of "good" processes, such as careful reflection, discussion with peers, consideration of moral argument, and so on. There are, however, many value changes that are the result of bias, or cognitive decline, or personality changes, rather than of genuine reflection. For example, if your income increases, you were to come to the view that there are no strong altruistic obligations, then you might justifiably suspect that your future self's moral views have been biased by self-interest.

Investment Returns

The final consideration we'll discuss is the rate of return that you can get by investing the money. The real rate of return of the S&P over the last hundred years has been about 7 percent; this is almost certainly higher than the expected return one can get going forward (because the S&P did unusually well in this time period, and there may be some very small annual chance of catastrophic losses that are not captured by one hundred years of data). However, the rate of return on investment is always positive on average, and so by investing the money in an index fund or other vehicle, you can therefore ultimately donate a much larger amount of money than you started with. This may seem like a simple consideration in favor of giving later. But the reality is actually fairly complicated.

It's been argued that, just as one gets a financial return from investing one's money, one gets a social return by donating;[17] making the extreme poor richer, for example, has compounding effects, both because making one person richer enables them to be more economically productive and because that person spends some of their money on assets, which themselves generate a return. Moreover, it's been argued that the rate of this social return is much greater than the rate that one can get by investing in the stock market. The existing studies suggest annual investment returns in the order of 7–48 percent for iron roofs, 30–39 percent for unconditional cash transfers, 18–21 percent for conditional cash transfers,[18] and 15–30 percent for donations targeting contagious diseases.[19]

If this were the correct analysis, then it would provide a strong argument for giving now. However, this analysis is not correct.[20] If you were investing to give later, then you would reinvest any financial returns you got in whatever was the highest-return investment. In contrast, you do not have control over the additional money generated by the social return; that money is in the hands of the beneficiaries, who are very unlikely to reinvest their gains in whatever has the highest social return. Instead, the positive effects of your donation spread out more and more over time, until eventually those effects will grow at the rate of world economic growth. The world growth rate, at about 2.25 percent per year, is lower than the rate of return that you can get from your investment.

Because of this, it doesn't make sense to think of social return as something that compounds over time. Though you should think of the indirect benefits of your donation as increasing the total value of your donation, you should think of it as a fixed benefit. The social rate of return doesn't provide an argument in favor of giving now, because it doesn't matter when the donation happens; you'll get similar indirect benefits from the donation either way.

However, the social rate of return might provide a consideration in favor of giving earlier if it's true that the *rate* of the social rate of return is going down over time. This may be true; if so then, in effect, it adds another wrinkle to the idea that the best giving opportunities are disappearing over time. If, for example, the best investment opportunities for the very poorest are drying up over time, and the multiplier effect is a large component of the total good that you do through your donation, that may mean that the most cost-effective opportunities are disappearing even faster than you might otherwise think.

It's also worth noting that, for some cause-areas, there is no social compounding of the benefits of one's donation at all. If one donates to mitigate species loss, or protect the natural environment, or to rescue animals from factory farms, then there may be no social compounding effect.

So far, I've suggested that the idea of a social rate of return does not provide an argument either way for giving now or later. This crucially relied on the assumption that the returns from the donor's giving are not captured by the donor, so they can't be reinvested in the best giving opportunities.

Interestingly, however, there is *one* sort of social return where you can "capture" the donation. This can happen if an organization is dedicated to fundraising (a "meta-charity") and raises at least $1 with every $1 it spends on fundraising. If so, then the organization functions like an investment vehicle, but where the money can often get a far higher return than it can in a typical financial investment. For example, Giving What We Can (disclaimer: which I cofounded and formerly ran) is an organization that encourages people to pledge to give at least 10 percent of their income to the most cost-effective charities, and has over its lifetime, raised millions of dollars for those charities. Its very lowest-bound estimate is that every $1 donated to Giving What We Can results in $6 donated to top-recommended charities (its best-guess estimate is that every $1 donated to it results in $100 of value to top-recommended charities).[21] If the money that it raised were simply directed to global poverty charities, then the fact that it acts as a multiplier on your donation would not give an argument for giving now rather than later. However, a significant proportion of the money it raises is subsequently donated back to Giving What We Can, which can then be used for further fundraising. As long as you believe that the donors that Giving What We Can raises money from have similar values and worldviews to you, or even if not will donate to similar charities that you would choose to donate to, then you are in effect gaining more money to donate later. You might not possess that money yourself, but it will be used in a similar way to how you wanted to use it.

Of course, this argument relies on there being such opportunities available. If donating to a meta-charity really can get such a great return, then many other people will also want to donate to that charity, and the available room for more funding may get used up.

A QUALITATIVE FRAMEWORK

In the previous two sections, we canvassed a number of considerations that impacted the decision to give now or save and give later. We found considerations relating to tax efficiency, future weakness of will, neglectedness, uncertainty and self-interest were fairly minor, but considerations relating to special obligations, changes in opportunities, knowledge and values, and investment returns were more major.

In this section, I propose a qualitative framework that encodes the major considerations, as outlined in table 7.1. In this framework, I propose that under "amount of money to donate" we bundle considerations relating to taxes, weakness of will and uncertainty as well as financial investment. Each of these considerations simply affects how large the total amount of money to be donated is; whereas the other considerations, in different ways, affect how valuable the expected donation opportunity is. That's why the idea that the total real value of money assigned to donations might decrease over time is not an idle one: if the weakness of will is a real concern (and a DAF is not an option), or if it's more tax-efficient to give now (and again a DAF is not an option), or if one is considering the question at an unfortunate point in time (such as during hyperinflation), then one would, in effect, have more money to donate now rather than later.

Table 7.1 Qualitative Framework for Major Considerations for Donating Decisions

Consideration	Score	Score Explanation
Special relationships	1	special relationships to people now
	4	no special relationships
	7	special relationships to people in the future
Changing opportunities	1	better opportunities now
	4	no change in quality of opportunities
	7	better opportunities in the future
Knowledge	1	better knowledge now
	4	no change in knowledge
	7	better knowledge in the future
Values	1	better values now
	4	no change in quality of values
	7	better values in the future
Movement-growth	1	donation creates many more like-minded donors
	4	no effect
	7	donation decreases the number of like-minded donors
Amount of money to donate	1	total real value of your money to donate will significantly decrease over time
	4	total real value of your money to donate will stay the same over time
	7	total real value of your money to donate will significantly increase over time

On this framework, a total score of 24 would indicate indifference to giving now versus giving later. A score of less than 24 would indicate that in general the arguments favor giving now. A score of greater than 24 would indicate that in general the arguments favor giving later.

However, because this framework is purely qualitative, you shouldn't put much weight on the total scores: the framework should be thought of as a way of thinking through the relevant considerations, rather than giving you a determinate answer. If, for example, we'd carved "amount of money to donate" as several different considerations—"investment opportunities," "weakness of the will," "tax efficiency," and so on—then, because each consideration is currently weighted equally, we would start weighing the "amount of money to donate" consideration several times as highly as we do in my framework.

It is my hope that future work can build on this chapter and develop a quantitative model, which could, at least in principle, give a determinate answer to the question of whether one ought to give now or later, for a given set of inputs. For the time being, I'd encourage each user of the framework to assign their own weights to each of the relevant considerations. If, for example, you think that values change is a particularly important factor, then you should weigh that consideration more heavily than the other considerations.

If we were to make this framework quantitative, what might we find about the weights of the different considerations? It's plausible to me that the final term—amount of money to donate—is actually the least important part of the equation, even though it's the one that tends to get the most attention in the discussion of giving now versus later (perhaps because it's the most quantifiable). Even using a 7 percent real rate of return, over thirty years, investing one's money increases the value of one's donation by only 7.5x. At 5 percent real return over thirty years, the increase in financial value of one's donations is only 4.3x. However, changes in the expected cost-effectiveness of one's donations, whether through changing opportunities, knowledge, or values, can be much larger. Let me illustrate.

Opportunities and Knowledge

It's plausible that the differences in cost-effectiveness between social programs can vary by a factor of tens or hundreds; paying for bednet distribution via a donation to Against Malaria Foundation is estimated to have a cost per life saved of $3,500,[22] whereas the marginal expenditure to save a life in the US by the government is about $7 million.[23] If we value all lives equally, then, for someone who is initially focused on lifesaving programs in the US, the value of the information that they could instead save lives by funding bednets is vast. And if there is such a large discrepancy between domestic lifesaving programs and international lifesaving programs, then perhaps the discrepancy between global health and some other cause-area might also be very great.

It's difficult to know how likely it is that we might make such discoveries. But our understanding of the most cost-effective programs is still in its infancy, the result of only a couple of decades of work. It's not implausible to me that we could very significantly improve our knowledge over time.

Special Relationships and Values

The additional weight you give to the interests of those you have special obligations to is an important factor in the equation. Non-consequentialist views on which special relationships have moral value can easily weigh the interests of family, friends, or co-nationals one hundred times as much or more as the interests of distant strangers. The ability to spend money to help those to whom one has a special obligation would therefore matter far more than the additional total amount of money one could donate if one saved in order to donate.

The potential for one's values to change over time is similarly important. For example, suppose that you currently value the interests of co-nationals one hundred times as heavily as the interests of people in other countries; for that reason, you think that the best domestic giving opportunities are about as cost-effective as the best giving opportunities to help the very poorest people in the world. However, suppose that you were to change your mind, and regard the interests of people living in other countries to be just as important as the interests of people living in one's own country. In which case, the best giving opportunities would now provide one hundred times as much value, with a given amount of resources, as you thought before.

Or suppose that you currently endorse a person-affecting view of population ethics, on which there is no value to creating new flourishing lives. For that reason, you think that global poverty is a more important area to focus on than mitigating the risk of human extinction. However, if you were to change your view and adopt the total view of population ethics, then you would come to believe that efforts to mitigate extinction risk were more important; moreover, because human extinction would involve the loss of hundreds of trillions of lives in the future, efforts to mitigate human extinction now, given that the total view is correct, would provide hundreds or thousands of times more value with a given amount of resources than efforts to improve the lives of people in poverty.

Again, therefore, the potential discrepancy in the amount of money one can donate over time is small compared to the possibility that you will rationally change your moral views.

CONCLUSION

In this chapter, I canvassed all the significant considerations that I know of that are relevant to the question of whether to give now or later. The most important considerations, in my view, are: whether one has the opportunity to invest in movementgrowth, and how good that opportunity is; the extent to which the amount of resources flowing into one's favored cause is increasing; to what extent one should expect one's ability to pick the most effective programs will improve over time; and to what extent one should expect one's values to improve over time.

Further work in this area would: (1) develop the qualitative framework that I have proposed into a quantitative framework; (2) apply this framework to a variety of different cause-areas; and (3) apply this framework to the *cause-neutral* donor—someone who is open to donating to any problem, and simply wishes to maximize the amount of good they do.

NOTES

1. Effective altruism is not merely limited to charity, but to any way of trying to make the world a better place. In particular, led by the organization 80,000 Hours, the movement places a heavy focus on career choice. There are now thousands of people around the world who have chosen their careers, at least in part, on the basis of effective altruist ideas: individuals have gone into scientific research, think tanks, party politics, social entrepreneurship, finance (in order to do good through donating), and nonprofit work in order to maximize the good they can do. "GiveWell's Money Moved in 2020," The GiveWell blog, November 12, 2021, https://blog.givewell.org/2021/11/12/givewells-money-moved-in-2020; "Our Global Effective Giving Community," Giving What We Can website, https://www.givingwhatwecan.org, accessed January 30, 2022; Holden Karnofsky, "Our Progress in 2020 and Plans for 2021," Open Philanthropy blog, April 29, 2021, https://www.openphilanthropy.org/blog/our-progress-2020-and-plans-2021.

2. For discussion of this issue by researchers within the effective altruism community, see Julia Wise, "Giving Now vs. Later: A Summary," *Effective Altruism Forum*, https://forum.effectivealtruism.org/posts/7uJcBNZhinomKtH9p/giving-now-vs-later-a-summary, and "Good Ventures and Giving Now vs. Later" (2016 Update), *Open Philanthropy Project Blog*, https://www.openphilanthropy.org/blog/good-ventures-and-giving-now-vs-later-2016-update.

3. Dan Moller, "Should We Let People Starve—for Now?" *Analysis* 66, no. 291 (2006): 240–47; Laura Valentini, "On the Duty to Withhold Global Aid Now to Save More Lives in the Future," *Ethics & Global Politics* 4, no. 2 (2011).

4. It is worth noting that in 2020, several foundations, led by the Ford Foundation, did in fact borrow funds in order to increase their grant-making during the pandemic, through "social bonds." See James B. Stewart and Nicholas Kulish, "Leading Foundations Pledge to Give More, Upending Philanthropy," *New York Times*, June 10, 2020, https://www.nytimes.com/2020/06/10/business/ford-foundation-bonds-coronavirus.html.

5. The relevance of weakness of the will to the question of giving now versus later is actually dependent on a contested normative assumption. According to *actualism*, you should take future weakness of the will into account in your decisions. On actualism, weakness of the will is therefore relevant to the question of giving now versus later. According to *possibiliism*, however, you should not take future weakness of the will into account. Possibilism endorses (whereas actualism rejects) the rule of deontic logic on which Ought(A & B) entails Ought(A) and Ought(B). Suppose it is true that you ought to both invest your money, and donate those savings at a later date, but that, as a matter of fact, you won't donate. According to possibilism, Ought(Save now & donate later) entails Ought(Save now), and the fact that you won't actually donate later is irrelevant. I don't dwell on this issue in part for focus and in part because I find actualism to be the far more plausible position.

6. John J. Havens, Mary A. O'Herlihy, and Paul G. Schervish, "Charitable Giving: How Much, by Whom, to What, and How," in *The Nonprofit Sector: A Research Handbook* 2nd ed., eds. Walter Powell and Richard Steinberg (New Haven, CT: Yale University Press, 2006), 542–67; Charity Navigator, "Giving Statistics," https://www.charitynavigator.org/index.cfm?bay=content.view&cpid=42.

7. *Giving USA 2021: The Annual Report on Philanthropy for the Year 2020* (Chicago: Giving USA Foundation, 2021).

8. Nicholas Herbert Stern, *The Economics of Climate Change: The Stern Review* (Cambridge, UK: Cambridge University Press, 2007).

9. James Andreoni, "Impure Altruism and Donations to Public Goods: A Theory of Warm-Glow Giving," *The Economic Journal* 100, no. 401 (1990): 464–77; Elizabeth W. Dunn, Lara B. Aknin, and Michael I. Norton, "Spending Money on Others Promotes Happiness," *Science* 319, no. 5870 (2008): 1687–88.

10. Note that if one were to act on this consideration, one would be departing from pure effective altruism, which treats all individuals' interests equally.

11. William MacAskill and Toby Ord, "Why Maximize Expected Choice-Worthiness?" *Nous* (2018); William MacAskill, "Practical Ethics Given Moral Uncertainty," *Utilitas*, 31, issue 3 (2019), 231–45.

12. "GDP per Capita, PPP (Constant 2017 International $)," The World Bank data, https://data.worldbank.org/indicator/NY.GDP.PCAP.PP.KD?end=2020&start=1990 &view=chart; data is from 1990 to 2020.

13. Max Roser and Esteban Ortiz-Ospona, "Global Extreme Poverty," Our World in Data, https://ourworldindata.org/extreme-poverty; data is from 1990 to 2017.

14. http://www.cbpp.org/research/poverty-and-inequality/a-guide-to-statistics-on -historical-trends-in-income-inequality.

15. http://data.worldbank.org/indicator/NY.GDP.PCAP.CD.

16. http://www.humanesociety.org/news/resources/research/stats_slaughter_totals .html.

17. http://blog.givewell.org/2011/12/20/give-now-or-give-later.

18. http://www.givewell.org/international/technical/programs/cash-transfers#Wha treturnoninvestmentdocashtransferrecipientsearn.

19. David H. Molyneux, "'Neglected' Diseases but Unrecognised Successes— Challenges and Opportunities for Infectious Disease Control," *The Lancet* 364, no. 9431 (2004): 380–83.

20. This point is made by Paul Christiano, "Giving now vs later," at https://ratio-nalaltruist.com/2013/03/12/giving-now-vs-later/.

21. https://www.givingwhatwecan.org/impact.

22. http://www.givewell.org/charities/against-malaria-foundation.

23. William MacAskill, *Doing Good Better: Effective Altruism and a Radical New Way to Make a Difference* (London: Guardian Faber Publishing, 2015).

Chapter 8

In Pursuit of Legacy

Digital Data and the Future of Foundations

Lucy Bernholz

> As soon as humans started using signs and symbols to represent the natural world, they pushed beyond that world.[1]

Perpetuity is a long time. As familiar as the idea is to us now, it's worth reflecting upon just how extraordinary it is as a framing idea for human enterprises. Of the basic structures of society—governments, markets, families, and civic or religious institutions—it is only in this last category that we find intentional designs forever.[2] And while these long-term aspirations are often manifest through grand buildings, it is really a web of legal conditions and cultural practices that provide the necessary support for institutional longevity. Philanthropic permanence, for example, is generally maintained by a mix of stated intentions, financial investment practices, and compliance with regulatory expectations on annual levels of activity. The regulatory requirements on US philanthropic foundations were tailored to protect the possibility of perpetuity, not to require it. These protections are legally fragile yet remain culturally powerful.

For generations, the legal conditions and institutional practices that guide philanthropy have been focused on the use of financial resources. Beginning about two decades ago, and continuing for the foreseeable future, philanthropists have also had the opportunity to manage digital resources toward their mission. Digital resources come in many forms—they include (at least) the records of foundation activity (grants and financial information), publications (evaluations, strategy documents, board materials, research reports, datasets), and communications records (email, social media, voicemails). They can include external digital infrastructure, institutional forms, and legal or technological frameworks designed to sustain and extend a social mission long into the future. Digital resources bring with them their own architecture of legal considerations, such as intellectual property and privacy laws, as well as telecommunications and security concerns. They raise new practical considerations, such as knowledge of records retention policies both in-house and of external vendors and require investment in digital security training and technology. As a resource to be managed toward mission, digitized data add to, and complicate, the more familiar resource categories of financial and human resources.

Philanthropists today and tomorrow have the opportunity to redefine their philanthropic legacy by capitalizing on the characteristics of digital data that differentiate them from financial resources. Doing so will require attention not only to the data but also to the surrounding architecture of networks, operating systems, legal conditions, and cultural norms.

The creation of institutions designed to last forever dates back at least a millennium.[3] Extending the intention of perpetuity beyond religious practices, people began to conjoin gifts of funds with material objects, endowing grand cathedrals, mosques, universities, and social service agencies. Monetary endowments intended for a general philanthropic purpose are a modern financial product, born from probate and estate planning practices, married to corporate law, and championed in the spirit of social progress.[4]

General-purpose philanthropic endowments are a creation of a political and economic time and place. Late nineteenth and early twentieth-century, US-based but globally influential financial fortunes were tied to an era of industrialization that also drove people from farms to cities, powered two world wars, and repeatedly redrew political maps. It was these fortunes—specifically those of Andrew Carnegie and John D. Rockefeller—that warranted the political and institutional innovation known as the general-purpose endowment, or modern foundation. It is today's wealth, born from and consisting of digitized data, that invites us to reconsider both the use of digital data by existing foundations and the potential for creating new institutions, purpose-built for managing digital resources for public benefit. Now is the time to imagine—and build—the twenty-first-century, digitally assumptive equivalent of the twentieth-century modern foundation.

The informed use of digital data as a philanthropic resource may allow us to focus on perpetual impact, not just the long-term maintenance of private fortunes. For this to happen, foundation leaders need to understand both the opportunities inherent in digital networks and the challenges of planning for long-term data use.

The chapter looks first at the nature of digital data as distinct from financial resources. It then considers examples of how financial endowments are using digitized information assets (data) to pursue their social missions and to extend the temporal reach of their monetary resources. Finally, it reflects on how digitized data can help us rethink our time horizons, essentially using these symbolic systems to extend beyond the natural world of financial permanence.

DATA AND ITS DISCONTINUITIES

Information comes in many forms. The media matters in ways distinct from the content. We are familiar with this in the natural sense, knowing that water as ice, liquid, or gas is still two parts hydrogen and one-part oxygen. But individuals and institutions are still coming to grips with the ways in which the structure of information (digitized or analog) opens up new opportunities.

To understand the impact of digitized data on institutions, we must start with the characteristics of the data that distinguish it from other resources. In this chapter, the term "data" will refer to any information held in digitized form—that is, the binary code (ones and zeros) readable by computers and stored on networked devices. While information can be stored in digital form and not connected to other devices, most of what we interact with today is networked together, so that is the default assumption for this chapter.

In economic parlance, networked digitized data is nonrival. It is accessible to many people at once and my use of it does not impinge on your use of it. This is true whether we are talking about the contents of a shared photo album, the information in an online spreadsheet, or the software code that powers our ability to manipulate either the photo or the spreadsheet. Political economists have long described such resources as public goods and societies have generally provided them via public funding.[5] The examples that readily come to mind are sewers, armies, and traffic lights.

But the advent of the internet and particularly the commercial provision of services such as search, storage, and communications upon it have shifted the relationships between governments, commercial institutions, other institutions (nonprofits, civil society organizations, or informal networks of people), and individuals. Digitized data are most often now created on and exchanged by a collection of commercial interests (the software company that sold you the tools and/or access to the internet), public infrastructure (the wireless spectrum or underground pipes licensed to run those connections), the institution at which the work is being done (commercial, public, or nonprofit), and the person or persons doing the data manipulation (you, your children, and your coworkers).

Digital data almost always have multiple creators, exerting multiple claims to ownership. These triangulated relationships, along with the nonrival nature of the data, distinguish it from money and time—the two resources that we've historically designed our institutions to manage. This feature alone is the reason to imagine the changes that digital data will bring to philanthropy, as clear boundaries of ownership and exchange are at the root of both charitable giving and volunteering.

The behaviors that networked digital data facilitate are now commonplace, even if the capacities that make it all possible remain opaque to most of us. Digital data are nonrival, remixable, generative, scalable, storable, and persistent. These characteristics matter.

For those who don't write software code, the interaction of algorithms and data sets remains deeply mysterious. Managing digital data does not require that everyone be able to write software, but it does rest on a shared understanding that our institutions are now shaped by continuous interactions between layers of code—software, organizational, and legal.

Turning again to perpetual philanthropies, we can begin to see the opportunity for considering the long-term management and impact not just of financial resources but of digital resources as well. The next section presents contemporary examples of digital data being used to extend our understanding of philanthropy, used in philanthropy, and for philanthropy. There are three distinct examples to consider: data about foundations, foundations' use of their own data, and foundations using data to extend the reach of their financial investments. Each is changing our understanding of, and the potential for, long-term philanthropic impact.

I begin with a brief look at how networked digital data are influencing our understanding of philanthropy as a sector.

DIGITAL DATA AND FOUNDATIONS

The Ruth Lilly Archives at Indiana University holds more than 800,000 tax records from US foundations, spanning two and a half decades from 1971 to 1997. The time period is telling. On the front end, it is bounded by the implementation of the 1969 Tax Reform Act, a piece of federal legislation often seen as a watershed in US philanthropic history. The Act required annual reports that included information on personnel, salaries, investment holdings, and grants that forever changed the scope and frequency of philanthropic reporting. What the Tax Reform Act did not include, although it had been proposed by Senator Albert Gore, was a forty-year time limit on foundations.[6] Instead, it required private foundations to meet distribution requirements, effectively paying out a percentage of the value of their endowment holdings each year.

Most nonprofit organizations have been filing information form 990 with the IRS since the mid-1940s.[7] The 1969 Act required public charities and private foundations (religious organizations have long been exempted) to report to the public (via the IRS) on their financial activity. In the early 1980s, nonprofit advocacy and research organizations began working with the IRS to use their information for research purposes. This led to the creation of the National Center for Charitable Statistics, which was housed for over a decade at the Independent Sector and transferred to the Urban Institute's Center on Nonprofits and Philanthropy in 1996.[8] Initial demand for this information came from scholars and advocacy organizations. The advent of the internet and societal expectations about information access motivated a push to make information ever more available. Thus, the end date of the Lilly Archive collection, in 1997, marks a transition driven not by regulatory or legislative action, but by new technological capabilities.

In 1999 the IRS started to use graphical user interface (GUI) technology to improve the quality checking of nonprofit tax records, and by 2002 the agency was scanning paper forms into digital images for use by examiners.[9] In 1994, before the IRS shifted to GUIs, Buzz Schmidt launched Philanthropic Research, Inc., and in 1996, the organization published the first *GuideStar Directory of American Charities* on CD-ROM. These discs provided financial reports on more than 35,000 public charities.[10] Guidestar's early value was not in changing the content of the tax information, but in simply making it more readily available.

This shift to digital images of paper tax forms meant that the Foundation Center (which had contributed its archive to Indiana University) no longer needed the hard-copy aperture cards on which it had been storing foundation tax records since 1971. Half computer punch cards, half microform, and aperture cards are a storage medium that only archivists could love. By the 1990s, paper tax forms could be run through optical scanners, turned into digital files, and made available to the public, first on CD-ROM and, before the end of the decade, on the GuideStar website.

This shift, first to digital and then to networked digital information, marked the beginning of a new age for foundations and nonprofits. The first part of the change is about access, not substance. The rules about what to report had not changed since 1969. But the practical expectations about who and how and when outsiders could access the information changed in 1996 and have kept changing ever since.

Paper files and aperture cards must be managed on-site by professionals who closely monitor the materials. As with all physical artifacts, access is limited by time and geography, which serve as natural barriers to use. The laborious process of using the materials means that sensitive information can be redacted on an as-needed basis. Both the contributors of the materials and those entrusted with their care can manage—actively or passively—the types of analysis that can be done with the materials. When access is closed, there is value simply in making the materials more open. We will see that, as access gets easier, the value depends on building upon and increasing the utility, content, or analysis of the raw information.

The advent of online collection and storage of these tax forms marks an important shift in how and when the public can access foundation information. Digitized, online records are inherently easier to use and more accessible than paper records in storage boxes. There are no "white gloves required" archive rooms and no research submission processes. The "natural controls" of time, space, and geography have given way to bandwidth limits and a researcher's facility with text extraction algorithms. Archivists and librarians around the globe have spent decades adapting their institutional practices and analog materials to networked digital capacities.

There's been a broader movement around open government data that has also influenced the datasets and data providers pioneered by Guidestar. Open data activists have successfully argued that government records should be available to the public in the most accessible ways possible. Tax records of nonprofits fall into this category. The movement for open access—making the tax records available in their most useful form—came to the nonprofit and foundation sector in 2016.

Most charitable US nonprofits and foundations file an annual tax return called a Form 990 (or 990-PF in the case of private foundations). Tax law requires public access to these forms. From 1969 to the late 1980s, this access was to be provided by request to the IRS. Beginning in 1986, organizations were required to provide such access directly, although they could require that both the request and the use be restricted to their premises. In 1998, access was expanded to allow for remote requests and charitable organizations and foundations were allowed to meet these requirements directly or through the widespread dissemination of this information via the internet.[11] The next major change in legal requirements to access came in President Obama's Fiscal Year 2014 budget, which included recommendations from the Nonprofit Data Project that nonprofits file their returns electronically and that the IRS make these files available "online, in machine readable format."[12] One lawsuit and three congressional sessions later, the House of Representatives approved the CHARITY Act and the Senate Finance Committee signed off on similar requirements in its Taxpayer Protection Act. In 2016, the IRS released approximately half of all charitable nonprofits' tax returns online.

This most recent change to nonprofit and foundation information was both technological and regulatory. Several years of advocacy by researchers and open-data supporters, investigative reporting by nonprofit media groups, and a lawsuit by a self-described "rogue archivist," pushed the call for change.[13]

Open files are searchable not just as images or static documents, but within each field on the form. The difference is enormous. You can search by field (i.e., all the organizations on whose boards Lucy Bernholz sits). You can pull all the similar fields from multiple files (all the oil or gas stocks held by the top 100 foundations). You can look for new relationships between fields (all the organizations on whose boards Lucy Bernholz sits that hold oil or gas stocks). Most important, algorithms can be written and software code deployed to access this information. Networked computers now do the equivalent of traveling to IRS headquarters on Constitution Avenue, requesting the files of all organizations, and manually searching across millions of pages of paper for names and stock holdings.

The IRS uploaded the first 600,000 open files in 2016, and more have been added each year. New uses of the data will be discovered, and the push for different types of information and the creation of complementary data sources will continue. Open data lowers the barriers between those whose information is on the forms and those who seek to make sense of it. It changes the dynamics of information use and control. This potted history of regulatory and technological changes is what led to our current system of accessible, networked, digital data on foundation philanthropy in the United States. This system enables research and innovation within and around philanthropy— everything from national donor-advised funds (DAFs) to impact investing to the research that informs tax policy—depends, to some degree, on this independent data system about philanthropy. It extends the reach and longitudinal understanding of the entire US philanthropic sector.

The digitization of tax reports has had many repercussions for foundations. Ready access to both legal and financial information on nonprofits allows for a much more streamlined grant-making process. Verifiability, an act that once took human staff, is now built into most grant management software packages. An ecosystem of capacity analysis has grown around the digitized tax forms— from software packages that enable financial comparison across nonprofits to online maps of different grant-making strategies and aggregation of strategies by multiple organizations. Because foundations file this tax information, the ecosystem also facilitates external examination of their work. Journalists, advocates, and members of the public have much greater visibility into individual foundations and the sector as a whole than was possible before this information was digitized. Some foundations wholeheartedly embrace this transparency, whereas others now seek to comply with the letter of the law but reveal nothing extra.

In the early days of Guidestar, users were mostly professionals who had previously relied on printed books of IRS-approved nonprofits. The CD-ROM and then web-based information made their jobs much easier. Slowly, over the next twenty years, the existence of an online source of digitized tax forms began to spark more expansive and creative uses of the information. The ability to check an organization's tax status electronically contributed to the growth of DAFs, for example, because the vendors of these products could automate the grant qualification process via a subscription to Guidestar. As the information became easier to access, more members of the public also chose to use it to check on the organizations to which they contributed.

There is no doubt that the easy and inexpensive availability of data on foundations has changed the nature of both the sector and the public's understanding of it. This publicly accessible repository of data on foundations built by the Foundation Center and Guidestar (which formally merged into one organization in 2019) also holds foundation-funded research, analyses, evaluations, issue maps, and other artifacts of foundations' work. By making this material publicly available in a single place the individual foundations extend their reach in place, on issues, and over time.

FROM STUDYING THE SECTOR TO INFLUENCING IMPACT

So far, we have looked at the qualities that make networked digital information different and the effects these changes have had on information about philanthropy as a whole. But what is the potential impact of digital data on individual foundations? And how does it intersect with questions of longevity and philanthropic time frame? That is where we now turn our attention.

There are a small number of foundation examples that show how digital assets might be managed toward the mission. In most cases, we find programmatic examples that reflect the understanding that digital resources can complement and extend financial strategy. The Hewlett Foundation's Open Educational Resources and The Gates Foundation's investments in open-access publishing are two good examples of programmatic strategies built on digital data. The second set of examples looks at the growing interest among foundations in transparency or openness policies and practices. A third manifestation comes from the F.B. Heron Foundation, which has found a way to use digital data to drastically reduce the reporting burden it places on grantees while simultaneously investing in their core organizational capacity. In this next section of the chapter, I consider each of these examples.

LICENSING FOR IMPACT

Nonprofit organizations dedicated to managing digital resources in new ways sprung to life in the mid-1980s. The Free Software Foundation (FSF) was founded in 1986, followed by the Electronic Frontier Foundation in 1990. These organizations came into existence separately, but their founders shared a deep understanding of the nature of digital data and how it would require new ways of thinking about intellectual property and civil liberties. More than a decade later, a small group of legal and engineering experts launched Creative Commons, a nonprofit organization dedicated to offering copyright licensing tools modeled after the GNU General Public Licenses for software that FSF initiated in 1986. These alternative licenses are designed to give authors, musicians, artists and others choices befitting the unique capacities of networked digital content. Creative Commons made its first such licenses available in 2002. Within five years, there were an estimated 90 million works using Creative Commons licenses.[14]

Creative Commons grew with foundation support. Early funders included the MacArthur Foundation and the William and Flora Hewlett Foundation, which each made grants of more than $1 million in the organization's first two years of existence. In 2011, ten years after its founding, Creative Commons had an organizational budget of $9.8 million, with foundation grants accounting for more than $9.3 million of that total.[15] In 2016, the Hewlett Foundation made a $10 million grant to Creative Commons.[16]

That same year, an independent study done by scholars at Harvard's Berkman Center on Internet and Society found that Creative Commons and other licensing schemes were slowly being adopted by foundations for their own work. A 2009 survey had found only three of the twelve foundations surveyed were requiring the use of alternative licenses by grantees. By 2011 that number had doubled, several more foundations encouraged (but didn't require) the use of the licenses, and many public funding agencies were beginning to mandate open or alternative licenses.[17]

Licensing practices are an important point of influence for grant-making foundations. They are embedded in the grant agreements—legal contracts—between the funders and the organizations receiving their financial support. As the 2009 Berkman survey noted:

> Funding from private foundations results each year in the creation of large numbers of works of all kinds, ranging from books, articles, reports and research summaries to educational materials and textbooks to photographs, works of visual art, films, videos, and musical compositions and recordings to software code, computer programs and technical systems to many, many others. These works include materials created by grantees with foundation support, works created for or on behalf of foundations by consultancies and contractors, and works produced by staff members of the foundation itself. Virtually all of these foundations-supported works are protected by copyright.[18]

Shifting the copyright claims made by foundations over these works had the potential to greatly increase the reach of their grant-making. Making it easier for funded work to be shared digitally extends the reach and visibility of these products. Since foundations usually rely on their grantees to distribute their own work, making it easier for them to do so was in both party's best interests.

Old practices are hard to change. Even as people and organizations became more aware of alternative licensing schemes, extant institutional practices and incentives that had been built around the traditional copyright system were slow to change. Academic publishing, for example, has been resistant to open licensing and publishing for most of the last decade. It is home to both some of the most radical innovations and some of the strongest forces of reaction. For some other foundations, their issue areas, such as indigenous cultural or medical practices, are already at odds with Western norms of marketplaces and intellectual property. Requiring these groups to use licensing practices that weaken their hand in negotiating in broader markets could be a step backward.

Though it has taken years, many government funders and large private foundations are now requiring digital licenses that facilitate access to and the sharing and repurposing of materials created with their financial support. It is a seemingly small, legalistic change, but one that recognizes two important opportunities: first, that the products of foundation funding can be created and distributed in ways that capitalize on their digital nature to achieve broader reach, and, second, that foundations can adapt their own administrative practices to make this possible. Rewriting grant agreements to incorporate alternative licensing schemes—especially those that make it easier to share the materials with more people in more places—is one practical way that foundations can extend the reach (in time and space) of the knowledge generated from their funding.

OPEN ACCESS AND OPEN DATA
AS PROGRAM STRATEGY

Foundations are not limited to adapting their administrative and legal practices to align with the digital age. Program strategies are being designed to take into account digital capacities as well. Two of these—the Hewlett Foundation's Open Educational Resources (OER) and the Bill and Melinda Gates Foundation's Open Access policy and open publishing platform—integrate the capacities enabled by alternative licensing throughout a program.

Since 2002, The William and Flora Hewlett Foundation has shaped its education grant-making to capitalize on the nature of knowledge sharing and access in the digital age. One of the key elements of this program strategy is to make high-quality academic materials available easily and affordably around the globe, and to demonstrate the connections between access to such materials and improved teaching and learning.[19] Building from some of the same principles that inform Creative Commons licenses, OER rests on the premise that digital data and networks allow for the creation, distribution, and local adaptation of resources on a global scale with greater ease and speed than ever before. Taking advantage of these digital capacities allows people everywhere to access materials created in elite universities and potentially unleash expertise, creativity, and development that might otherwise lay fallow. The information flow is bidirectional, allowing the universities to benefit, and is also increasingly reaching beyond higher education to secondary schools.

Of course, doing so challenges existing practices and business models. Free, global access to information was initially viewed as counterproductive to the incentives that shape faculty tenure decisions, although in reality they may be well aligned. It also cuts into the revenue models of publishing houses, testing companies, and accreditation bureaus, and might cause other unpredictable changes in the educational marketplace. Powerful vested interests had little initial desire to experiment with the potential of open information. For these reasons, much of the Hewlett Foundation funding for OER focused on the ecosystem itself.

In keeping with this systemic focus, and in trying to match its own practices to the values of the open educational space, the Foundation began to "open" up its grant-making around OER. One example of what this looked like in action was to allow applicants to see proposals from other organizations. The foundation would receive proposals, strip them of confidential information such as budgets and salary information, and repost the sections that defined the problem and proposed solutions. Since every proposal required statements on these issues, this was a way to help individual organizations working in the system to know what their peers (and, yes, competitors for funding) said, build on each other's work, and try to construct a shared sense of the ecosystem, its problems and challenges. This was, in technological terms, a very small step but one which ran counter to almost all norms of proposal submission. It was a significant cultural shift that required educating the applicant organizations, as well as legal attention to who owns the information in a proposal and with whom and how it could be shared.

The Hewlett Foundation's OER experiment continues to be an early step toward using digital capacities—in this case, websites—to foster a collective discussion and understanding of an issue area. Over time, this has become a much more common goal. It is now easier than ever to open data sets and share methodological approaches. This has led to new norms for publishing scientific studies, such as the rise of open-access publishing and new online resources such as the Public Library of Science (PLoS). Foundations have played a significant role in funding PLoS and other science commons, and, led by public funders in the United Kingdom and the United States, the aim of making these materials open for sharing is being built directly into the funding requirements. The Wellcome Trust in the United Kingdom and the Bill and Melinda Gates Foundation in the United States have both taken steps to require research grantees to share their data, their findings, and their final analysis through public and open portals. In 2014, the Hewlett Foundation adopted an open licensing policy for its own grant-making. In 2016, the Gates Foundation recognized the challenges these open demands created for some scholars and launched an open publishing platform to help support grantees in fulfilling the foundation's requirements. These examples demonstrate a commitment to aligning financial resources with digital strategy and seeking ways to structure the resources so as to increase impact.

In order for these approaches to succeed in extending the reach of foundation investments, they need to account for future technological changes. The rate of change in software and hardware is familiar to anyone who may have recently tried to access documents stored on floppy disks or even CD-ROMS. Archivists and librarians are very knowledgeable about the challenges of preserving digital resources over time. This knowledge—and the costs associated with implementing it—are critical components of foundation-driven efforts to maintain digital records into the future. It represents a new dimension to our understanding of the intersection between philanthropy and considerations of temporality.

DIGITAL OUTSOURCING AND
FOUNDATION PRACTICE

The F.B. Heron Foundation in New York has taken steps to use digital resources in ways that reimagine program strategy and administrative practice. When Clara Miller became president of the foundation, she made the bold move of declaring that all of the foundation's resources would be directed to its poverty-alleviating mission. This mandate required the foundation staff and board to reconsider all of its practices—from investment policies to grant evaluation and monitoring. In doing so, the foundation recognized an opportunity to restructure the reporting requirements it places on its partners.

Idiosyncratic application processes and burdensome reporting requirements have long been both a mainstay of foundation practice and a burden on their partners. As the Heron Foundation sought to analyze all of its investments, expenditures, and grants through the lens of impact, it found that the data sources it needed to assess potential grantees had more in common with those used by investors. If it could align the data sources it needed to analyze grant opportunities with those it used for investment opportunities, the foundation would be better positioned to assess the whole of its portfolio. This, in turn, led the foundation to support the use of operational and programmatic metrics that its nonprofit partners already used and tracked. Heron invested in third-party structures that could serve the analytic, benchmarking, and reporting functions of the organizations it worked with. Two organizations in particular center this strategy—the Sustainable Accounting Standards Board (SASB), which is developing social and environmentally aware accounting mechanisms and CoMetrics, a cooperatively owned platform that aggregates performance data for cooperatives. These two investments allow Heron's grantee partners to monitor their own performance in line with peer organizations. When Heron needs information to inform either a potential investment or grant choice, or to monitor the progress of a partner, it turns to these third-party sources. The result: a stronger digital data infrastructure for the fields in which Heron works, an ability to look at the sector-level impact, and less time wasted on reporting.[20]

Both SASB and CoMetrics rely on the core properties of digital data and infrastructure. Participating organizations can easily and affordably collect and store their own information, manage and control it as they see fit, and compare themselves to peers using shared standards and collective data sets. The data and analytics are those which good operational managers need to run their businesses, and there is no additional special data collection or reporting required by the foundation. In addition, the process ensures that everyone is using the same data, both for purposes of organizational comparison and longitudinal monitoring. This advances the foundation's programmatic goals with less redundancy and time burden for both grantees and foundation staff.

DIGITAL INSTITUTION BUILDING

From changing claims of copyright to investing in grantee organization's digital capacity, these are early signs that foundations recognize the importance—and complementary characteristics—of digital data and infrastructure to achieving their missions. It is this opportunity—to use digital data as both an amplifier and an additional philanthropic resource—that offers new ways to think about impact over time and the nature of philanthropic legacy.

Foundations have long invested in creating institutions—from the Rockefeller's University of Chicago to Carnegie's public libraries. In both cases, the legacy of these donors, and the impact of these financial investments, was extended by their requirements for matching funds and commitments to these projects. We are beginning to see some examples of data being used in a similar way. For example, funders and nonprofits in the UK are experimenting with shared repositories of digital data from government agencies. These are called data trusts or data labs and serve as trusted intermediary institutions to allow multiple uses of existing datasets. One example involves funders of social impact bonds in the UK that are looking for efficient ways to meet the evaluation requirements of their investments. By pooling government data on relevant issues such as prison recidivism or school achievement into one repository, and then negotiating the evaluators' use of that data in line with agreed-upon principles of privacy and access, the bond partners are assured of both quality and consistency. The data trust can also be used by others, leveraging the initial investment. As Carnegie helped build physical libraries for future generations of learners, these data trusts are virtual libraries of data, protecting them and making them available in the future.

The Mellon Foundation (among others) piloted an early version of these data trusts with the creation of JSTOR and ARTSTOR in the 1990s. Both organizations represent trusted intermediaries for digital information, JSTOR focusing on academic journals and ARTSTOR working with the digital rights to artistic works. The purpose of the intermediary is to serve as a searchable repository for data from multiple sources as well as a single portal of entry for multiple users. Overseeing the web of intellectual property, digital ownership, and digital rights management challenges becomes the responsibility of the intermediary. Both of these examples operate within the academic universe, whereas the data lab example sits at the nexus of governments, nonprofits, and social investors. Two of the next frontiers are repositories of corporate or private digital data that can be accessed for social purpose and repositories of algorithms and analysis. Carnegie Mellon's LearnSphere project, which makes more than 400,000 hours of student data available for analysis and encourages the sharing of individual research algorithms and findings as well, is an example of this second structure.[21]

INVESTING IN THE DIGITAL INFRASTRUCTURE FOR CIVIL SOCIETY

There is another level at which foundation philanthropy could invest. Every civil society organization that uses email or cell phones is digitally dependent. The tools that they rely on are, for the most part, commercially manufactured and serviced, and government surveilled. Given the extent to which modern organizations and associations use these digital tools—in many cases for the generation, management, storage, and protection of all of their information—it is not an exaggeration to say that digital service providers effectively act as landlords to today's civil society associations. All of the information assets of today's foundations and networked nonprofits exist within their software and hardware. There's a wonderful opportunity for today's foundations—individually and collectively—to recognize this relationship and act to ensure that the sector's records will live on, independent of decisions made by software vendors. This requires actively shaping a "digital infrastructure for philanthropy"—which includes institutions, regulations, norms, and software code—that will make sure that the digital artifacts of today's philanthropy are protected and preserved for tomorrow. Otherwise, as foundation work becomes ever-more software dependent, the individual histories of foundations and the collective story of the field will be locked away inside the software code and on the servers of their technology vendors.

Because a good deal of commercial software incorporates open-source code, a significant amount of the software that powers philanthropy and civil society is dependent on open-source contributions and contributors. Given this dependence, philanthropists committed to perpetuity should consider the fragility of the open-source ecosystem. If this software code breaks, everything that depends on it also breaks. For example, in 2016, an open-source software coder who had written an eleven-line piece of code, removed it from the online repository where others accessed it. These few lines of code had been integrated into major pieces of software across the world. The result of his decision? Programs stopped running around the world, or, in the parlance of the day, the removal of his work "broke the internet."[22] It took several hours to get things running again. While most foundation executives aren't likely to understand their network architecture in any depth, they need to realize the extent of their dependency on these systems, as well as the dependency of their grantees. In a world where an individual and a few lines of code can bring down the internet, foundations with interest in long-term change also have interest in ensuring the durability and sustainability of the software that underpins their work. A Ford Foundation report, called *Roads and Bridges: The Unseen Labor Behind our Digital Infrastructure*, underscored both the values and frailties associated with institutional and sector-wide software dependence.[23] Certainly, as we become ever more reliant on digital tools, it will become more necessary for the pursuit of perpetuity to protect the digital infrastructure on which our institutions and investments depend. In 2019 the Ford and Alfred P. Sloan Foundations, recognizing this challenge, launched a research program to investigate the role of open source as part of philanthropy's critical digital infrastructure.

REDEFINING PERPETUITY

Foundations are starting to understand how to use digital data as a resource toward their mission. At a practical level, this has involved some fairly basic, often operational, changes such as the use of online application systems, sharing information via websites and emails, and using social media to broadcast information. These practices are not groundbreaking, but they are necessary first steps in changing philanthropic behavior.

The types of changes likely to lead to more lasting influence must capitalize on the innate characteristics of networked digital data and the legal constructs that guide their use. Using digitally native intellectual property constructs such as Creative Commons or other alternative licensing schemes is an important example. Foundations both invested in building the system of Creative Commons licensing and are now beginning to use it.

Once these legal constructs for the use of digital data are recognized, the next step forward is aligning them with foundation funds. Open publishing, open data, and open-access policies are all examples of this alignment. The Heron Foundation's investment in external data systems—designed by and for grantees—and its willingness to reimagine its institutional practice to fit this changing ecosystem, iterates on this idea. Data labs and data trusts are another piece of this emerging external digital data infrastructure.

All of these examples demonstrate how foundations can use digital data and the accompanying legal and institutional architecture to extend their reach across both space and time. Because these structures largely exist outside of the foundation (or as guide rails for how data move in and out of the foundation) they allow us to reimagine the bounds—both physical and temporal—of philanthropy.

One observation seems obvious—the more a foundation is willing to invest in digital structures and practices that extend the use and life of digital data, the more likely the data will continue on even after the funding ends. This has implications for all foundation programs. Asking how to incorporate digital practices into grant-making programs to extend the reach of financial resources should become a core question for all strategy development.

It also has implications for our conception of perpetuity and philanthropic legacy. If the digital strategy can be used to extend the impact of financial resources, then we can decouple the potential for perpetuity and legacy from foundation investment practices. Used well, digital resources and capacities can extend the impact and influence of a foundation beyond its financial resources, and beyond, perhaps, the existence of its endowment.

Once they recognize the power of digital data, philanthropists can apply to it the same intentionality they bring to their financial strategies. The calculations will be different because of the characteristics of digital data, but the end goal should be the same—the pursuit of the mission. Smart philanthropists will begin to look for strategies that utilize the power of both money and digital data. Those who care about preserving their legacy will recognize that using digital data in networked, generative, open, and accessible ways extends the reach of their dollars, both during and after a funding cycle.

These possibilities are not without risk. If, as the adage states, information is power, then foundations that can align their financial and digital resources have the potential to vastly increase their influence. Such power merits scrutiny and oversight.

The pattern demonstrated by the examples of Creative Commons, OER, open access, and CoMetrics offers a good model for thinking about sector-wide change. Foundations can foster the creation of digital systems—licenses, repositories, governance norms—that fit the values of civil society. They then can lead by example, by aligning their financial commitments with these digital opportunities, and by advocating for others (public and private funding peers) to do so as well. Once these capacities and expectations take hold, the foundations can begin to redesign their internal practices, seeking both efficiencies and stronger sector infrastructure (as seen in the Heron Foundation and CoMetrics example). Investments in data about philanthropy, such as that provided by Candid (the merged enterprise made of Guidestar and the Foundation Center), represent a part, but by no means all, of this infrastructure.

The experiments with data labs and new intermediaries suggest some of what a digitally extended philanthropic infrastructure will contain. These repositories of digital data will enable foundations and nonprofits to outsource some of their current internal functions to scalable and networked third parties. They may also come to represent a new form of philanthropic actor, one in which the resources being deployed consist exclusively of digital data, algorithms, and analysis. Given the persistent nature of digital data and the complicated terrain of personal privacy and public interest it encapsulates, we have a lot of work to do to create the best legal conditions and cultural norms for such activity.

Just as nonprofit organizations and foundations are set apart from business corporations by codified restrictions on the use of their financial resources, it is logical to assume parallels to the use of digital data. What will be the equivalents to nonprofit corporate nondistribution clauses and restrictions on private inurement regarding digital data? These questions are being addressed at individual organizations, and through some collaborative efforts around data governance within spheres such as humanitarian aid or human rights advocacy. Developing practices that can inform new policies or legal requirements are becoming ever more urgent, especially as the regulatory landscapes for certain kinds of digital data, such as student records, continue to change.

Another step will be to look specifically at the legal constructs that guide philanthropic practice. The 1969 Tax Reform Act represented a regulatory compromise that promoted philanthropic financial plans that could attend to current spending and the pursuit of perpetuity. The regulatory frames that will shape how digital data are used—by philanthropic actors for public purposes—need attention to ensure that the digital resources of philanthropy also contribute to and are available for long-term public benefit. These frameworks are not likely to be found in tax law. They are currently resident in a mix of laws and regulatory bodies covering consumer protection, intellectual property, privacy, and telecommunications practices.

In the last decade, we have seen how ready access to mobile devices, along with algorithms that use, analyze and generate ever more networked digital data, can fundamentally alter services and markets as distinct as urban transport, recorded music, journalism, healthcare, and political protest. Philanthropic enterprises are still, for the most part, scratching the surface of what's possible by integrating some of this capacity into their existing organizational practices. Efforts to open access to data, to share and reuse materials funded by philanthropic dollars, or to reimagine core funder-grantee reporting relationships are early steps toward reimagining philanthropy in the digital age. Digital data trusts, contributions to data commons, shared algorithms and open analysis, and investments in the maintenance of the digital infrastructure itself—all of which require fundamental reconsiderations of a foundation's institutional and temporal boundaries—are the next step forward. These types of opportunities shift control, demand more transparency (and an accordant willingness to be publicly engaged), and will no doubt, result in both mistakes and failures. But they also point the way toward philanthropic practice that equates legacy and influence more with impact than simply with assets under management.

NOTES

1. Elizabeth Kolbert, *The Sixth Extinction: An Unnatural History* (New York: Picador, 2014), 266.

2. Author interview with TJ Bliss, February 2, 2017.

3. See Rob Reich, *Just Giving: Why Philanthropy Is Failing Democracy and How It Can Do Better* (Princeton, NJ: Princeton University Press, 2018).

4. There are legitimate questions about the proper relationship between permanent wealth and democratic values. See, for example, Rob Reich, *Just Giving*.

5. This is one reason that networked digitized data have revived interest in the commons form of resource management.

6. Eleanor L. Brilliant, "The Peterson Commission," in *Philanthropy in America: A Comprehensive Historical Encyclopedia*, Volume 1, ed. Dwight Burlingame (Santa Barbara: ABC-CLIO, 2004), 372.

7. Paul Arnsberger, Melissa Ludlum, Margaret Riley, and Mark Stanton, "A History of the Tax-Exempt Sector: An SOI Perspective," Internal Revenue Service, *Statistics of Income Bulletin, Winter*, 2008, https://www.irs.gov/pub/irs-soi/tehistory .pdf, p.124

8. National Center for Charitable Statistics, "About NCCS," nccs.urban.org/ about.index.cfm.

9. Arnsberger, Ludlum, Riley and Stanton, "A History of the Tax-Exempt Sector," 122.

10. "GuideStar: A Brief History," https://learn.guidestar.org/about-us/history.

11. Public disclosure requirements contained within *H.R. 4328 the Omnibus Consolidated and Emergency Supplemental Appropriations Act of 1999, Public Law 105-277.*

12. See timeline of the Nonprofit Data Project at https://www.aspeninstitute.org/ programs/program-on-philanthropy-and-social-innovation-psi/nonprofit-data-project -updates/

13. Key steps in this process include the release of an Aspen Institute report, "Information for Impact: Liberating Nonprofit Sector Data," in 2013, the creation of the Nonprofit Explorer Tool by ProPublica that same year, and a lawsuit against the IRS by self-described rogue archivist Carl Malamud, *Public.Resource.org vs. IRS,* (N.D. Cal, Jan 29, 2015).

14. See https://creativecommons.org/about/history/ and https://wiki.creativecom-mons.org/wiki/History. For more on the Free Software Foundation see Sam Williams and Richard Stallman, *Free as in Freedom (2.0): Richard Stallman and the Free Software Revolution* (Boston, MA: Free Software Foundation, 2010).

15. All financial information taken from Creative Commons 990 forms and from the Independent Auditors Report, Creative Commons Corporation, Good and Fowler, LLP, December 31, 2011. Documents accessed online at https://wiki.creativecom-mons.org/wiki/Public_reports#Annual_reports.

16. See Grants, Hewlett Foundation, http://www.hewlett.org/grants/creative-com-mons-for-general-operating-support/.

17. Phil Malone, "Foundation Funding: Open Licenses, Greater Impact" (Cambridge, MA: The Berkman Center for Internet and Society at Harvard University, February 2011), iii–v.

18. Phil Malone, "An Evaluation of Private Foundation Copyright Licensing Policies, Practices, and Opportunities" (Cambridge, MA: The Berkman Center for Internet and Society at Harvard University, August 2009), M2.

19. www.hewlett.org/programs/education/open-educational-resources.

20. Author Interview, Clara Miller, January 18, 2017.

21. See http://learnsphere.org/about.html.

22. Keith Collins, "How One Programmer Broke the Internet," *Quartz*, March 27, 2016, https://qz.com/646467/how-one-programmer-broke-the-internet-by-deleting-a -tiny-piece-of-code/.

23. Nadia Eghbal, *Roads and Bridges: The Unseen Labor behind our Digital Infrastructure* (New York: The Ford Foundation, 2016).

Part III

PRACTICE

Chapter 9

Time-Limited Foundations

Comparative Perspectives from Europe

Helmut K. Anheier and Sandra Rau

Time-limited, spend-down, or spending-out foundations have existed in the United States for some time.[1] Yet this form of institutionalized philanthropy has emerged only recently in a handful of European countries, especially the United Kingdom, Germany, France, and Switzerland.[2] Academic reflections and comparative perspectives on this institutional form remain rare. The present chapter seeks to address this shortfall by examining time-limited philanthropic institutions in various European countries and contrasting them, both historically and contemporarily, with their counterparts in the United States.

In both the United States and Europe, the growth of time-limited foundations can be seen as a reaction to four largely independent pressures that have affected institutional philanthropy in the course of this decade, especially. These are: (1) the pursuit of financial sustainability: maintaining or growing endowments to meet objectives; (2) striving for historical consistency: the desire to honor donor intent; (3) shifts in management objectives: dealing with the rise of performance and impact measures; and (4) changing growth patterns: a boom in the establishment of smaller foundations.

Combined, these pressures put stress on conventional foundation forms, and particularly on grant-making institutions that are established in perpetuity. While these pressures have been present in the world of institutionalized philanthropy throughout the past decades, they coalesced more powerfully in recent years and gained greater importance among policymakers and foundation representatives.

Specifically, in both the United States and Europe, historically low interest rates since the 2008–2009 global financial crises have required greater efforts to yield adequate returns on asset investments in order to maintain grant-making activities at a constant level and to avoid the erosion of nominal endowment values.[3] In such a situation, philanthropists might prefer spending down assets over a given period to achieve the desired impact sooner, and would do so by allocating greater sums in the shorter term rather than through smaller sums stretched out into an indefinite future.

However, unlike in the United States, the foundations in Europe do not face any payout rule. Instead, they typically adhere to the legal requirement of asset protection to ensure the sustainability of their operations. This means that foundations in Europe are somewhat less affected by low interest rates as long as yields are at or above inflation. It also makes European foundations more conservative in their asset management, as the principle of asset protection leads to risk aversion.

What is more, Europe has a much larger share of operating foundations than the United States (see below), many of which have small, sometimes nominal endowments while earning a much higher share of recurring revenue through service provision. Thus, not only are low interest rates less important for European foundations than in the United States, such financial pressures also apply to a much smaller share of foundations, namely only to the grant-making ones.

In both the United States and Europe, foundations established in perpetuity face built-in tensions between the original donor intent and its interpretations over time. Boards may question the practicality and even the relevance of deeds formulated for an indefinite time period. At the core of such tensions are questions about whether private funds of considerable size can address public purposes better if donor intent can be reinterpreted and changed in part or completely over time, even against the original stipulations of the deed, or if trustees can, even against the donor's wishes, decide to spend down at a later stage.[4]

The third development that has placed more pressure on foundation leaders to consider spending-down applies, like the first, somewhat less to Europe: the rise of strategic philanthropy with an emphasis on measurable shorter to medium-term results and impact.[5] This approach invites a culture of entre-preneurialism less interested in asset growth and long-term sustainability, and perhaps best illustrated by terms like venture philanthropy[6] or catalytic philanthropy[7] as well as approaches under the umbrella of social investment.[8] These approaches may well require the mobilization of greater funds for shorter periods of time in the near future rather than at some unspecified time decades away.

Thus, a foundation might spend a significant share of its endowment in realizing a shorter-term strategy toward the set objectives, or even deplete its assets altogether. However, while strategic philanthropy has gained currency in the United States, it is far less common in Europe. A recent study reported that only one in five of the about twenty thousand foundations in Germany practice some kind of strategic philanthropy.[9] There are two main reasons why strategic philanthropy in Europe is less pronounced: the greater presence and economic weight of operating foundations (see table 9.1 for Europe and table 9.2 for Germany) combined with a smaller number of larger, grant-making foundations; and the lower degree of professionalization of philanthropy when compared to the United States.

Fourth, the United States and Germany, the country with the largest foundation sector in Europe, have in common a disproportionate rise of smaller foundations, many with endowments of less than $100,000 in assets.[14] The social ecology of institutional philanthropy is changing, which brings up two central questions. The first is one of efficiency, and how to deal with growing numbers of smaller foundations that may not be well-managed in terms of financial performance and governance. The second is one of effectiveness: How can smaller foundations still achieve some impact and maintain relevance and legitimacy over time?

Time-limited foundations can be seen as one answer to these pressures. Representing a different form of institutional philanthropy, they innovate by attaching to the endowments of grant-making foundations a dual conditionality. In terms of purpose, they are usually dedicated to addressing more

Table 9.1 Number and Types of Foundations in Selected Countries, Various Years

Country	Number	Relative Share of Grant-Making Foundation	Relative Share of Operating Foundations	Mixed Type
Austria	3,310[10] (2014)	Few		Majority
Belgium	1,049[11] (2012)	Few		Majority
Britain	~12,400 (2013)	Majority	Few	few
Denmark	~14,000			
Finland	2,830 (2016)	50%	30%	20%
France	4,315[12] (2015)	Few	Majority	
Germany	19,800 (2014)	~50%	~25%	~25%
Greece	~380 (2015)	Few	Majority	Few
Ireland	40 (2015)	27%	70%	3%
Italy	6,220 (2011)	15%	39%	43%
Liechtenstein	1,239 (2014)		Majority	
Luxembourg	230 (2013)		Majority	
Netherlands	7,500 (2013)	Majority		
Norway	7,311 (2014)			Majority
Portugal	401 (2010)		Majority	
Spain	8,866 (2013)	5%	95%	
Switzerland	13,075 (2015)	5%	Majority	Many
Turkey	3,320 (2015)			Majority
Comparison: United States	87,142 (2012)	Majority	6%	Few

Source: Anheier, 2001; Anheier and Daly, 2007; Philanthropic Foundations Canada, 2015; European Foundations on Research and Innovation, 2015, Foundation Center, 2016; Donors and Foundations Network in Europe, 2016.

Table 9.2   German Foundation Types by Size and Approach

N = 952[13] (100%)	*Small Foundations* (Budget < 100,000,- EUR)	*Large Foundations* (Budget ≥ 100,000,- EUR)
Operating and mixed foundations	Niche providers (29%) 1% of total expenditures	Services providers (15%) 43% of total expenditures
Grant-making foundations	Engagement foundations (42%) 2% of total expenditures	Professional philanthropists (14%) 54% of total expenditures
	676 (71%)	276 (29%)

Source: Anheier et al., 2017

specific deeds and to reaching clear objectives. In terms of time, they seek to do so in a set period, after which the funds are fully expended and the foundation is wound down before it eventually ceases to exist. Among the eminent examples of time-limited foundations in the United States are Atlantic Philanthropies and the Bill and Melinda Gates Foundation, set to expire twenty years after the death of its namesakes.

There are also smaller spend-down foundations like the Beldon Fund, set up in 1982 to support environmental policy (which closed its doors in 2009), and family foundations set up as time-limited trusts to avoid "dynastic" developments over generations.

A LOOK AT HISTORY: FOUNDATIONS EVOLVING

The historical development of foundations in Europe is an important reason why the pressures mentioned above have a different effect on the relevance of time-limited foundations than in the United States. Politically, the issue of time limitation in Europe has played a more central role in the past than in recent decades. Indeed, since the Enlightenment and lasting well into the twentieth century, there has been a long-standing debate revolving around the question of perpetuity. As Rob Reich notes in this volume, the eighteenth-century French economist and statesman Turgot formulated perhaps the most forceful critique of perpetuity when he pointed to the dead-hand problem, that is, the ineffective use of sunk capital by landed elite and their vast real estate holdings organized as foundations. Combined with anticlerical sentiments at that time, he arrived at a scathing indictment of foundation failures.[15] Kant was also critical of foundations. In "The Metaphysics of Morals" and the chapter "On the rights of the state in relation to perpetual foundations for the benefit of its citizens," his principle of utility for the public good stipulated state primacy in allocating foundations to best public use, as a way to counteract much-feared obsolescence.[16]

As a matter of course, foundations in Europe have changed significantly in form, role and position over the centuries, and did not remain in the condition lamented by Turgot or Kant. As Smith and Borgmann suggest, the role and raison d'être of foundations in Europe underwent several dramatic changes between the sixteenth and the twentieth centuries.[17] The Reformation era did away with the medieval ideal of community and triggered the complex process of state building, in which foundations were no longer part of a *res publica christiania*. Instead, foundations had to compete for space in an increasingly secular public sphere. Only some foundations succeeded in this task, and many, if not most, became victims of the forced secularization of the Napoleonic era and the state expansion of the nineteenth century.

At the same time, new foundations continued to emerge, fueled by the interests of the emerging middle class, particularly urban merchants and industrial entrepreneurs. In the nineteenth century, the urban middle class supported much of the growth in the number of foundations, whether under aristocratic or autocratic regimes. This was the case in Britain, Scandinavia, the Netherlands, Germany, the Austro-Hungarian empire, and Italy. Mostly, these foundations remained local in character and often served well-defined circles of beneficiaries.

As the nation-state developed, the role of foundations changed from that of a traditional, largely religion-based charitable institution to a somewhat more pluralist provider of quasi-public goods, used by special groups and to serve particular interests. The numerous guild-based and trade-related foundations in eighteenth- and nineteenth-century London, Amsterdam or Vienna illustrate how foundations became a private tool for serving the needs of specific and more circumscribed publics and professional groups. These foundations were established to serve both short-term (sickness) and longer-term (old age) social needs. Foundations required sustainability through cash flow flexibility for the former and permanent funds in the form of an endowment for the latter. The state welcomed these institutions as they fulfilled important social security functions and provided long-term stability for the operations of craft, trade, and professional groups.

In much of the nineteenth century and early twentieth century, the development of foundations in Europe depended on achieving a political balance between the aspirations of an expanding and frequently struggling nation-state on the one hand, and the interests of a more pluralist civil society on the other. The latter included the new economic elite, the urban middle class and the professions. These groups were major forces in the establishment of foundations.

In some countries, like France, the state succeeded in establishing itself as the primary representative of the public will *and* in keeping foundations at bay through anticlerical, anti-liberal policies.[18] In such cases, the question of time-limited foundations did not arise at all, as any foundation form was discouraged if not outright illegal. Yet not all nation-states were as successful as France in establishing a hegemonic regime across and against diverse political and cultural interests. More frequently, the emerging nation-state remained weak, failed in its attempt to consolidate power, and had to forge political compromises with existing power bases and their institutions. As a result, traditional foundations remained strong in nation-states such as Italy and Spain, and many new ones emerged in Switzerland and Germany. Early forms of private-public partnerships began to emerge between state and foundations, leading to a general expansion and consolidation.

These foundations required sustainable finances either in terms of an endowment or recurring revenue through fees and charges. For example, the Bodelschwingh´schen Anstalten Bethel, founded in Germany in the 1880s by a Protestant entrepreneur to serve the welfare needs of the growing urban population, soon operated with a mix of public and private funding as Bismarck's social insurance reforms were introduced in the 1880s. Today, Bethel is a nonprofit holding company of four separate operating foundations: Stiftung Bethel, Stiftung Nazareth, Stiftung Sarepta, and Hoffnungstaler Stiftung Lobetal. They are church-related foundations established under private law governed by the Evangelical Church of Westphalia, a public law corporation under ecclesiastical law. They comprise numerous institutions and are among the largest social, health and educational service providers in the country, with thousands of employees and a combined budget of several billion euros.

Today, foundations are mostly accepted institutions within a political landscape that has become much less restrictive and more enabling of philanthropy over time. Even countries like France, traditionally opposed to independent foundations, have passed laws encouraging philanthropy, and especially endowment funds (see below). The overall result of this complex historical development across Europe is a great diversity of foundation forms (e.g., public and private law foundations, ecclesiastical foundations established under canonical law), modes of operations (grant-making, operating foundation, mixed) and governance (e.g., foundations owning corporations, corporations owning foundations, family foundations).[19]

The American experience has been very different.[20] While Europe's foundations initially faced great uncertainty and then developed cooperative relationships with the emerging welfare state, American foundations moved to the forefront of organized philanthropy as an independent force. Although foundations in various forms have existed throughout American history, the emergence of large-scale philanthropic foundations associated with corporate titans such as Andrew Carnegie and John D. Rockefeller was an especially important development.

Historians like Barry Karl and Stanley Katz have shown that the first of these new foundations did not adopt the more traditional charity approach of addressing social and other public problems through direct giving.[21] Instead, they aimed at systematically exploring the causes of these problems with the aim of generating long-term solutions for the elimination, rather than just the alleviation, of the problems' visible manifestations.[22] The first of these foundations came to symbolize a new era of institutional philanthropy that pushed the more traditional elements of foundation activity to the background. The rise of general-purpose grant-making foundations in the United States in the early twentieth century neglected, if not outright discarded, the service delivery function that was, and remains, one of the major raisons d'être of European foundations.

FORM DIVERSITY

In contrast to the United States and the United Kingdom, where the trust concept rests on the relationship between endowment and trustees, foundations in the civil law countries of Europe are typically defined in the civil code as a specific form of a corporation: In Germany, for example, the great majority of foundations are civil law foundations regulated in §§ 80 of the Civil Code, which establishes a very broad, open definition and states three necessary conditions for establishing a foundation: (1) specification of the purposes in the statutes; (2) the identity of a legal representative for foundation transactions; and (3) the availability of assets to provide for a sustained fulfillment of set purposes. In particular, the third requirement—the principle of asset protection—came to imply that foundations are established in perpetuity.

The Swiss Civil Code in §§ 80–89 provides the legal framework for foundations, albeit without a fixed legal definition. A foundation requires assets endowed for specific purposes. Foundation types include conventional/ ordinary foundations, ecclesiastical foundations, foundations concerning employee benefit schemes, family foundations, corporate foundations, and fiduciary, dependent funds. Foundations pursuing public benefit purposes are tax-exempt. The legal default is that foundations are established in perpetuity, but they can spend down if they determine and establish temporal limits and if the regulator, that is, the cantonal authorities, consent.

Table 1 suggests that only a few countries are in a position similar to that of the United States, where the emergence of time-limited foundations presents a major form of differentiation.[23] There are two main reasons for this difference.

First, the more pronounced presence of operating foundations and mixed foundations in Europe creates less pressure on endowments. Most of the revenue of operating foundations is not based on interest payment or returns on investments, but on fees and charges. These foundations are typically service providers in the fields of social services, education, health and culture, and as such, complement the welfare state provision for which they receive compensation of some sort. Additionally, their assets are more likely in the form of real estate (e.g., buildings and physical infrastructure, or land) than in monetary investments and cash.

Second, as already mentioned, European foundations have no payout requirement and must adhere to the principle of asset protection instead. They can become dormant or inoperative without any negative consequences from regulators or tax authorities as long as their asset values are maintained. As a result, in terms of asset management, foundations primarily aim at compensating for any erosion of wealth that inflation might bring. They have no legal incentive to do more. In other words, they are locked into a narrow range characterized by asset protection without necessarily having to meet expectations of asset growth at one end and the strict avoidance of asset consumption and erosion at the other (see table 9.1).

The German case illustrates what the greater share of operating foundations relative to larger grant-makers means for the potential space available for time-limited foundations. In this context, it is useful to look at two essential distinctions: grant-making versus operating and mixed foundations; and two size categories of annual budgets, yielding four foundation types (see table 9.2).

According to table 9.2, the larger grant-making foundations represent 14 percent of the German philanthropic sector and 54 percent of estimated total expenditures of over €13 billion. When considering grant-making foundations as a whole, with their total annual budget of €7.1 billion, the large grant-making foundations account for 96 percent of total grant-making expenditure. The larger operating and mixed foundations are essentially service providers and account for 15 percent of the sector but contribute a major share of all financial resources (43 percent). The smaller operating and mixed foundations are largely niche providers and represent 29 percent of all foundations while accounting for only 2 percent of total expenditures. Finally, the combined budget of the small grant-makers (engagement foundations) makes up just 2 percent of the total expenditures, yet they represent more than 4 out of 10 foundations.[24]

Operating foundations can be divided into two groups (see table 9.2). The first consists of relatively large social enterprises, such as the von Bodelschwingh´schen Stiftungen Bethel. Such operational foundations often have millions of euros in annual budget at their disposal (28 percent). The second group among operating foundations, the niche providers, are mostly run by volunteers and focus more on the gaps in public social service provision. One example of such a niche provider is the Alfred und Toni Dahlweid Stiftung in Germany. With an annual budget of €41,000, the foundation runs a small recreation center for the elderly and offers Yoga courses.

The small grant-makers are labeled as engagement foundations to signal the pronounced role of volunteer boards. Being almost entirely volunteer-run, these foundations engage mainly at the local level and support community-related causes with relatively small budgets. For instance, the Ellen Schad-Stiftung in Frankfurt am Main supports the local branch of the German Association of Hearing-Impaired People (Deutscher Schwerhörigenbund e.V.). Engagement foundations are mainly young and founded after 1991 (77 percent). They work mostly without paid staff and have five volunteers on average.

The smaller foundations have grown disproportionately in recent years, which has brought up the question of how effective and efficient such smaller endowments are in actually meeting their objectives. There are two arguments that have to be weighed against each other: one suggests that small foundations are less efficient in terms of asset and grants management than larger foundations, and hence mergers or some form of cooperation, even pooling of resources, should be encouraged. The second argument states that small foundations are an expression of civic engagement and are better viewed as institutions of civil society. It is the intent that counts, the expression of commitment to a location or cause, and less so the actual efficiency and effectiveness of their operations.

Clearly, the first argument would suggest time limitations on economic grounds, while the second would remain largely neutral in this respect and stress the civil and cultural-institutional effects of philanthropic engagement: support for smaller foundation could signal caring for a particular cause or a community well beyond the lifetime of the initial donors, and constitute a bond that provides a certain continuity across generations. Larger grant-making foundations in Germany also employ volunteers but operate with a larger base of paid staff to provide direct or indirect financial support to grant recipients. They come close to a modern understanding of professional philanthropy that does not distinguish between an exclusively operative or grant-making approach. Foundations of this type were also founded mainly after 1991 (62 percent). These kinds of foundations have seventeen paid employees and twenty-three volunteers on average.

The option of time-limitation or a spend-down mechanism is not relevant to operating and mixed foundations, because financially, they thrive on third-party payments and are well integrated into a system of welfare state provision. However, it could, in principle, apply to grant-making German foundations. Here, we have to keep in mind the legal framework that prefers perpetuity of assets over time limitation, that is, the principle of asset protection.

How much this principle influences foundation behavior becomes clear in a survey conducted by the umbrella organization for German foundations, Bundesverband Deutscher Stiftungen. When asked, "How important are the following principles of foundation work," 92 percent of foundation founders answered that maintaining the foundation's endowment was "important" or "very important."[25] By contrast, 55 percent responded equivalently to the importance of ensuring the effectiveness of their activities. In other words, for many German foundation officials, asset protection is more important than performance. Yet, the same survey showed that 2 percent of respondents did in fact opt to spend-down and that time limitation is an ex-post option for 13 percent of founders.[26] At least for the time being, the form of time-limited spend-down foundations remains a generally marginal phenomenon in Germany.

CURRENT TRENDS

There is no general trend toward time-limited foundations in Europe, nor are such foundations a major issue in policy debates throughout the continent. Yet this aggregate view ignores the fact that the relevance and political salience of time-limited foundations varies substantially across countries. In Germany, the 2013 civil law reform that introduced time-limited options for philanthropy was not controversial, and parliamentary records do not indicate a debate about the introduction of time-limited foundations that went beyond legal technicalities and minute tax issues. In Switzerland, local policies at the cantonal level deal with foundation matters in flexible ways, including any time limitations. In France, the various foundation reforms and especially the introduction of the endowment fund (see below) passed without much debate. In Italy, other topics dominate public discourse on philanthropy, especially the governance of the foundations of banking origins after the Amato Law (1990), which privatized local savings banks.

Assuming that the four pressures outlined at the beginning of this chapter were to intensify, what could this mean for time-limited foundations? Developments in four select countries can be summarized as follows (see table 9.3).

In Austria, there are few foundations, and the institution is not the subject of controversy or vigorous debate. Nor does the state attempt to control them. One exception is the "*Privatstiftung*" or "private foundation," that is, foundations established to protect family fortunes, while allowing the dedication of part of the endowment to charity. As part of a politically sensitive policy,

Table 9.3 Scale of Foundation Sector and Degree of Politicization of Policy Environment by Sample Countries

	Smaller Scale	Larger Scale
Lower Politicization	Austria Pressure: low Solution: time-limited private foundations	Germany, Switzerland Pressure: low Solution: consumption foundation (G), flexible regulations at cantonal level (CH)
Potentially Higher Politicization	France Pressure: higher (fiscal) Solution: endowment funds	Italy Pressure: higher (Banking foundations) Solution: not an issue so far

the Austrian government grants beneficial fiscal treatment to private family fortunes in order to prevent capital flight mostly to neighboring Lichtenstein and Switzerland. Depending on the design of its statutes, a Privatstiftung can be either perpetual or time-limited. Since the contested introduction of the law on Privatstiftungen in 1993, subsequent policies have reduced longer-term tax-related benefits, which not only quelled much of the political controversy, but emphasized the time-limitation of funds over perpetuity. An original decision for perpetuity can be revoked by unanimous decision of the board, if the foundation's aims are achieved or no longer achievable, the founder objects to its work or other reasons stipulated in the statutes. Thus time-limits for Privatstiftung serve two purposes. For the foundation, they give boards greater flexibility. At the political level, they take pressure off claims that Privatstiftungen are vehicles of tax avoidance and ways to fortify family fortunes.

France too can claim a few foundations. However, more recently, endowment funds (*fonds de dotation*) have emerged as a parallel system to regular public benefit foundations (*fondation reconnue d'utilité publique*) which continue to be highly regulated. As opposed to traditional foundations, endowment funds are a flexible instrument to encourage philanthropy. In 2008, seeking to mobilize private funds for public purposes in times of fiscal austerity and in the context of restrictive foundation regulations, the Law on Modernization of the Economy introduced the endowment fund (*fonds de dotation*) as a new legal and nonprofit entity.

Endowment funds can be time-limited or perpetual. While endowment funds benefit from similar tax regimes as the public utility foundations, they generally cannot receive public funds. The registration of such funds is handled at the local prefectural level, and not by the central government, as is the case for regular foundations. This reduces the time period for establishing endowment funds from previously up to two years to just about one month. A total of 2,125 endowments funds were registered in 2013, and over 2,500 as of September 1, 2016.[27]

This growth has to be seen in a broader context: until the 1980s, legal hurdles interdicted almost all efforts to establish foundations in France.[28] The Development of Philanthropy Act (1987) introduced and defined the term "foundation" as a perpetual institution, and adjustments regarding legal requirements and processes were subsequently made in 2003 and 2005. Regular foundations must be irrevocable in nature and can only be recognized as nonprofit and for public benefit by a decree of the Ministry of Interior. Thus, the existence and activities of these foundations are highly regulated. However, corporate foundations (*fondations d'entreprises*) and fiduciary foundations (*fondations abritées*, incorporated in recognized "shelter" organizations, for example, *Institut de France, Fondation de France, Fondation pour l'Enfance*) could be established as time-limited entities.

With about twenty thousand foundations, Germany is home to the second largest foundation sector after the United States. As we have seen, foundations there are guided by the principle of sustainability and asset protection. This conventional model of permanent foundation assets in perpetuity is complemented by recent policy changes that aimed at strengthening civic engagement and volunteering. The Law to Support Voluntary Activities (*Gesetz zur Stärkung des Ehrenamts*) reformed the perpetuity rule so that foundations can be established for a limited period of activity and with a minimum of ten years (Civil Code §80 [2]). Specifically, there are now foundations established in perpetuity, time-limited foundations (*Verbrauchsstiftung* or "consumptive foundation"), and mixed foundations with permanent and flexible assets (the flexible components can be spent and/or replenished). Any time-limited assets are tied to objectives as stipulated in the deed or articles of incorporation. Each model requires a minimum endowment size, which, however, varies across the various federal states. Yet tax regulations continue to favor permanent over temporary assets, which helps explain how rarely the time-limitation option has been taken up.

In Switzerland, time limitations for foundations are receiving more attention as interest rates have remained low. Compared to Germany, Switzerland offers a more flexible treatment of time-limited foundations. While the form of a spend-down foundation is not explicitly recognized in law, the praxis at the cantonal level, which regulates foundations, has been very flexible in allowing the establishment of time-limited foundations. Determination of the endowment use (and not just the returns on investments) rests with the foundation board, which can also lead to annulment of the perpetuity rule. Overall, as in Germany, politicization of the issue of time-limited foundations seems low.

In Italy, on the other hand, the foundation environment is generally politicized, given continued and long-standing tensions between foundations of banking origins (based on the Amato Law of 1990, which privatized local savings and loans and created relatively large charitable foundations in the process) and the provincial and national governments which prefer more control over both endowments and spending.[29] This conflict dominates the political discourse about foundations, and discussions of time limitations remain marginal at best.

Thus, the policy environment in which time-limited foundations emerge, and the nature of their introduction and reception, depend largely on two aspects: the scale of foundations in terms of numbers and economic size, and the degree of politicization of philanthropy generally in a country. Reforms are being introduced that, even when fundamental (e.g., the French endowment funds), operate at a technical rather than an ideological level. The foundation form seems no longer questioned in principle, nor subject to stricter and more far-reaching regulatory control. Instead, European reforms aim at enabling rather than restricting philanthropy, even though the steps taken seem small and even half-hearted at times, as the German case illustrates. The Italian case is at least a partial exception, awaiting the political settlement of the banking foundations.

TIME-LIMITED FOUNDATIONS IN EUROPE

While time-limited foundations exist, their absolute numbers are small in the two largest European foundation sectors: estimates suggest around thirty to forty spend-down foundations in the UK and about four hundred so-termed consumption foundations (*Verbrauchsstiftungen*) in Germany.[30] They are more common in Switzerland, with more than two thousand,[31] and in France in the form of endowment funds, of which about 2,226 exist as of 2016.[32] The relatively high number of Swiss time-limited foundations stems from flexible foundation law implementation on a case-by-case basis at the cantonal level that allows maximum donor intent; in other words, even though the default setting of creating a foundation in Switzerland establishes the endowment for perpetuity, time-limited forms are allowed if a reasonable case can be made to cantonal administrators. The French case is different and a recent result of a new law that makes it possible to establish philanthropic funds outside the otherwise rigid regulation of foundations. Beyond these four, however, time-limited foundations are rare across other European countries, even in those with a sizable foundation sector like Spain or Italy.

In the UK, the concept of a time-limited, spend-down foundation, while well-established, has received little support. Overall numbers remain small relative to a total of over twelve thousand foundations existing in the UK in 2013 (see table 9.1). A number of time-limited foundations and trusts were initiated decades ago. While such foundations seem to reflect explicit donor preferences, they appear unrelated to the four pressures mentioned above. Examples include:

- **Four Acre Trust (1995–2015)**: John Bothamley created Four Acre Trust as a vehicle for providing financial support to operating charities in the field of children and youth work registered in the UK. Since 2010, the trust has been closed to new applicants.
- **Diana, Princess of Wales Memorial Fund (1997–2012)**: After the death of Princess Diana in 1997, public donations to Kensington Palace with a total volume of £34 million were channeled into a fund, along with Sir Elton John's £38 million donation from sales of *Candle in the Wind* (1997) and £66 million from investments, commercial partnerships, and exhibitions. As a grant-making charity, the fund aimed at creating a lasting legacy for Diana's humanitarian work in the UK and abroad. After the fund was closed in 2012, legal ownership was transferred to The Royal Foundation of The Duke and Duchess of Cambridge and Prince Harry to assign further incoming donations to charitable work.
- **Tubney Charitable Trust (1997–2012)**: This grant-making trust supported charities in the field of preserving species listed in the UK Biodiversity Plan (UKBAP) as well as the welfare of farmed animals both nationally and internationally. Its founders, Miles Blackwell, retired chairman of the Oxford-based bookseller Blackwell Limited, and his wife Briony, left no heirs. The funds totaled approximately £50 million at that time, and the spend-down approach was in line with the founders' wishes.
- **The Rootstein Hopkins Foundation (1990–2008)**: Rick and Adel Hopkins had considered a time-limited charitable fund as early as 1984 in the context of the sale of their business that designed and manufactured mannequins. The foundation's main field of activity was the visual arts in the UK. Over its lifetime, the foundation awarded £8 million to artists, art students, art galleries, and colleges of art and design.
- **Anglo-German Foundation (1973–2009)**: The Anglo-German Foundation for the Study of Industrial Society was based on an endowment provided by the German government and subsequent contributions by both governments. It aimed at supporting the exchange of knowledge and policy-related processes in Britain and Germany by funding comparative research on economic, environmental, and social issues. Its joint patrons were HRH the duke of Edinburgh and the president of the Federal Republic of Germany. The Anglo-German Foundation closed down in 2009 following the expiration of its Royal Charter.

Until 2013, time-limited foundations in Germany remained few in numbers due to legal hurdles. If they existed, such foundations generally addressed special issues or problems that were, for various reasons intrinsically, time-bound or involved political urgency:

- **Stiftung Erinnerung, Verantwortung, Zukunft (2000–2007)**: The German government and a consortium of corporations endowed the foundation with D-Mark 10 billion (about 5 billion euros) to indemnify forced laborers during World War II.
- **Beatrice und Rochus Mummert-Stiftung (2001–2007)**: The foundation operated a stipend program to support young talent in the area of business management from EU-accession and EU candidate countries in Central and Southeastern Europe (mid-1990s to 2003). The foundation later merged with the Robert Bosch Foundation and ceased to exist as an independent institution.
- **Hessnatur Stiftung (2015–)**: The foundation was set up by the natural and fair-trade eco-textile company *Hessnatur* on the occasion of its fortieth anniversary. It supports research and development in applied sustainability. Given the urgency the founding corporation attached to ecological issues, the foundation was established as an operating spend-down foundation, providing grants and commissioning projects. Although the foundation has no specified life span, the board can spend all or parts of its endowment but at least 10 percent annually.

In France, time-limited endowment funds or *fonds de dotation* became legal in 2008. The first fund was recognized in March 2009, and the *Journal Officiel* had registered about 2,500 endowment funds by September 2016. Unlike in the UK and in Germany, time-limited foundations in France are less the result of donor intent or time limitations arising through specific circumstances. Rather, they reflect a new financial instrument to allow donors to circumvent an otherwise restrictive regulatory environment for foundations with a demanding registration process. Examples include:

- **Credit@People (2009–)**: Christophe Casabonne initiated the fund to support people in need. It uses micro-credits to improve access for women and children to labor markets, education, and natural resources (water, food, first aid) in rural India.
- **Fonds de Dotation de l'Adie pour l'Entrepreneuriat Populaire (2009–)**: In response to the economic crisis in 2009, l'Adie created the fund to support micro-entrepreneurs in France by providing financial startup funds and support services.
- **Fonds de dotation de l'association Théodora (2009–)**: The fund supports the work of the Théodora association, founded in 2000, to support the quality of life of children undergoing medical treatment. Specifically, it engages clowns to entertain children.

- **Fonds de Dotation Generation Solidaire (2012–)**: The fund funds citizen initiatives to support efforts on behalf of intergenerational solidarity and increasing the quality of life of the elderly. It received an initial time-bound donation of company shares worth about €70,000 for three years.

CONCLUSION

In contrast to the United States, the pressures resulting from low interest rates, the high valuation of donor intent and the rise of new ways and means to practice philanthropy are less acute in Europe, especially for some foundation types. As we saw above, compared to the American situation, the European foundation landscape is more differentiated, with a greater form variety besides the perpetual grant-making foundation that dominates US philanthropy. In particular, the pronounced presence of operating foundations with often significant shares of earned income relative to returns on endowments means that relatively fewer foundations are exposed to all four pressures with equal force.

What is more, European foundations have no equivalent to the minimum payout requirement that US foundations are subject to. Rather, in civil law countries, regulations are aimed at the preservation of the initial endowment, and trustees are required to maintain its nominal value. In Germany, according to § 80(2) of the Civil Code, endowments shall ensure perpetual and sustainable fulfillment of the purpose. In France, sustainability is one of the three criteria[33] regulators apply to public utility foundations. This regulatory context implies that foundations are both relatively more risk-averse, and their performance is tied to asset preservation rather than goal achievement.

However, a few countries introduced policy changes over the last decade to accommodate time-limited forms of foundations and funds, most notably France and Germany. As already mentioned, France established the endowment fund in 2008, which constitutes a new organizational form of institutionalized philanthropy in the country. In 2013, Germany changed existing regulations and introduced the so-called *Verbrauchsstiftung* or consumption foundation as a variant of the foundation established in perpetuity, the latter continuing to serve as the prevailing standard form.

In their analysis of American foundations, Hammack and Anheier suggest how much the roles and contributions of formal philanthropy have changed over time, passing through several distinct phases.[34] Indeed, they apply the label "versatile" to signal that philanthropic institutions have evolved, and continue to do so, by accommodating changes in politics and society at large. The question of time-limited, spend-down foundations has yet to assume a full sense of salience in Europe, both among policymakers and philanthropists.

The model of the foundation established in perpetuity continues to dominate for the time being. However, there are initial signs that Europe´s foundation landscape will continue to evolve as well, and in the future, will see the arrival of a new form in greater numbers: time-limited foundations, either as formal organizations or as a version of the French *fonds* model.

NOTES

1. See Loren Renz and David Wolcheck. "Perpetuity or Limited Lifespan: How Do Family Foundations Decide?" (*The Foundation Center and Council on Foundations*, 2009); "Making Change by Spending Down" (Foundation Center, 2015); Francie Ostrower, "Limited Life Foundations. Motivations, Experiences and Strategies" (Urban Institute, 2009); David La Piana, "Recommendations for Foundations Seeking to Exit a Program Area or Close Down Responsibly," *Stanford Social Innovation Review*, August 20, 2004; John R. Thelin and Richard W. Trollinger, *Time Is of the Essence: Foundations and the Policies of Limited Life and Endowment Spend-Down* (Washington, DC: Aspen Institute Program on Philanthropy and Social Innovation, 2009); on the topic of "limited life" and "spend down" philanthropy, the Duke Sanford Center for Strategic Philanthropy and Civil Society assembles information, research and documents, see https://cspcs.sanford.duke.edu/time-limited-philanthropy.

2. Such as Barbara Meyn, *Stiftung und Vermögensverzehr: Zivil- und spendenrechtliche Auswirkungen des Ehrenamtsstärkungsgesetzes für Verbrauchsstiftung & Co. Stiftung & Sponsoring*, 2013 and Nina Leseberg and Karsten Timmer, *Stifterinnen und Stifter in Deutschland Engagement - Motive - Ansichten* (Berlin: Bundesverband Deutscher Stiftungen, 2015) for Germany; Beate Eckhardt, Dominique Jakob, and Georg Von Schnurbein. "Swiss Foundation Report 2016" *CEPS Forschung Und Praxis* 13 (2016) for Switzerland; "Spending Out: Learning Lessons from Time-limited Grant-making" (Association of Charitable Foundations, 2010) and "THE POWER of NOW. Spend Out Trusts and Foundations in the UK" (Institute for Philanthropy, 2010) for the UK; and Fondation de France 2014 for France.

3. Paul Brest and Hal Harvey, "Dealing with Hard Times: Advice for Foundations," *The Chronicle of Philanthropy*, November 13, 2008; "An Overview of Philanthropy in Europe" (Fondation De France, 2015), https://www.fondationdefrance.org/sites/default/files/atoms/files/philanthropy_in_europe_2015.pdf.

4. Jeffrey J. Cain, *Protecting Donor Intent: How to Define and Safeguard Your Philanthropic Principles* (Washington, DC: Philanthropy Roundtable, 2012); Susan Gary, "The Problems with Donor Intent: Interpretation, Enforcement, and Doing the Right Thing," *Chicago-Kent Law Review* 85, no. 3 (June 2010), 977–1043.

5. Paul Brest, "Strategic Philanthropy and Its Discontents," *Stanford Social Innovation Review*, April 27, 2015, https://ssir.org/up_for_debate/article/strategic_philanthropy_and_its_discontents; Christine W. Letts, William P. Ryan, and Allen S. Grossman, "Virtuous Capital: What Foundations Can Learn from Venture Capitalists," *Harvard Business Review*, March/April 1997, https://hbr.org/1997/03/virtuous-capital-what-foundations-can-learn-from-venture-capitalists.

6. Michael E. Porter and Mark R. Kramer, "Philanthropy's New Agenda: Creating Value," *Harvard Business Review* (November 1999), 121–30.

7. Mark R. Kramer, "Catalytic Philanthropy," *Stanford Social Innovation Review*, Fall 2009, https://ssir.org/articles/entry/catalytic_philanthropy#.

8. "Social Investment," *Global Studies Encyclopedia*, vol. 5, eds. Helmut K. Anheier and Mark Juergensmeyer (London: Sage, 2012).

9. Helmut K. Anheier et al., *Stiftungen in Deutschland* 1: Eine Verortung (Heidelberg: Springer, 2017).

10. The number includes about 2,400 private interest foundations, which decimates the number of public benefit foundations to 701 as of 2014.

11. The number includes 558 fiduciary funds that are overseen and managed by King Baudouin Foundation.

12. The number includes endowment funds (*fonds de dotation*).

13. As of 2016, the German foundation sector includes about twenty thousand organizations in total.

14. For the disproportionate rise of smaller foundations, cf. Foundation Center for the United States; for Germany see Anheier et al., *Stiftungen in Deutschland*; and for Switzerland, see Eckhardt, Jakob, and Von Schnurbein, "Swiss Foundation Report 2016."

15. Keith Baker, "The Old Regime and the French Revolution," in *University of Chicago Readings in Western Civilization 7* (Chicago: University of Chicago Press, 1987).

16. Immanuel Kant, *Die Metaphysik Der Sitten* (Berlin, 1797).

17. James A. Smith, Karsten Borgmann, and Peter Walkenhorst, "Foundations in Europe: The Historical Context," in *Foundations in Europe: Society, Management, and Law*, eds. Andreas Schlueter, Volker Then and Peter Walkenhorst (Gutersloh, Germany: Bertelsmann Stifttung, 2001).

18. Edith Archambault, *Le Secteur Sans but Lucratif: Associations Et Fondations En France* (Paris: Economica, 1996).

19. Anheier et al., *Stiftungen in Deutschland*.

20. David C. Hammack and Helmut K. Anheier, *A Versatile American Institution: The Changing Ideals and Realities of Philanthropic Foundations* (Washington, DC: Brookings Institution Press, 2013); Helmut K. Anheier and David Hammack, *American Foundations: Roles and Contributions* (Washington, D.C: Brookings Institution Press, 2010). Stefan Toepler, "Charitble Foundations," in *International Encyclopedia of the Social Sciences*, 2nd ed. (Farmington Hills, MI: Macmillan Reference/Thomson, 2007).

21. Barry Karl and Stanley Katz, "Foundations and Ruling Class Elites," *Daedalus* 116, no. 1 (Winter 1987), 1–40.

22. Martin Bulmer, "The History of Philanthropic Foundations in the United Kingdom and the United States," in *Private Funds, Public Purpose: Philanthropic Foundations in International Perspective*, ed. Helmut Anheier and Stefan Toepler (New York: Kluwer Academic, 1999); Kathleen McCarthy, "Philanthropy in the Reagan Years," *Nonprofit and Voluntary Sector Quarterly* 18, no. 3 (Fall 1989).

23. In contrast to the United States, comparable data on foundations in Europe are still patchy and suffer from a lack of comparability due to different legal definitions, tax treatment, and cultural differences.

24. Anheier et al., *Stiftungen in Deutschland*.

25. Nina Leseberg and Karsten Timmer, *Stifterinnen Und Stifter in Deutschland Engagement—Motive—Ansichten* (Berlin: Bundesverband Deutscher Stiftungen, 2015), 111.

26. Ibid., 113.

27. Foundation Center, "Foundation Directory Online," Foundation Center, accessed February 12, 2016, http://foundationcenter.org/products/foundation-directory-online.

28. Archambault, *Le Secteur Sans but Lucratif*.

29. Gian Paolo Barbetta, "Foundations in Italy," in *Private Funds, Public Purpose*.

30. Neither the German umbrella association for foundations, Bundesverband Deutscher Stiftungen, nor the fiscal authorities collect information on the number of *Verbrauchsstiftungen* through registry offices. Estimates, based on a survey (n = 575, sector size: about 20.000 foundations), show that only 2.4 percent have indeed established a time-limited foundation, whereas 12.7 percent of the respondents indicated a general interest in this form. Yet, transition from perpetual to time-bound endowment is bureaucratic and rather complicated. See Leseberg and Timmer, *Stifterinnen Und Stifter in Deutschland Engagement*, 88, 91, 112–13. Institute for Philanthropy, "THE POWER of NOW."

31. The number is a calculated estimate based on a survey (n = 110) by the Swiss Centre for Philanthropy Studies where 23 percent of the respondents indicated their status as spend-down organizations. David Hertig and Georg Von Schnurbein, "Die Vermögensverwaltung Gemeinnütziger Stiftungen. State of the Art?" (Centre for Philanthropy Studies, 2013), 13.

32. Centre Francais de Fondations, "Les Derniers Chiffres Sur Les Fonds Et Fondations En France," http://www.centre-francais-fondations.org/fondations-fonds-de-dotation/le-secteur/les-derniers-chiffres-sur-les-fonds-et-fondations-en-france.

33. The criteria are: (1) sufficient endowment to fulfill the purpose, (2) be nonprofit in nature and aim at public benefit purposes, and (3) sustainability in terms of perpetuity and an endowment that guarantees a stable and steady stream of income.

34. Hammack and Anheier, *Versatile American Institution*.

Chapter 10

Is It Really a Matter of Time?

*Rethinking the Significance of Foundation Life Span**

Francie Ostrower

THE DEBATE OVER PERPETUITY

Most private foundations are perpetual endowments, and perpetuity has been called a "key feature" of foundations, so pervasive that "it is hard to imagine any other type of charitable giving" associated with such institutions.[1] Nonetheless, perpetuity has also been subject to criticism and controversy for hundreds of years. In the 1830s, philosopher John Stuart Mill criticized the irrationality that makes "a dead man's intentions for a single day, a rule for subsequent centuries."[2] In the United States, early in the last century, Cleveland lawyer Frederick Goff developed the community foundation form in part to release future generations from the "dead hand" of donor control.[3] At the start of this new century, Ray Madoff, coeditor of this volume, decried the assumption that "people can make intelligent decisions about the use of resources in the distant future."[4] Critics have also objected that perpetuity leads foundations to focus on organizational survival and asset preservation at

* This chapter is based on the article "Perpetuity or Spend-Down: Does the Notion of Lifespan Matter in Organized Philanthropy?" published by the *Nonprofit Quarterly* on March 31, 2016, and draws substantially from Francie Ostrower, *Limited Life Foundations: Motivations, Experiences and Strategies* (Washington, DC: Urban Institute, 2009), with permission from the Urban Institute, https://www.urban.org/sites/default/files/publication/30121/411836-Limited-Life-Foundations-Motivations-Experiences-and-Strategies.PDF, and Ostrower, *Sunsetting: A Framework for Foundation Life as Well as Death* (Washington, DC: Aspen Institute, 2011), with permission from the Aspen Institute, https://www.aspeninstitute.org/publications/sunsetting-framework-foundation-life-well-death/. The author thanks Benjamin Soskis for comments on this chapter.

the expense of mission, and that foundations could more effectively address pressing problems by spending those assets.[5]

Interestingly, while some criticize perpetuity for giving too much control to donors, others object that perpetual foundations *undermine* donor intent. On this view, perpetual foundations tend to drift away from the donor's wishes as these are forgotten, become less intelligible in changing circumstances, or as trustees and staff substitute their own priorities for those of the donor.[6] Peter Frumkin, for instance, writes that many donors would be appalled by their foundations' subsequent fate and argues that donors opting for perpetuity should have either a broad philanthropic purpose or a readiness to have their specific purpose be reshaped.[7]

An assumption made by critics and supporters alike is that life span is an organizational characteristic with considerable consequences for foundation practice. Even those that take no official position in the debate contend that the very act of thinking about life span enhances foundation strategy and effectiveness.[8] But are these assumptions true? How salient is life span to foundation attitudes and practice? To answer this question, we need to go beyond the abstract character and frequent reliance on anecdotal illustrations that characterize much of the debate on perpetuity and examine systematic research on foundation practice. This chapter does so by integrating findings from three studies for which the author served as principal investigator.[9]

Based on the results of those studies, this chapter questions assumptions about the impact of perpetuity as an organizational characteristic per se and calls for refining and reframing the debate. If one sought an organizational characteristic to predict foundation practice, one would be better off having information about other characteristics such as asset size. Life span generally appears to be less a predictor of foundation practice than a reflection of the values and norms of the trustees and donors making decisions about life span. Relatedly the impact of a decision to forgo perpetuity and embrace limited life is deeply shaped by *why and how* foundation leaders approach the decision to sunset and the details of its implementation.

THE SIGNIFICANCE OF LIFE SPAN:
WHAT THE DATA TELL US

If perpetuity has a significant impact on foundation functioning, there should be considerable differences between perpetual and limited-life foundations. Yet comparisons of the attitudes and practices of private foundations that had opted for limited life versus perpetual life in a 2003 Urban Institute survey revealed few such differences.[10]

Although this survey was not originally designed to examine life span, it asked respondents about their longevity plans, and therefore permitted comparisons of a wide range of attitudes and practices. A further advantage of the study was that foundations were identified independent of their longevity plans, since the survey was sent to all staffed grant-making foundations in the United States that could be identified. It therefore captured a varied group of foundations, including some that were highly public about their plans to sunset, and others whose longevity plans were not well publicized. The following comparisons are based on the 710 private independent foundations in the study that had decided to limit their life (70 foundations) and those that decided to continue in perpetuity (640 foundations).[11]

Perpetuity generally was not correlated with what foundations viewed as important to being effective, or to their practices when it came to grant-making goals, criteria, or style. Perpetuity was not correlated with self-perceptions of effectiveness with respect to grant quality, impact, and staffing or grantee relations (although limited-life foundations were less often satisfied with their asset management performance).[12] Consider the results when survey respondents were provided with a list of ideas about what makes a foundation effective and asked to rate how important they thought each is for a foundation such as theirs (some examples were "establish focused and limited grantmaking areas," "maintain a broad grants program," "adhere to founding donor's wishes," "conduct formal evaluations of funded work," and "collaborate with external groups/organizations").[13] On fully fourteen of the seventeen items, there were no statistically significant differences between responses from limited-life and perpetual foundations.[14] An eighteenth item, maintaining family unity, was asked only of family foundations, and here too no significant differences were found between perpetual and limited-life family foundations.

Sunsetting foundations were, however, more donor-centric in certain respects. In the first instance, limited-life foundations were more likely to have a living donor than perpetual ones (50 versus 21 percent). A striking area in which limited-life and perpetual foundations differed was in their attitudes concerning donor intent. Respondents from foundations planning limited life more often characterized adherence to the founding donor's wishes as very important to achieving foundation effectiveness (87 versus 66 percent of perpetual foundations). To consider whether this difference simply reflected the more frequent presence of a living donor in limited-life foundations, comparisons were made separately for foundations with and without a living donor. Indeed, among foundations with a living donor, longevity plans made little difference (82 percent of limited-life and 75 percent of perpetual foundations with a living donor characterized adherence to the donor's wishes as very important to effectiveness). Among foundations *without* a living donor, however, a considerably higher percentage of limited-life foundations rated adhering to the donor's wishes as very important to foundation effectiveness (91 versus 65 percent). This attitudinal difference endured even after foundation size and age were taken into account.[15]

The other two areas of attitudinal differences were the importance of publicizing the foundation and its work and having a strong organizational infrastructure. While neither limited-life nor perpetual foundations often characterized publicizing the foundation and its work as very important to effectiveness, a higher percentage of perpetual foundations did so. The pattern with respect to organizational infrastructure is somewhat different and reveals greater polarization among limited-life foundations than among perpetual ones. Thus, while comparable percentages of limited-life and perpetual-life foundations see a strong organizational infrastructure as very important, a higher percentage of limited-life foundations said it is not important.[16]

When we turn to practices, the situation with respect to donor orientation is somewhat different. Sunsetting foundations did say more often than perpetual ones that the donor's interest in a cause was a somewhat or very important criterion in foundation grant-making decisions during the past two years (85 versus 67 percent). This difference was not statistically significant, however, once the presence of a living donor and foundation age were taken into account. Put otherwise, over time, plans to sunset per se apparently offered no greater likelihood of using the donor's interest in the cause as a grant-making criterion.[17] In sum, having a living donor increased the likelihood of this being an important grant-making criterion, foundation age decreased the likelihood, and longevity plans were unrelated.

Donor control is at the heart of the debate over perpetuity. Some argue that perpetuity grants too much control to donors by letting their wishes dictate for all time. Others contend that perpetuity undermines donor authority over time. The findings of the 2003 Urban Institute survey are consistent with the view that limited-life foundations are more donor-centric—up to a point. Such foundations are more likely to have a living donor involved and to express attitudinal support for the importance of adhering to donor wishes. However, the findings also raise questions about whether that attitude continues to influence practice over time. To further explore these attitudes, we turn in the next section to interviews with CEOs and trustees of sunsetting foundations. The results invite additional questions about the current conceptualization of donor control in debates over foundation life span.

The Significance of Life Span According to CEOs and Trustees

Between 2007 and 2008, the author conducted in-depth personal interviews with CEOs and/or trustees of twenty-two sunsetting foundations that had participated in the earlier survey.[18] Interviews explored the motivations, experiences, and strategies associated with sunset. The decision to sunset was deeply reflective of donor values and the donor-centric outlook discussed earlier. In most cases (fifteen out of twenty-two) the donor decided to sunset. In other cases, the decision was made by a surviving spouse, child, or nonfamily trustee. The reason most frequently given for the decision to sunset was the preservation of donor intent. One donor, for instance, felt that foundations are often "captured" by trustees that diverge from the donor's plans. Said another donor, "A foundation represents something that a human being feels. I never felt anyone could adequately represent what I feel." Interestingly, some trustees cited a desire to preserve donor intentions as the motivation even when the donor in question did not leave guidelines expressing their intentions. Said one trustee: "[The donor] left no guidelines. We have been governed by his likes and dislikes. The further away we get, the less influence that has on trustees."

Whatever the reality, many of these donors and trustees of sunsetting foundations believed that perpetuity undermines donor intent rather than perpetuating donor control and decided to sunset to avoid that outcome. Said one, "The key here is not sunset. We were concerned about staying faithful to donor intent . . . that becomes difficult over time, not necessarily because the donor's intent becomes difficult to fill, but because trustees change their minds." Our findings are consistent with those of another survey, of family foundations, in which 89 percent of those creating foundations with a sunset provision cited a concern with the preservation of donor intent as a reason.[19]

Yet the way that people spoke about donor intent suggests that it should be conceptualized more broadly than strictly a question about whether the foundation will adhere to, or deviate from, specific donor wishes or instructions. Rather, the comments express a particular normative or cultural outlook concerning the role of the donor, and of foundations as organizational vehicles. In addition to wanting to preserve donor intent, interviewees repeatedly expressed an aversion to the perceived institutionalization resulting from perpetuity. In their view, over time, perpetual foundations become bureaucracies more focused on their own future survival than on philanthropy. One such individual expressed concern that "some foundations are perpetual and [take on] a life of their own and may lose sight of what they were founded for." In this view, perpetual foundations become bureaucracies more focused on self-preservation than on philanthropy. Thus, one donor observed, "You can't maintain things without institutionalization. . . . I don't want to create something that's primary purpose is to maintain itself." Explaining her family's decision to limit foundation life, another trustee said, "The overriding reason was the desire not to create a self-perpetuating bureaucracy." She observed that over time foundations become "so stagnant" and "spend a lot on offices and staff but not giving much." As such comments suggest, time considerations may factor in to decisions about life span not only with respect to giving (e.g., the relative merits of giving sooner rather than later) but also with respect to attitudes about the impact of time on foundation evolution.

Creators of the modern foundation embraced the corporate form as a flexible and independent vehicle that could be created with broad purposes to respond to changing social and cultural needs long after the death of the original donor.[20] The individuals that chose to sunset in this study, however, frequently exhibited an aversion to the very idea of the foundation as an organization with an existence and purpose independent of the donor. On this view, the passage of time has negative consequences leading foundations to shift attention away from donor intent and philanthropic priorities, toward institutional survival as an end in itself. As we shall see, however, donors and trustees may still be concerned about leaving a philanthropic legacy to live beyond the life span of the organization, while rejecting the creation of a perpetual foundation as a vehicle for achieving that goal.

Taken together, the survey and interview findings suggest that debates and criticisms regarding donor control and intent can become too narrowly or literally focused on perpetuation of donor directives. Instead, our findings underscore the importance of a broader normative orientation toward the role of the donor and of foundations as organizational vehicles. Those in limited-life foundations regard philanthropy in a more personalistic way, view foundations as an expression of the donor, and have an antipathy toward institutionalized philanthropy, which they believe represents an organization taking on a life of its own detached from the intentions and will of the donor.

In some cases, the decision to sunset was more of a default choice—for instance, when the donor had no children, or when children did not share the donor's interests, or when the family didn't get along. Very few interviewees chose sunsetting because they believe it offers strategic advantages or greater impact.

To this point, we have discussed the reasons given for sunsetting, but some respondents also pointed to different *consequences* of sunsetting. The most commonly cited of these was that the foundation gave more funds away as its leaders did not have to be concerned with preserving the foundation as an entity. Said the head of one foundation board:

> Some foundations are perpetual . . . and may lose sight of what they were founded for. They may protect their assets and give less. . . . You don't have to worry about that when you plan limited life. So if there is a downturn in the market we can still say, "let's give the same amount anyway."

Yet while some felt greater freedom to vary and tailor their giving level to philanthropic objectives because of sunset, this was not always true. For instance, one foundation said they continued to adhere to the 5 percent annual spending rate prevalent among perpetual foundations and would defer spending larger sums until close to their termination date. Thus, the significance of time frame in relation to philanthropic practice may shift over the foundation's life. This is one reason we opt for the terms "sunset" or "limited life" over "spend down."

A significant minority (over one-third) felt sunsetting had no influence on practice at all. Apart from giving away more, most did not perceive an impact on what or how they gave. Many of the foundations did little planning for their ultimate closure. Over half said they had done no planning, and the majority felt no immediate pressure to do so. Some had not established a termination date. An interviewee who had been involved with two sunsetting foundations observed, "You wouldn't see [them] any differently than other foundations on a day-to-day basis because of the fact that they are spending down. You couldn't discriminate . . . based on their grantmaking."

The lack in many cases of planning, a fixed termination date, or perceived alterations in foundation operations and grant-making indicate that "sunsetting" and "perpetuity" are not necessarily rigid or dichotomous categories with clearly laid-out imperatives regarding the timing of giving. For instance, one family foundation in the study is spending at a rate that they know will ultimately result in spending down the endowment, but they have not set a termination date and don't incorporate sunsetting into their decisions. One executive commented, "We have no formal spend down plan. . . . The family is flexible. . . . They focus on what's needed for this year, not on where the foundation should be 5 to 10 years from now." A family foundation survey conducted around the same time found that many foundations have no life-span directive in their charter and a 2015 survey finds that fully 42 percent of family foundations had not yet decided.[21] While more research is needed to understand why, these foundations may not have a definite attitude toward the temporal dimensions of giving—or the founders may have decided to leave the decision to family members sometime in the future.

In sum, the findings take us away from our initial focus on life span as an organizational attribute and back to the attitudes and values of those who make and execute decisions about foundation longevity. Does that mean then that the decision about longevity has no impact on how a foundation operates? No—but that impact is not automatic or predetermined. Instead, it depends on *how and why* foundation leaders approach and implement a sunset plan.

While most foundation leaders did not characterize sunsetting as a philanthropic strategy, some did and consciously approached sunsetting as a way to achieve both personal and philanthropic goals. We turn to these atypical foundations in the next section.

SUNSETTING AS A PHILANTHROPIC STRATEGY: CASE STUDIES

In a third study, conducted between 2008 and 2010, the author conducted in-depth case studies of four foundations that explicitly connected having a limited lifetime to their philanthropic strategy.[22] The case studies are based primarily on sixty personal interviews (with trustees, staff, and the donor in the case of the sole foundation with a living donor), supplemented by archival materials (such as board minutes, internal memos, and other documents). The author also interviewed foundation grantees (and community residents in one case). The cases were selected because they were unusually deliberative and strategic about their sunsetting plans, linking them closely to other dimensions of foundation operations. They illustrate what it looks like when a foundation makes life span a focus on an ongoing basis, and we turn to examples of two foundations that closed during the study, the Beldon Fund and the Mary Flagler Cary Charitable Trust.[23]

In 1998, John Hunting, the creator of the Beldon Fund, increased the Fund's assets from $10 million to over $100 million—and announced the foundation would pay it all out over the next ten years. In 2009, reflecting back, Hunting wrote, "The decision reflected my belief in the urgency of this mission and a strong sense that making large investments over a shorter period of time would be more effective than making smaller grants over many years." That mission was "to help build public and policy support for environmental protection."[24] Hunting's reasons involved personal, philosophical, and strategic considerations, including those related to time: He wanted to see the results of his giving, felt today's donors should solve today's problems, and believed perpetual foundations too often do not follow the original donor's intent. He linked his time frame to his philanthropic focus on the environment, asking, "Given all the environmental problems besieging our planet today, how can I not give away all of the foundation's assets in the very near future?"[25]

Following the original decision, trustees and staff saw an additional rationale emerge. Specifically, they felt that because they were able to spend so much more, sunsetting permitted the foundation to have the visibility and impact of a foundation many times its size. Said one, "We were spending at the rate of a much larger organization, and thus had the influence of a larger foundation. So you can play with the big boys." Grantees agreed, including one that explained, "They weren't that big . . . so being able to give larger amounts with that kind of focus, it probably had more of an impact than if they had been slowly giving out $25,000 grants." To achieve the goal of coming as close to "zeroing out" as possible, great attention was given to financial planning, which interviewees said required different investment models than those required by a perpetual foundation.

Beldon's strategy was not simply to give a lot of money within a delimited period, but to do so in a highly focused manner and to link decisions about grant-making to their time frame. The Fund narrowed its scope to two major programs oriented toward building support for environmental advocacy. Trustees and staff felt the federal policy climate was not conducive to the reforms it hoped to achieve and could not assume that climate would change during its ten-year lifetime. They therefore focused on the state level. Likewise, they pulled back from initial grant-making concerned with global warming because, given the timing, "it would be problematic for us to do anything impactful." Interviewees said that their ten-year termination date kept them focused. Said one, "The advantages [of sunsetting] were staying committed and true to a strategic approach."

While the foundation did not seek its own long-term sustainability, it tried to create structures with sustainability to continue after its closure. Trustees and staff believed the way to do this was to provide large, ongoing funding to strengthen grantees' capacity and the environmental movement more broadly to help them be more effective advocates for policy change. Said one trustee, "There were a set of enhancement grants . . . that were made, because we understood that we were going out of business and needed these organizations to be able to thrive after we were gone."

Beldon and the other three foundations in the report differed in many ways, but all made four similar decisions: They adopted highly focused philanthropic purposes, gave long-term funding to grantees, tried to strengthen grantees to carry on the foundation's work after it had closed its doors, and gave a high level of attention to donor intent. The four foundations' approaches and trajectories were not simply determined by the decision to sunset, but by the values and norms trustees and donors brought to their decisions about why and how they would sunset. It was not life span per se, but how foundation leaders approached and used that life span that, in the end, led sunsetting to impact not only when the foundations ended but also how they operated when in existence.

Another foundation studied, the Mary Flagler Cary Charitable Trust, took a different approach to sunsetting but one that also illustrates these dynamics. The Trust was established in 1968, in accordance with the will of Mary Flagler Cary, with initial assets of approximately $72 million. The will directed that funds be spent within fifty years.[26] Although the will does not explain the reasons for her decision, she reportedly adopted it because she was "not enamored of perpetuity" and was concerned that foundations drift away from donor intent over time. She charged trustees with overseeing the donation of certain property, but left them wide latitude and discretion over grants. Trustees sought to honor her "wishes and at the same time respond to new societal and cultural needs which the trustees believe she would have supported." In doing so, they observed that the Trust's fifty-year life span "imparts a sense of urgency in using the Trust's resources to establish a lasting legacy."[27]

As noted, the Trust was charged with transferring substantial property and with charitable grant-making. With respect to its grant-making, over time, the Trust came to feel that it was too diffuse and fragmented and therefore focused the scope of its giving on conservation and music, two fields of interest to the donor. The trustees focused further within each of these fields—on coastal preservation and small innovative contemporary music groups in New York City.

While regularly giving away more than the legally required 5 percent, this foundation did not aim to gradually spend down. Instead, it planned to distribute principal at termination, mainly through gifts of endowments. Said one trustee, "If you're concerned about whether an organization will survive in the future, you should give an endowment." The foundation made annual grants for general operations and sought to strengthen grantee organizations to enable them to receive and independently manage an endowment. They considered but rejected an incremental spend-down approach in favor of holding the principal to distribute at the end. Explaining their reasoning, one interviewee attributed the decision to their concern with the impact on grantees, saying:

> Just making larger grants for ongoing operations of the grantees is not compelling, because once you stop doing it, then what do you do? And what do the grantees do? Suppose we didn't hold on to the principal, but increased the grant size—And then you stop, but the charitable institutions become twice as dependent on us.

The lifetime limit sparked a sense of purpose. One interviewee observed, "If you don't have the discipline of a date certain [for closing], you have in mind a set of long-term operations of a foundation and you're not thinking of a date at which you have to account for results." By contrast, under limited life, the interviewee explained, "It's a discipline, so you think in terms of things that you can complete by a certain date. It's a big psychological difference. Foundations that go on in perpetuity don't have that." Grantees also believed that the foundation's plan to terminate had a substantial impact on their approach. Said one, knowing that the Trust would close created "an urgency on our part, and on theirs, to really set this program apart and set it up for the future without the Cary Trust." Another also commented, "They wanted the foundation's work to endure long after the Cary Trust dissolved. . . . Cary never lost its focus because it knew it had that date certain. . . . You never had to worry about, what seminar has [Cary staff] been to this year? What's the flavor of the month? Foundations can tend to do that."

Feeling that most of its purposes had been accomplished, the Cary Trust made its final grants in 2009, nine years prior to its fifty-year limit. A trustee explained, "There's a cost to operating the Trust, so if there is a cost, and the purposes are accomplished, you might as well pay out the principal to the recipients." Additionally, given the trustees' ages it seemed unlikely they would be in their position for the full fifty years, and they did not think it was a good idea to leave the Trust in the hands of new individuals with no connection to the original people who knew the donor. During its lifetime, it had overseen the disposition of property and major collections the donor wanted to be preserved for charitable purposes and awarded grants of $334,245,969.[28]

Earlier sections of this chapter suggested that the presence or absence of perpetuity does not necessarily distinguish how foundations implement or experience their philanthropy. For these foundations, however, it did—but this was not preordained by the decision to terminate. Key elements appear to be focused and well-defined grant-making goals, rooted in expressed donor interests, along with a strong interest in finding ways to preserve the foundation's work. With respect to this last characteristic, we have seen that a time-limited horizon with respect to foundation operations can coexist with an orientation toward the future in terms of grantee sustainability, when limited-life foundations think about ways to give during their lifetime that will have an ongoing value after they close.

The desire for sustainability, coupled with the fact that the foundation itself would end, promoted a style of philanthropy heavily invested in strengthening grantee organizations. When difficulties arose, the foundations tried to work with grantees to correct problems. That is not to say they would never stop funding a program. They did, however, have strong incentive to search for a solution first, and felt they had a personal stake in doing so. Their approach and position, in turn, served to lessen conventional grantee-grantor relationships of dependency, in favor of a more partnership-oriented approach in which each party is more acutely aware that the other has something it needs. Grantees repeatedly characterized their relationships with these foundations as unusually respectful, open, and collaborative. Some contrasted the foundations' approach with current trends of foundations developing their own initiatives and then using grantees as "instruments" for carrying these out.

For sunsetting foundations, on the other hand, the foundation is the instrument, and by definition, a temporary one. In conventional philanthropy, foundations often give an organization enough to complete a project, but do not provide a level of support that will truly leave the grantee in a stronger and more independent position after the grant ends. Yet these foundations' approach to sunsetting gave them a strong reason to do just that.

For these foundations, sunsetting was integral to thinking and planning across a wide array of foundation operations. This was no automatic result of a plan to terminate the foundation, however, but the result of how those charged with making decisions chose to approach and implement their sunsetting plans.

CONCLUSION

Most foundations are created, or function by default, as perpetual endowments. Perpetuity has long been a subject of intense criticism in some quarters, and in recent years, the option of sunsetting has attracted growing attention. One assumption made by critics and supporters is that foundation life span is an organizational characteristic that has considerable consequences for foundation practice. This chapter makes no claim to offer a comprehensive empirical comparison of limited-life and perpetual foundations, an undertaking that would benefit from future research intentionally designed to examine that issue. The data this chapter offers from a rich and varied set of studies do raise questions about whether assumptions of the significance of life span stand up to empirical scrutiny.

The findings suggest that longevity plans per se are not a particularly telling indicator of foundation practice. They are more so indicators of the values, interests, and norms of those making the decision to sunset. Foundations can make the decision to sunset and then function for their remaining years in ways that are not necessarily dissimilar to perpetual foundations, until they terminate. More generally, many foundations seem to have no restrictions concerning their life span built into their charters, and the decision to sunset may often be made later due to the donor or trustees changing attitudes regarding perpetuity and donor intent. Orientations toward time in relation to giving can differ among foundations with similar life span plans, and even change over the life course of the same foundation.

Our findings suggest that the debates and criticisms regarding donor control can become too narrowly or literally focused on perpetuation of specific donor directives. Rather, the evidence suggests a broader understanding of the relationship between foundation life span, time orientation, and giving is needed. Limited-life foundations conceptualize philanthropy in a personalistic way, as an expression of individual donors, and often have an antipathy toward institutionalized philanthropy, which they see as representing an organization taking on a life of its own. This reflects a larger evaluative and cultural orientation toward organized philanthropy that is consistent with why some trustees invoked motivations related to the preservation of donor intent, even in cases where the donor left no apparent wishes or preferences. It is also consistent with the fact that some foundation leaders could simultaneously embrace a shorter time horizon with respect to foundation life while considering the future sustainability of the foundation's philanthropic purposes in grant-making.

In sum, this discussion redirects us from our initial focus on life span as an organizational attribute and back to the attitudes and values of those who make and execute decisions about foundation longevity. Sunset can be adopted as a strategic choice, as in the case studies presented here. Decisions about longevity can profoundly impact how a foundation operates and can open up alternative strategies for foundations. But that impact is not guaranteed. In the end, it depends on the ways in which the individuals opting for and managing the sunset bring their values, interests, and thinking to bear on how the decision to sunset is carried out.

NOTES

1. Kenneth Prewitt, "Foundations," in *The Nonprofit Sector: A Research Handbook, Second Edition*, ed. Walter W. Powell and Richard Steinberg (New Haven, CT: Yale University Press, 2006), 365; Ray Madoff, *Immortality and the Law: The Rising Power of the American Dead* (New Haven, CT: Yale University Press, 2010), 102.

2. John Stuart Mill, "The Right and Wrong of State Interference with Corporation and Church Property," in *Dissertations and Discussions* (Boston: W.V. Spencer, 1868 [1833]), 6.

3. F.H. Goff, "The Dead Hand: An Address Delivered at Hotel Astor, May 24, 1921, before the New York Association of Trust Companies," Cleveland Trust Company, 1921, https://issuu.com/clevelandfoundation/docs/cleveland-foundation-1921 -dead-hand?e=9760645/5495178; John J. Grabowski, "Frederick Harris Goff," in *Notable American Philanthropists*, ed. Robert T. Grimm (Westport, CT: Greenwood Press, 2002), 121–24.

4. Madoff, *Immortality and the Law*, 106.

5. Thomas Billitteri, *Money, Mission, and the Payout Rule: In Search of a Strategic Approach to Foundation Spending* (Washington, DC: Aspen Institute, 2005); Waldemar Nielsen, *Inside American Philanthropy: The Dramas of Donorship* (Norman: University of Oklahoma, 1996); Francie Ostrower, "Donor Control and Perpetual Trusts: Does Anything Last Forever?" in *Philanthropic Giving: Studies in Varieties and Goals,* ed. Richard Magat (New York: Oxford University Press, 1989).

6. Peter Frumkin, *Strategic Giving: The Art and Science of Philanthropy* (Chicago: University of Chicago, 2006); Nielsen, *Inside American Philanthropy*; Ostrower *Limited Life Foundation*s; "Adam Meyerson, President, Philanthropy Roundtable Donors and Philanthropic Intent," PND News Philanthropy Digest, November 29, 2006, https://philanthropynewsdigest.org/newsmakers/adam-meyer-son-president-philanthropy-roundtable-donors-and-philanthropic-intent.

7. Frumkin, *Strategic Giving*.

8. Billitteri, *Money, Mission, and the Payout Rule*; Frumkin, *Strategic Giving*.

9. Francie Ostrower, *Attitudes and Practices Concerning Effective Philanthropy* (Washington, DC: Urban Institute, 2004), https://www.urban.org/research/publication/attitudes-and-practices-concerning-effective-philanthropy-0/view/full_report; Ostrower, *Limited Life Foundations*; Ostrower, *Sunsetting*.

10. See Ostrower, *Attitudes and Practices Concerning Effective Philanthropy;* Ostrower, *Limited Life Foundations*.

11. Another 135 private independent foundations in the study said they were undecided about their longevity plans and thus are excluded from the current discussion which is focused on comparisons between foundations planning limited or perpetual life. The balance declined to answer the question about foundation longevity plans.

12. Twenty-four percent of limited-life foundations rated themselves as excellent versus 37 percent of perpetual foundations when it came to asset management. This was a prominent interview theme, with interviewees explaining that as termination approached, they had to move into lower risk, lower yield investments leaving them with fewer investment options.

13. For the survey instrument, see Ostrower *Attitudes and Practices Concerning Effective Philanthropy*, appendix B.

14. Throughout, when we term something statistically significant, it means $p < .05$.

15. In a logistic regression (with whether or not adhering to the donor's wishes is considered very important as the dependent variable) the parameter estimate for whether the foundation is limited life (1 = yes) was 1.7 (SE = .61, $p < .01$). For foundation age it was $-.002$ (SE = .004) and for assets -0.0000000000821 (SE = .0000000187). Age and assets were not significant.

16. Sixteen percent of perpetual foundations versus 4 percent of limited-life ones felt publicizing the foundation and its work is very important to achieving foundation effectiveness. Turning to organizational infrastructure, 48 percent of limited-life foundations (and 52 percent of perpetual ones) say this is very important, but fully 34 percent of limited-life foundations as compared with only 18 percent of perpetual foundations say it is not important. The balance (18 percent of limited-life foundations and 31 percent of perpetual foundations) say it is somewhat important.

17. The parameter estimate for whether the foundation is limited life was .5268 (SE = .369), for foundation age it was $-.011$ (SE = .004, $p = .011$) and for whether the donor is alive (1 = yes) was 1.05 (SE = .283, $p < .001$).

18. Ostrower, *Limited Life Foundation*.

19. Loren Renz and David Wolcheck, *Perpetuity or Limited Lifespan: How Do Family Foundations Decide?* (New York: Foundation Center, 2009).

20. James Allen Smith, "The Evolving American Foundation," in *Philanthropy and the Nonprofit Sector in a Changing America*, eds. Charles Clotfelter and Thomas Ehrlich (Bloomington: Indiana University, 2001).

21. For the former, see Renz and Wolcheck, *Perpetuity or Limited Life span*; for the latter see Elizabeth Boris, Carol J. DeVita, and Marcus Gaddy, *National Center for Family Philanthropy's 2015 Trends Study: Results of the First National Benchmark Survey of Family Foundations* (Washington, DC: National Center for Family

Philanthropy, 2015), https://www.ncfp.org/export/sites/ncfp/knowledge/reports/2015 /downloads/Trends-in-Family-Philanthropy-Full-Report-NCFP-2015.pdf.

22. The foundations were: the Mary Flagler Cary Charitable Trust, the Beldon Fund, the Jacobs Family Foundation, and the Pear Foundation, a pseudonym used because this foundation requested anonymity. Ostrower, *Sunsetting.*

23. The following are drawn from Ostrower 2011, where additional information and discussion of the cases may be found.

24. John Hunting, "Why Spend Out: A Message from John Hunting Founder and Chair," http://www.beldon.org/spend-out-strategy.html.

25. John Hunting, *Beldon Fund President's Report* (New York: Beldon Fund, 1997), 4–5.

26. Last Will and Testament of Mary Flagler Cary, March 22, 1962, p. 12.

27. Mary Flagler Cary Charitable Trust Twenty-Year Report 1968–1988, p. 29.

28. See Heidi Waleson, *A Trust Fulfilled: Four Decades of Grantmaking by the Mary Flagler Cary Charitable Trust* 2009, p. 88. This report, commissioned and published by the Cary Charitable Trust, gives a detailed history of its grant-making.

Chapter 11

Value, Time, and Time-Limited Philanthropy

*A Theoretical Approach Applied to Two Real Examples**

Tony Proscio

Foundations limit their life spans for any number of reasons, many of which are based on personal preferences rather than on any hard calculation. Donors may want to be involved in grant-making while they're alive, for example, or to witness the results firsthand. Or they may fear that a permanent institution would eventually stray from its mission or lose its sense of urgency. Or they may believe that the causes that interest them (the environment, say, or stopping an epidemic) simply can't wait for solutions. Some foundations might prefer to make very large grants for big projects, in amounts greater than can be earned year-by-year on a lasting endowment. These choices may be the result of research and deliberation, or they may simply reflect personal preferences and beliefs. But either way, they aren't hard to explain or understand.

Sooner or later, however, many time-limited philanthropies assert another, more objective rationale for spending out their assets—one that seems simple on the surface but is actually a good deal more complicated than the others. They argue that putting philanthropic money to use in the near term produces a greater benefit to society than investing smaller amounts over a longer time. Chuck Feeney, the founder of The Atlantic Philanthropies, put the case succinctly in 2011 when he wrote to Bill Gates that "intelligent philanthropic support and positive interventions can have greater value and impact today than if they are delayed."[1] In effect, this suggests that the amount of social benefit that can be generated from $1 today is greater than what can be generated by the same dollar *plus investment returns* in a few years. For philanthropists and foundation managers weighing the possibility of setting a

---
* This chapter has been adapted from a longer report with the same title, prepared for and funded by the Atlantic Philanthropies under a grant to Duke University.

time limit on their philanthropy, this is an important claim that would benefit from closer scrutiny.

IS TODAY WORTH MORE THAN TOMORROW?

For some causes, the argument for a concentrated burst of near-term giving may seem almost self-evident. An epidemic may be so virulent that if it is not stopped quickly, the human and societal costs will be catastrophic. The same argument might apply to preserving a natural wilderness that would otherwise be lost forever, along with its wildlife, to approaching development. But for many purposes, the proposition is not so clear-cut. Is an apartment for a homeless person today inherently more valuable than for someone who becomes homeless in the future? Is a work of art produced in our own time more desirable than one produced for our children or grandchildren? Is society necessarily worse off with a secure provision for future needs than with an all-out dedication to current ones?

The answer depends, of course, on the type of activity to be funded and on the kind and timing of the value it produces. Weighing the value of philanthropy now versus later amounts, in business terms, to a cost-benefit comparison: an assessment of the value that can be produced today, along with any costs avoided, minus the cost of producing it, compared with the net present value of what could be produced in the future. The "value" in question would presumably include not only the immediate benefits at the moment a result is produced, but the continuing or compounding value of those benefits, if any, as time goes on.

For example, the gift of a scholarship to a student who would otherwise not have been able to afford an education produces more social benefits than just the value of the schooling it purchases. The young scholars who benefit may well go on to live more satisfying lives, produce more, earn more income and pay more taxes, raise more secure and healthy families, and educate their own children better than if they had been deprived of an education. All of those ripple effects are part of the value produced. And they might well compound at a high rate over time—the successful recipients might establish businesses that employ other people, or might produce products or services of high value that in turn enrich the marketplace. Their healthier, better-educated children may go on to raise additional healthy, well-educated, and productive generations. And so on.

A financial adviser to Chuck Feeney's time-limited foundation, The Atlantic Philanthropies, summed up the concept using the language of investment analysis: "If you're able to put money into projects that generate a social return, and that return compounds at a higher rate than your financial assets would," then that would be a persuasive argument for putting all one's resources to rapid use now, rather than investing them and spending only the earnings over an indefinite period.

Admittedly, it's unlikely that those who hold this view take such an explicitly mathematical or even analytical approach to the issue. For many, including Mr. Feeney, the belief that present achievements outweigh future ones is more intuitive or aspirational: *Surely,* a donor might reason, *with some wisdom and hard work, one can score at least a few big wins whose enduring value will far exceed the normal earnings on an endowment, or even the future value of social achievements that those earnings might someday buy.* And this general impression is beguiling enough that audiences rarely question the argument or its evidentiary basis.

In reality, it is an essentially mathematical claim, even if many of the numbers needed to perform a complete calculation are unavailable or difficult to estimate. And the results of the math are far from obvious. The proposition that today's philanthropy can produce more value than tomorrow's—at least for certain purposes, in certain fields, given certain circumstances—is an argument about social utility, rates of return, and the compounding or erosion of value over time. It implicitly describes a complex interaction of different variables that's worth spelling out and examining in some detail, with real philanthropic projects as examples.

In the interest of inciting more debate about this proposition, I will offer two illustrations, drawn from actual grant-making by The Atlantic Philanthropies, a group of charitable foundations that ceased operations in 2020. I spent more than a decade chronicling Atlantic's final decisions as it brought its work to a close, and these examples are drawn from cases I studied in the course of those years. The examples suggest how a limited-life philanthropy might choose its goals and projects with an eye toward generating a greater return from a comparatively short-term investment than it could achieve by preserving its assets indefinitely and spending more slowly. Although Atlantic did not explicitly conduct a formal analysis of this kind, much of its reasoning in these examples was a careful, if implicit, judgment about how and where its expenditures would generate the greatest long-term value for the countries where it operated, and how that value would increase over time.

VALUE IN FIXED TIME VERSUS
VALUE IN PERPETUITY

Before considering the examples, it helps to disentangle the elements of the underlying idea—first, as a way of making the whole argument for time-limited giving explicit, and second, as a means of illustrating how and under what conditions that argument would be the most persuasive. At the most basic level, a foundation's "value" to society comprises four core elements:

a. The direct outlay that it is able to inject into public-interest activities (a function of its total resources—financial, human, and reputational—plus its earnings on those resources, and the rate at which it pays them out)
b. The social value that those dollars purchase directly (the experiences that students get from an after-school program, the discoveries resulting directly from a scientist's research, a meal or shelter bed for a homeless person), which might become greater over time if the foundation becomes more skillful, influential, or effective in supporting this work
c. The ripple effects of those direct purchases—the beneficial aftershocks that arise when something accomplished today provides the key to even greater accomplishments tomorrow, compounding the benefits year over year
d. The durability of the value and the ripple effects over time: Does the value produced with the foundation's money continue indefinitely (as, for example, with the purchase and protection of environmentally sensitive land), or will it fade as time passes (as with the construction of a building, which will depreciate)? Do the ripple effects, if any, continue to compound, or might their rate of expansion gradually slow, stop, or even reverse in the future?

To say that "philanthropic support can have greater value and impact today than if delayed" is to make an implicit assessment of all four of these elements, and to judge that they will be greater—at least in some fields, with some forms of intervention—if the foundation makes an all-out effort in the short term than if it instead were to preserve its assets indefinitely and make a much longer stream of smaller grants.

This test is fairly demanding. Let's grant, for the sake of argument, that a foundation operating in perpetuity would produce less value year by year than it could have produced by spending more and depleting its capital. And let's imagine, further, that it may become a less driven, creative or productive organization in its later life, as some donors fear. Even so, because it has many more years in which to generate a lower annual level of value (in theory, an infinite number of years), it might eventually be able to amass, albeit slowly, a formidable stockpile of good results. If we assume that future beneficiaries are no less important to humanity than those of today, then the perpetual institution, simply by persevering, would eventually be expected to benefit more people directly than its time-limited counterpart. It isn't hard for the tortoise to beat the hare if the hare quits the race.

At this point, some skeptics might be tempted to invoke the time value of money. Even if future beneficiaries matter just as much as today's, they might say, the value of any *benefit* to those future lives would have to be discounted before it could be compared with any comparable benefit in the present. The applicable discount rate could be debated, but they would argue it should not be zero. By this line of reasoning, anything achieved in the future would be less valuable than the same achievement today, simply because a given amount of money loses value over time. Benefits in the very distant future would become trivially small after a long discounting.

That is a mistake, as Michael Klausner of Stanford University pointed out in a 2003 article. The perpetual foundation would be earning returns on its endowment year by year, and those returns would be increasing its ability to do good in the future at approximately the same rate as its future achievements would be discounted to the present. If a foundation could produce $1 of social benefit today or else hold that dollar in its endowment and earn a 10 percent return, it would have earned enough to produce $4.18 worth of benefits in fifteen years' time. Discount that back to the present at a rate of 10 percent, and you get exactly what you started with: $1. In other words, as Professor Klausner wrote, the simple time-value argument "amounts to inflating and deflating the foundation's assets at the same rate, which results in a wash."[2]

But if we do not resort to an artificial discounting of future benefits, the time-limited institution would seem to be at an insuperable disadvantage. A perpetual institution would almost always outperform a time-limited one of the same size *eventually*—just because, as John D. Rockefeller is rumored to have remarked, perpetuity is a long time, and even small successes would mount up year after year after year. That would be the end of the discussion, were it not for the third element of value described above: the ripple effects. If the limited-life foundation put all or most of its resources into activities whose good results would set additional positive forces in motion, compounding the beneficial effects over the years, then—as the Atlantic financial adviser put it—its "return" would "compound at a higher rate than [its] financial assets would."

If, for example, a foundation could provide the means to wipe out malaria in a generation, as the Bill and Melinda Gates Foundation hopes to do, then surely the benefits of that achievement—more than 600,000 lives saved every year; massive health-care costs averted and the money redirected to other needs in poor societies; and a wave of human productivity set loose from disease[3]—would compound at a rate far beyond what could be earned in the financial markets. The good thus achieved would accumulate faster than virtually any endowment could grow, thus making it far less likely that the foundation could have achieved as much by husbanding its resources and spending them later.

Still, as the malaria example suggests, this is a calculation that rests on probabilities, not certainty. Many unpredictable factors make it necessary to base this reckoning on the likelihood of various outcomes—the pace of research progress, perhaps, or the availability of other organizations to play a role in implementing a solution. It is possible that hundreds of millions of dollars could be spent on research without producing a cure or vaccine. In that case, if the foundation had meanwhile exhausted all its resources (something the Gates Foundation has not yet begun to do, despite its stated intentions), it would have no money left to soldier on and keep trying. The funder would have to hope that the progress it supported had significantly hastened the day when the disease would in fact be conquered, and the ripple benefits of the overall effort would thus be postponed but not forgone. Even so, the argument for an all-out, short-term use of funds would then be at least attenuated.

Also, it is unlikely that the massive benefits from halting malaria would continue compounding at the same rate forever. This is where we encounter the fourth element of value described earlier: the durability or erosion of benefits, and the nature and extent of the ripple effects over time. The ripple effects may not all be positive—for example, the indisputable good achieved through lifesaving vaccines and medicines might nonetheless also lead to greater societal costs later, if a larger surviving population leads to additional demands on health services, food supplies, or other limited resources. Future events (a new disease or other catastrophes in sub-Saharan Africa, for example) could undermine the social progress resulting from the conquest of malaria, and thus halt or reverse improvements in lives and societies. In that case, the tortoise might still win the day by outlasting the hare: By doing less each year, but surviving to battle new problems, the perpetual institution might eventually accumulate greater social value with smaller spending over a longer term in which it can learn, adapt, and become more effective.

MATCHING GOALS TO TIME LIMITS

So it would seem that the choice to put a whole charitable fortune to use in a limited period would amount to a bet on the efficacy of the work to be supported in the available years, and on the probability that the initial results will compound as the benefits ripple through the lives of the beneficiaries, across their communities, and into future generations. Choose the right intervention in the right field, and this calculation makes eminent sense—the dollars wagered would generate, in Mr. Feeney's words, "greater value and impact today" than if they were held for later action. But the key to that result is not merely a willingness to act quickly; just as critically, it takes a careful selection of goals, objectives, and methods.

Admittedly, neither Mr. Feeney nor the other Atlantic trustees made the decision to limit the foundation's life explicitly in these terms, or with such a specific calculation in mind. They did, however, set out in 2002 to focus the foundation's remaining years of grant-making (then expected to be about fifteen years) on a few areas of effort that seemed ripe to produce significant benefits in the time available. That choice was based partly on the lasting impact they expected to achieve and the probability that successes would pay mounting dividends long after Atlantic had ceased to exist. At least implicitly, they were looking for points of intervention that would both yield the most net benefit in the near term and then compound that benefit at a high rate over a long period without severe erosion or reversals.

They chose to focus on improving the lives of children and youth, the health of disadvantaged populations, the quality of life of older people, and the protection and promotion of human rights and reconciliation. Effort in each of these areas was focused not solely on benefits to individuals, but on systemic reform—changing the way large segments of public and private activity worked together to promote (or impede) opportunity, health, and fundamental rights. By dealing with systems rather than discrete services or programs, they reasoned, Atlantic would have the opportunity to help create widespread and permanent—or at least very long-lasting—improvements for large numbers of people. And those improvements would be likely to expand as children entered adulthood, as older people enjoyed more productive later lives, as healthier people raised healthier families and built healthier communities, and as more just and harmonious societies extended opportunity more broadly to all their members. Although their reasoning almost never took an explicitly mathematical form, the thought process was very much like that of an investor seeking the highest value and greatest prospects for growth.

The examples that follow show how the variables in this implicit equation interacted in two actual Atlantic initiatives and how the foundation formed its expectations about the intensity, duration, and compounding of the benefits it hoped to achieve.

Example I: Better Services for Children in Ireland

An early Atlantic strategy paper, written soon after the decision to operate on a limited life, observed that "Ireland has relatively few early childhood programs—no equivalent of America's Head Start program exists—and highly variable standards. Thus, truly early intervention, from birth to five-year-olds, is a priority. . . . Across ages, there is little understanding of what really works. . . . Therefore we will support the implementation of pilot projects that showcase proven approaches. . . . To improve the lives of disadvantaged children, the state must adopt a prevention policy and support promising prevention programs."[4]

At the time, most government programs that served children and families in Ireland were untested, and many seemed unlikely to have much of a lasting effect. Worse, these programs tended to respond to problems only after they had progressed and become both difficult to reverse and expensive to treat. For lack of some basic, early improvements to children's nurturing, health, or learning, the state ended up paying far greater sums later, for adjudication and punishment of crime, remedial education, mental health care, and other post-hoc reactions to problems, which too rarely helped young people reach a more successful adulthood.

So as its main thrust in improving the lives of children and youth in Ireland, the foundation undertook a campaign to bring about a thoroughgoing change in the way public agencies choose which services to fund for helping young people in poor or troubled families. Atlantic believed that the Irish government could be persuaded to focus on preventing children's behavioral or learning problems, or deal with them at a very early stage, and to rely mainly on methods that had been proven to work in rigorous experiments.

The result, foundation staff believed, would be a giant leap in the cost-effectiveness of family services, saving both public money and, far more important, children's lives. The foundation sought to work with the state to test both the effectiveness and affordability of this approach, combining a suite of newly conceived services with a barrage of sophisticated evaluations to assess the effectiveness of each component part. If the government adopted the most successful approaches, the social benefits for the children of Ireland, for their communities and families, for the public sector, and for the children's later offspring would likely grow exponentially over a very long time.

The exceptional size of Atlantic's financial commitment to this undertaking—close to $162 million—was fundamental to the project. Because of the expense involved in substantially reconfiguring services in a variety of underprivileged communities, plus the high cost of conducting sophisticated randomized controlled trials on every new service in each area, it would have been nearly impossible—or at best, of little use—to attempt this effort on a much smaller budget. The point was not to change services only in a few places, or just to introduce one or two new methods. It was to upend the way the government selected, paid for, and evaluated all services for all vulnerable children. For that, a demonstration of considerable size, with all but irrefutable evaluations of their results, was the only choice. In short, it was the kind of very large, time-limited commitment for which limited-life philanthropy is ideal.

Here, it would seem, is a nearly exact case of the kind of calculation we have been envisioning: If Atlantic and its grantees succeeded, it would achieve a social return far greater than what it could earn in a permanent endowment. With a "big bet" now, it could reap a monumental benefit—one that could actually be calculated, and whose later compounding could be estimated—that would be enriching Irish lives long after the foundation itself had faded from memory. Thanks to cost-benefit research in other countries, it was possible for Atlantic to estimate—or at least to imagine—the possible scale of the social benefits Ireland might expect with this strategy.

To examine this calculation up close, consider just one of the early-intervention models Atlantic supported in Ireland: a program known as Incredible Years, which offers a suite of effective early responses to children's behavioral problems.[5] Research in the United States and elsewhere was already beginning to demonstrate that children who develop behavioral problems—even relatively minor ones—early in life would be at a significant and lasting disadvantage later. A team of evaluators from the National University of Ireland–Maynooth cited evidence pointing to "poorer educational attainment, increased criminal activity, reduced labour market success, and poorer adult mental health."[6]

These are costly outcomes, both for children and families and for the state. Atlantic's hypothesis was that a substantial expenditure on programs like Incredible Years would reduce these harmful effects—thus saving costs to the educational, health, mental health, and criminal justice systems. Better still, more children would overcome their behavioral problems and go on to more successful education, employment, and adult life, thus contributing to the economy and society and improving their own chances of raising children with fewer problems and greater opportunity.

Although this principle had been tested successfully in other places, that did not, by itself, prove that it would work equally well in Irish communities. Another early-intervention model, the highly regarded (and meticulously evaluated) American program called Nurse Family Partnership, registered almost no success when it was later transplanted to the United Kingdom.[7] Though the reasons for that disappointment aren't clear, it strongly suggests that cultural context matters, and that results from one place cannot be presumed to apply identically elsewhere. In any case, persuading the Irish government to upend decades of entrenched practice in funding children's programs would surely require some homegrown results that Irish officials could observe for themselves, in places they know well and regard as high priorities.

To test the idea in Ireland, a team of evaluators selected families whose children scored above a clinical threshold on the Eyberg Child Behavior Inventory (ECBI), a standard screening instrument for conduct problems in children. The families were randomly assigned either to a treatment group that participated in the program immediately (93 parents) or to a six-month waiting list that served as the control group (39 parents).[8] The study found that "Significantly more of the treatment group had obtained ECBI scores below the clinical cut-off following the intervention (60 percent for the treatment group vs. 35 percent for the control group)." Children of parents who received the Incredible Years training were much less likely to need costly treatment from physicians, nurses, speech therapists, and social workers or to require special education.[9] The evaluators compared the cost of delivering the Incredible Years training with the savings in reduced use of other services, and found a very high probability that the program would be cost-effective.[10]

But that was just in the near term. To complete the cost-benefit analysis, the researchers added conservative estimates of the longer-term costs of three likely outcomes from early behavioral trouble: remedial or repeat schooling, entanglement in the criminal justice system, and periods of unemployment. International research provides estimates of the percentage of children with behavioral problems who are likely to incur these costs in later life, and Irish government data supply the actual cost of the necessary responses (for example, in 2007 the average cost of keeping a prisoner in Ireland was roughly $130,000). Incorporating the cost of various forms of remedial action, both near-term and longer-term, and the probability of a child requiring such action, researchers compared that probable cost for children who had benefited from Incredible Years with those who had not. With that comparison, they estimated a total government savings in these three areas that resulted from the beneficial effects of the program. The present value of these savings over a child's lifetime was at least $4,000 per child. Measured against the cost of delivering the services (just under $2,000), they found that Incredible Years generated an internal rate of return (IRR) of 11 percent.[11]

This is, the evaluators note, a very conservative estimate. A full calculation of social benefit would likely be as much as three times greater, they suggest. For starters, it is nearly certain that the harmful effects of early behavioral problems extend beyond just the three realms whose costs were estimated in this analysis (education, criminal justice, and employment). "These outcomes," the authors acknowledge, were chosen because they "were most easily valued in monetary terms." However, "other benefits, such as improvements in second- and third-level educational attainment and associated increases in productivity and earnings capacity, reductions in substance abuse, decreased teenage pregnancy, benefits to victims of reduced crime, and benefits accruing to the parents and/or other siblings as a result of the program were omitted and are likely to push the estimated returns higher."[12]

The research does not address the even more distant social benefits—what we have loosely referred to as ripple effects—that might well flow from Incredible Years. For example, improved education and reduced rates of criminality and imprisonment, of unemployment, ill health, addiction, and teen pregnancy would seem highly likely to result in more successful parenting—and thus a more successful life for the subsequent generation, with even less need for remedial services. Classroom learning might be expected to improve for all students if behavioral disruptions were significantly reduced, so that other students *not* enrolled in Incredible Years might experience some benefit, as would their teachers and schools. Increased lifetime incomes would presumably have follow-on benefits for the wider economy. And so on.

These extended benefits were important considerations for Atlantic for at least two reasons. First, while an 11 percent IRR is encouraging, it is not beyond what some astutely managed endowments have earned in the past. In other words, this conservative estimate of the social yield of Incredible Years might not, by itself, be enough to "compound at a higher rate than [the foundation's] financial assets would." It would be an interesting, but not necessarily convincing argument for the foundation to mount an all-out effort to change Irish government policy in a limited time and then go out of business. (Then again, in the leaner financial markets of the early twenty-first century, the prospect of achieving 11 percent returns consistently might indeed seem remote enough to swing the argument toward favoring the near-term commitment to Incredible Years, just on these conservative results alone.)

However, if the real benefit is double or triple the conservative estimate—if it encompasses other areas of social gain plus the ripple effects on the rest of society and future generations—then the argument for a limited-term effort becomes much stronger.

This leads us once again to the fourth variable mentioned earlier, which can easily undermine the more enthusiastic calculations of near-term achievement: How durable are the results, or how likely are they to erode or disappear over time? The evaluation is persuasive that Incredible Years leads to measurable improvements in children's early behavior, which can raise the odds of a successful adulthood. But many of the children in Atlantic's demonstration live in disadvantaged and turbulent communities where external difficulties may intervene in young people's lives even after a comparatively successful start. Some American longitudinal research—notably by James J. Heckman, a Nobel laureate in economics at the University of Chicago—has shown "substantial positive effects" of early childhood interventions "long after the interventions ended,"[13] which provides reason for optimism about the lasting value of Incredible Years. Still, further study will be necessary to determine how sturdy the gains have been in an Irish context, in the face of surrounding social and economic headwinds.

Political complications may also have a profound effect on the durability or erosion of benefits. Although the government was an active partner with Atlantic in all the experiments with prevention and early intervention in children's services, and although several senior government figures are committed to adopting and broadening the use of this approach, governments change, budgets and economies fluctuate, and policy choices often change with them. It will likely be many years before anyone can say with confidence whether the principles of prevention and early intervention have taken firm root in Irish policy and practice, or whether more traditional, largely unscientific means of funding children's services remain the norm.

Nonetheless, nearly all the most interesting and important goals in philanthropy amount to a calculation not only about value and impact, but about risk. For foundations that do not intend to survive indefinitely, risk becomes an even more critical factor in their calculations about value than it is for perpetual institutions. The perpetual institution, after all, can adjust course later, learn from its failures, and try a different approach. The time-limited institution is, in effect, placing all its chips on a single expected set of outcomes. If some of its efforts pay off especially handsomely—with exceptional compounding of benefits far greater than what could be achieved in financial markets with the same amount of money—those successes may compensate for disappointment in some other lines of work. But then, in calculating the foundation's overall return on its social investments, losses from less-successful projects must be subtracted from the gains that flow from the best performers.

At the time Atlantic ended its work in Ireland, Incredible Years appeared to have been a sound bet. It was evidently yielding fairly high near-term returns, with persuasive odds of compounding the value of those returns over time, especially if its approach is put to wider use across Ireland. In 2017, for example, parts of the program were introduced nationwide in schools that serve large numbers of disadvantaged students.[14] Still, the risks of erosion or even reversal remained a concern. Whether the investment ultimately meets the standard set forth by Chuck Feeney—that grants should have "greater value and impact today than if they are delayed"—is a judgment that must await several more years of effort and observation.

Example II: Increasing the Supply of Nurses in South Africa

In a 2011 report on primary health care in South Africa, Professor Stephen J. Reid of the University of Cape Town prefaced his analysis with the story of a Zulu grandmother, 68-year-old Thembelihle Ndlovu, from a tiny mountain village in northeastern KwaZulu-Natal. Having lost all five of her children to AIDS, Ms. Ndlovu was providing a home for her grandchildren and other village orphans, roughly a dozen children in all, until she became ill with severe headaches early in 2011.

After making the five-kilometer trek to the nearest clinic and waiting there all morning, she learned that the clinic's one professional nurse was on leave. She was seen by a nursing assistant who, without examining her, prescribed an over-the-counter pain reliever. After a week of unrelieved head pain, Ms. Ndlovu returned to the clinic.

This time the registered nurse, back from holidays, examined her and found her blood pressure dangerously high. Unaware of her previous visit, the nurse scolded Ms. Ndlovu for not coming sooner and referred her to a hospital, since it was not known when a doctor would next be in the village. The hospital was almost a day's journey away, and the trip alone cost \$8, a substantial share of the household's monthly budget. Meanwhile, the children were on their own.

After three full days in the hospital, she returned home with some pills but, because the doctor did not speak her language, with no more understanding of her condition than she'd had before. She took the pills until they ran out, and the headaches returned. Afraid of being scolded again, she did not return to the clinic, and instead took a folk remedy that brought some minor relief. After months of severe hypertension and pain, she suffered a massive stroke that has left her paralyzed and helpless.

"And so," Professor Reid concluded, "a key resource person in the community with a preventable illness is effectively rejected rather than enrolled by the health system. . . . Thembelihle's saga is not extraordinary in South Africa: A multitude of missed opportunities pass through the public health service every day that require minimal resources to redirect and avert costly outcomes."[15]

As Professor Reid and other health policy experts in South Africa frequently point out, the problem was not official indifference or ill intent. As early as 2005, the South African Parliament had passed what appeared to be a far-reaching Nursing Act, providing most of what analysts and practitioners were prescribing as a way to narrow the country's gaping health disparities. Later policies and initiatives by the national Ministry of Health gave the impression of a serious movement toward reform. In general, progress in the realm of official government policy seemed steady and positive. Unfortunately, as a high-ranking health official put it, the problem with delivering actual results to poor, rural South Africans like Thembelihle Ndlovu was "not the policies, which are some of the best in the world. It's the execution, which is too often totally lacking."

Atlantic had already begun a concerted effort to improve health policy and implementation in South Africa in the early 2000s. But at that point it was focused mostly on overcoming the government's opposition to distributing antiretroviral drugs in the public health sector, which were making headway against HIV/AIDS everywhere else. Although Atlantic also funded other projects aimed at health equity more broadly, it was only when the grassroots campaign for access to antiretrovirals finally succeeded that the foundation focused its attention squarely on nurses, who make up 70 to 80 percent of the country's health professionals.[16]

Starting in 2008, the foundation set out to strengthen the faculty and curriculum at a range of nursing colleges and university departments, with the goal of increasing the number of qualified nurses in the workforce, improving their skills, retaining them in the public sector, and encouraging more of them to work in poor and rural areas. It also focused attention on key institutions in the nursing field beyond colleges and universities—particularly the South African Nursing Council (a statutory body that both certifies nurses and accredits nurse-training programs), the largest nurses' union, and professional associations of nursing educators.[17] Other parts of the strategy ranged more broadly, emphasizing management and staffing of district health systems; the capacity of organizations that formulate, analyze, and promote reforms in health policy; and the grassroots social movements that advocate for health equity. But beginning in 2008, enriching the workforce of nurses and midwives was effectively the top priority.

The challenge, as in many less-wealthy countries, was not only to boost the quality and quantity of nurses' education and training programs. Harder still would be persuading the better-trained nurses to remain in South Africa, and to serve its remote, neglected, and desperately poor rural communities, rather than emigrating to wealthier cities and to countries with better pay and working conditions. This was, as a team of researchers later put it, an "area traditionally ignored by other players" working in the health sector.[18]

Here, then, was a pattern similar to the one in Ireland's services for disadvantaged children:

- a gap in policy—or in this case, in the implementation of policy—that systematically disadvantages large numbers of people in ways that shorten their lives or reduce their prospects for a healthy and productive future
- a waste of public resources on ineffective practices, or a failure to employ effective practices whose cost would be readily offset by the resulting benefit

- an apparent moment of readiness in which public officials appear disposed to committing public resources toward a solution, but where the solutions are not yet well formed, understood, or fit to be implemented
- the prospect of enormous social returns on investment, or the avoidance of brutal societal costs, from bringing about a successful reform.

In theory, it should not be difficult to quantify the economic harm being done to South Africa from the failure to care adequately for the health of millions of its residents. Even more than in the case of Ireland's children's services, the evidence of lost income and productivity, of stunted future opportunity, and of the bleak prospects for a succeeding generation of orphaned or uncared-for children should be obvious. Better yet, calculating these costs might be politically useful in demonstrating the potential national wealth being squandered on a defective and inequitable primary health-care system. In practice, however, these were simply not the kinds of questions South Africans or Atlantic were principally interested in answering. The cost in human well-being and the affront to basic justice in South Africa's broken health-care system were more than sufficient grounds for action, without the added trouble and expense of gathering economic data on the consequences of success or failure. As a result, data to assess these particular kinds of benefits have not been available.

However, the scarcity of such data was not merely the result of an emphasis on other priorities. Until Atlantic's involvement in health-care reform, South Africa sorely lacked the ability to communicate, assemble, and use health-care data to improve, or even to fully understand, the quality of care its citizens were receiving. With a stream of grants to organizations dedicated to improving health-care analytics and policy formation, Atlantic helped to bridge the analytical gaps as well as those in the frontline delivery of care. Meanwhile, the collection and use of data on the allocation of health resources, both in the Health Ministry and the National Treasury, have grown substantially. It is becoming more feasible in South Africa to ask and answer the kinds of empirical cost-benefit questions about health care that were raised in Ireland. If those are not normally the highest-priority questions on policymakers' minds, that is understandable. But the reality is that, not so long ago, it would not have mattered what the priorities were; the questions would have been nearly unanswerable. That is changing, and the time may yet come when these more-theoretical discussions will have an eager audience.

In the meantime, this example cannot proceed with even rudimentary data and a hypothetical discussion of returns on investment or cost-benefit analyses, as the earlier one did. Still, although the data are lacking, it is fair to say that any likely calculation of benefits would be enormous: Rural poverty in South Africa encompasses nearly 17 million people, almost 30 percent of the national population.[19] Atlantic's aggregate investment of $32.8 million in nursing reforms would surely prove tiny in comparison with the present value of a decade or more of improved care and healthier lives for even a sizable fraction of such a large and neglected group of people.

What we do know of the achievements so far in the effort to enrich nursing in South Africa is highly encouraging. An evaluation completed in 2015 reported a significant rise in government funding and official commitment to nursing education and a "steady growth in the number of nurses being trained."[20] The number of nurses graduating each year rose dramatically between 2005 and 2014, including in the least advantaged and historically poorly staffed provinces: a 90 percent increase in Limpopo (142 graduates in 2005 and 271 in 2014); a 180 percent increase in Mpumalanga (52 to 145), and 160 percent in Ms. Ndlovu's home province of KwaZulu-Natal (243 to 630).[21] Most promisingly, the brain drain among South Africa's nurses appeared to be slowing—partly, perhaps, because of rising pay and working conditions under the country's gradually improving policies toward the profession. Compared with an out-migration of more than 3,900 nurses in 2001, just 378 left the country in 2012.[22]

Atlantic was also instrumental in supporting the formation of Nurse Professional Associations by, among other things, purchasing offices for them. Zola Madikizela, Atlantic's program executive for health in South Africa, explained that these associations "became more visible, influenced nursing policy, and became activist advocates for nurse educators. This could not have been accomplished with less funding over a longer time." If health and longevity in poor areas continue improving at anything near the rate at which the supply of nurses appeared to be rising in 2014, the social benefits—both in human and economic terms—will be enormous.

As in the Irish case, some caveats are in order. Obviously, the march toward a thorough reform will be very long, fraught with risks, and highly susceptible to eroded effectiveness or outright backsliding in the future. Inclusive, democratic government is still very young in South Africa, and the process of political change has been turbulent and erratic. All of this adds considerable uncertainty to any calculation about future achievements, their timing, and the social benefits they might, or might not, produce. If a cost-benefit calculation had been made at the moment when Atlantic entered the field—or, for that matter, even at the moment when it exited—a substantial "risk premium" would have had to be added to the discount rate to reflect the uncertainty about outcomes and the volatility of results over time.

A second caveat has to do with timing and time limits. One important reason to be optimistic about future improvements in South Africa's nursing profession is the long-term involvement of other donors in South Africa's push toward reform—including some that collaborated with Atlantic and that now continue to soldier on because they are not time-limited. The government's designation of a chief nursing officer in the National Department of Health, whose office is dedicated to leading and promoting nursing issues, will also be critical in sustaining the momentum into the future. These players, remaining on the scene, can carry on the effort that Atlantic's major funding helped to jump-start, and they can persevere along the long and still-unpredictable path to a better health-care system. If Atlantic's large investment can be thoroughly justified based on its likely social payoff, it must be acknowledged that that payoff is expected at least partly because other funders have taken a different, slower, more sustained approach than Atlantic did. Still, the fact that the South African government substantially increased investment in nursing as Atlantic was departing shows the lasting impact that the foundation's big bet in this field may have fueled.

In short, this is not a story that justifies one model of time and philanthropy over another. Instead, it demonstrates how the two can intersect with beneficial outcomes for both kinds of foundations. Still, it is at least arguable—and might, someday, be demonstrable—that Atlantic's large and disruptive investment in a field ripe for improvement, where social need was pronounced and potential benefits huge, created "greater value and impact" than if the investment had been delayed, and that the resulting value could be expected to "compound at a higher rate than [its] financial assets would."

CONCLUSION: SOME LESSONS AND QUESTIONS

William Bruce Cameron, an American sociologist of the 1950s and 1960s, warned that "not everything that counts can be counted,"[23] and that caution applies with particular force to this chapter. The purpose of this discussion is not to attempt a substantive evaluation of what Atlantic's grants achieved, much less to pin a precise monetary value on those achievements. To begin with, it is not yet possible to make a definitive pronouncement on the ultimate success or failure of any of them, all of which face countless hurdles on the way to their ultimate goals. More fundamentally, there are many things about these initiatives that are profoundly important but not readily enumerable— that is, they count but cannot be counted.

Instead, the point is to elaborate, with some roughly financial reasoning, on why a foundation might share Chuck Feeney's belief that it can produce "greater value and impact" by putting all its resources to use in a limited period of time than by creating a lasting endowment. Some critics have argued, fairly enough, that this belief is rarely spelled out in sufficient detail so that it can be analyzed and debated. In fact, the lack of such detail and analysis puts the whole idea at risk of caricature: Stated only in the simplest and most general terms, it becomes easy prey to the suggestion that advocates are merely privileging the needs of today over the needs of tomorrow, as if the latter were inherently less important. The essential purpose of this discussion is to escape that trap, and to provide a somewhat fuller articulation of the logic for large-scale, near-term giving—one that tries to be free of any generational bias—and then to invite a discussion about its merits.

Among the implications of this approach and the samples offered here, at least five stand out as hypotheses deserving further inquiry and elaboration:

1. The choice of a limited philanthropic time-horizon should be, at least in part, a decision about how and when to achieve the greatest social benefit.

If there is nothing inherently more valuable about solving today's problems than tomorrow's, then one reason to prefer immediate action over long-term action must be that immediate action *produces more aggregate value* for society—both today and tomorrow—than could be produced by conserving resources and employing them later. It seems obvious that this is not always true. But if there are conditions and assumptions under which near-term action yields more value, then a philanthropist might well look for ways to identify those conditions and assumptions and recognize the opportunities to which they point.

Presenting Atlantic initiatives as if they had been the subject of that kind of inquiry was a thought experiment only. The foundation did not, in reality, analyze and choose the programs in that way, nor were its expectations about their success rooted in calculations about social utility measured in dollars, euros, or rand. Nevertheless, the more intentionally analytic approach in this chapter may be a useful way of formulating decisions about the best size and timing of a philanthropic effort: big vs. small, now vs. later.

2. The search for very high social returns on a large, short-term investment might make particular sense when a foundation's goal is to improve the performance of big public systems.

One choice Atlantic did make explicitly, and which has become something of a trademark in its approach to philanthropy, was to place what it calls "big bets" on major changes in public systems and policy. It is no coincidence that both of the examples described in these pages were, at heart, attempts to change the way governments dealt with vulnerable populations. In both cases, the motive was to win widespread, lasting improvements in the life prospects of large populations—something that can, under certain circumstances, be accomplished with a large philanthropic effort over a limited period of time.

3. Even the most carefully chosen "big bet" will take time to get right; "limited timespan" is not necessarily the same as "short-term."

A foundation may determine that a successful initiative could indeed result in an escalating value that would far exceed what it could achieve with a slower, more limited expenditure of its resources. Yet even so, it might take a long time to reach a point where that kind of success is likely. Early years must be spent in forging relationships, gathering information and formulating strategy, cultivating (or building) strong frontline organizations, and recovering from missteps along the way. Both of the examples cited here began with years spent preparing the ground, assembling the means of intervention (often at several levels, involving many different kinds of grantee organizations— grassroots, research, legal, media, public relations, and more), and adjusting to lessons learned as the initiative was taking shape. Estimating how much time all this will take, and making allowances for uncertainty about that time estimate, are at least as critical in committing to a limited life as is the selection of the goal, the estimation of its long-term value and durability, or the decision about how much money to allot to it.

There may also be cases when the marginal return on philanthropic investment actually declines as the size of that investment rises above some inflection point, thus delaying the hoped-for achievement of large-scale social value even longer. As a foundation pursues its big bet, the best, most ready objectives may be met first, leaving only harder and harder challenges to be tackled thereafter. Or the amount or quality of talent in a field may decline once the earliest and best-prepared people or institutions have been put to work on a problem, leaving only less expert people or weaker institutions to be enlisted afterward. For example, in setting out to bolster nursing education in South Africa, and to train significantly more nurses, Atlantic needed to support not only the nursing departments of major universities, which were relatively well prepared to manage large grants and undertake major new initiatives. It also needed to support the smaller, less well-funded nursing colleges where poorer, more rural students were more likely to enroll. These less-advantaged schools needed much more time and assistance in building up enrollment, adding courses and faculty, and otherwise meeting the challenges that Atlantic was helping them to tackle. The investment is showing promise, but it has taken longer, and performed less robustly in the early years, than originally projected.

In short, the bigger the bet, the more time may be required to achieve the desired payoff, and the less benefit may be reaped with each additional dollar expended.

4. When estimating the likely social return on a philanthropic investment (even implicitly), it is often necessary to discount the expected future benefits at a higher-than-normal rate, given that social initiatives face many kinds of risk—especially when aimed at prompting long-term changes in large, complex systems.

The calculations we have been discussing have tended to focus on the value of what is expected to be achieved, and how that value would grow in the future. But the longer the time horizon, the more volatile these returns can be. For example, the suggestion that public policy changes offer particular opportunity for higher, fast-growing returns masks the risk that those changes may not be lasting. Atlantic, for example, helped build what became a policy bandwagon behind reforming school discipline in the United States so as to curb excessive suspensions and expulsions—practices that seriously impeded the educational prospects of poor, minority, and disabled young people. The US Departments of Education and Justice ultimately endorsed these reforms in the federal Supportive School Discipline Initiative,[24] which helped spread them nationwide—until a new administration reversed course beginning in 2017, and the bandwagon stalled.

5. The decision about how and when to set a time limit on a philanthropic initiative is not a challenge exclusive to limited-life institutions.

Weighing the balance of time and money, of relatively brief, big bets versus smaller-and-steadier use of resources, is a decision not just about how to structure a foundation. It is really a decision about how to maximize social value in a given period of time. As such, it should be at least an implicit part of any decision about the size and duration of a foundation program—even in foundations that are committed to operating in perpetuity. If larger expenditures can reap greater returns in a shorter amount of time, and those returns "compound at a higher rate than your financial assets would," as the Atlantic financial adviser puts it, it would be worthwhile to consider how to enlarge and accelerate the outlays. If not, or if uncertainty about future conditions imposes a severe risk premium on the expected social benefits, then it would make sense to proceed more slowly, at least until the uncertainty can be reduced.

For a perpetual institution, the two initiatives described here might have been just as appealing as they were for Atlantic. They would still have called for a large commitment of resources over a short time period, to launch something on a significant scale, to capture the attention of leaders and thinkers across the field, and to build a case for far-reaching change. In these cases, a big bet with a ten- or fifteen-year time horizon (at least for assessing cost-effectiveness and determining how to move forward) would have been as worthwhile for the perpetual funder as it was for Atlantic. But the perpetual funder would have the additional advantage of being able to soldier on, beyond the initial time limit, if it saw continuing prospects for large social returns or concluded that the returns needed more time to become stable and durable.

In short, estimates of future social returns—even very general, non-quantitative estimates—rest on a presumption that one can predict future conditions in the marketplace or at least estimate the probability of favorable or adverse changes. That is, in practice, rarely possible. But some informed suppositions about the future are usually part of a foundation's decisions (conscious or not) about where to put its money and for how long. Those rough predictions then become essential variables in the foundation's calculation about the social return it expects to reap on its charitable investments—whether that calculation is intentional and explicit or just intuitive. The difference between the estimate of these probabilities at a perpetual institution and at a time-limited one is that the perpetual funder can treat them as mere surmise and revise them later at will. The limited-life foundation, by contrast, will face a proximate day of reckoning when all its bets are final, and in time the future will render a quantifiable verdict on what its grants have achieved.

NOTES

1. Chuck Feeney to Bill [Gates], February 3, 2011, The Giving Pledge website, https://givingpledge.org/pledger?pledgerId=195.

2. Michael Klausner, "When Time Isn't Money: Foundation Payout Rates and the Time Value of Money," *Stanford Social Innovation Review,* Spring 2003, p. 54.

3. "Malaria," WHO Fact Sheet, 2006, at https://www.who.int/news-room/fact -sheets/detail/malaria.

4. 'Disadvantaged Children and Youth Programme Strategy,' the Atlantic Philanthropies, internal document, June 2005, pp. 21 and 26.

5. Incredible Years website, http://incredibleyears.com/about/incredible-years -series/program-previews/.

6. Donal O'Neill, Sinéad McGilloway, Michael Donnelly, Tracey Bywater, and Paul Kelly, "A Cost-Effectiveness Analysis of the Incredible Years Parenting Programme in Reducing Childhood Health Inequalities," *European Journal of Health Economics* 14:1 (February 2013), 85, 91.

7. Olga Khazan, "Why a Health Program that Works in America Failed in Britain," *The Atlantic,* October 23, 2015, at http://www.theatlantic.com/health/archive/2015/10/nurse-family-partnership/412000/.

8. O'Neill, et. al., "A Cost-Effectiveness Analysis of the Incredible Years," 86.

9. Ibid., p. 89.

10. Ibid., p. 90.

11. Ibid., p. 91.

12. Ibid.

13. James J. Heckman, "The Case for Investing in Disadvantaged Young Children," in Big Ideas for Children: Investing in Our Nation's Future, First Focus, 2008, p. 51, at http://heckmanequation.org/content/resource/case-investing-disadvantaged-young-children.

14. Hayley Halpin, "'It reduces stress': This Program Is Helping Teachers Support Children With Behavioural Difficulties," *The Journal.* ie, Oct. 10, 2017, at https://www.thejournal.ie/incredible-years-programme-schools-3636992-Oct2017/.

15. Steve Reid, "Opinion Piece for Atlantic Philanthropies: Population Health in South Africa," Primary Health Care Directorate, Faculty of Health Sciences, University of Cape Town, July 2011, pp. 1–2.

16. Marcia Smith and Le Nhan Phuong, "Update: Population Health Strategic Review," memorandum to the Board of Directors, The Atlantic Philanthropies, 24 February 2009, p. 201.

17. Ibid.

18. Nelouise Geyer, "Promoting Excellence in Nursing Through North-South Partnerships," undated PowerPoint presentation to The Atlantic Philanthropies, slide No. 4.

19. See "South Africa Rural Poverty 1960–2022," Macrotrends, at https://www.macrotrends.net/countries/ZAF/south-africa/rural-population; "South Africa—Poverty Headcount Ratio at Rural Poverty Line as Share of Rural Population," Knoema, at https://knoema.com/atlas/South-Africa/Rural-poverty-rate; and "Ranking by Population," Data Commons, at https://datacommons.org/ranking/Count_Person/Country/africa?h=country/ZAF.

20. Ibid., slide 12.

21. Ibid., slide 15.

22. Ibid., slide 18.

23. The quotation is often attributed to Albert Einstein, but there is no evidence of Einstein's having said anything of the kind. The earliest published use of the phrase appears to have been in Cameron's *Informal Sociology: A Casual Introduction to Sociological Thinking* (New York: Random House, 1963), eight years after Einstein's death.

24. Leila Fiester, "Tilling the Field: Lessons About Philanthropy's Role in School Discipline Reform," *The Atlantic Philanthropies*, 2014, pp. 22–23, at https://www.atlanticphilanthropies.org/wp-content/uploads/2015/07/Tilling-the-Field-AP.pdf.

Chapter 12

The Myth of Payout Rules

Where Do We Go from Here?

Brian Galle and Ray Madoff

We begin with a thought experiment. Suppose Congress offers a $10 billion reward to any donor or group of donors who will enter into a binding commitment with Congress. The terms of the commitment are that the donors will pledge to spend $15 billion on good works, works of charity that "lighten the burdens of government," at some point in the future. The pledge does not specify a date by which the money must be spent. The donors sign the commitment, set aside the funds, and collect their $10 billion. One hundred years later, or two hundred, the $15 billion has grown in value, but nothing has been spent. Did Congress get a good deal?

Private foundations play a critical role in the charitable landscape and American society as a whole. These are entities formed by an individual, family, or corporation for the purpose of providing financial support for charitable activities that are typically carried out by others. As we write, private foundations hold about $1.3 trillion in assets.[1] Some private foundations are very large and well known—such as the Bill and Melinda Gates Foundation and the Ford Foundation—but the vast majority of foundations are family foundations with total assets of $1 million or less.

As our opening hypothetical suggests, private-foundation status is a sort of pact between Congress and private donors. There are significant tax benefits associated with creating private foundations, and the bulk of these are granted at the time a donor contributes assets to the foundation. However, because private foundations are created and controlled by a small number of individuals, and because they are not dependent on outsiders for funding, there is little natural oversight of these organizations' activities. Because of this, Congress enacted rules that impose additional requirements on private foundations (as opposed to other charitable organizations) in an attempt to ensure that they are serving the public good on an ongoing basis, rather than just in the future.

The Tax Reform Act of 1969 enacted payout rules as a central component of the private-foundation regulatory regime it established in order to counteract the problem of private foundations accumulating rather than spending their charitable assets. Congress was concerned that the accumulation of wealth resulted in undue delay between the time of tax benefits and the time the public benefited from charitable spending. To address this, Congress enacted rules that require (and here we simplify a bit to spare the reader the indignities of tax minutia) that private foundations spend at least 5 percent of their assets each year on charitable endeavors—most typically by making grants to other charitable organizations.[2]

The 5 percent rule quickly secured strong roots within the nonprofit sector, experiencing only an occasional challenge from either inside or outside the sector, through congressional proposals or lobbying efforts.[3] Indeed, the 5 percent payout rule has become widely accepted and widely touted (by the foundation world, among others) as a reasonable compromise that allows private foundations to exist in perpetuity while ensuring that a portion of their funds be put to current charitable use. Even more importantly, the 5 percent payout rule has served to legitimate private foundations to the public by giving foundations a readily recognized role of providing steady sources of capital to charitable organizations. All of these things make it seem that the 5 percent payout rule is well established as both a practical and theoretical matter.

However, despite the apparently robust nature of the 5 percent payout rule, in this chapter, we argue that the 5 percent payout rule operates more as a fig leaf than as a meaningful control on private-foundation spending. Analyzing how the rule operates fifty years after its enactment, it has become increasingly evident that the meaning of the term "payout" has become so elastic that the rule cannot be relied upon to fulfill its stated purpose of ensuring the current flow of dollars to charitable activities. In particular, the ability to meet payout requirements by (1) paying unlimited administrative expenses of the foundation (including salaries and travel expenses for family members), (2) making unlimited contributions to donor-advised funds (DAFs) (which themselves have no further payout requirement), and (3) making certain investments in for-profit companies (provided the payments meet the very liberal definition of a program-related investment [PRI]), give private foundations ample opportunity to skirt the purpose, while still fulfilling the letter, of the law governing payout.

Should the hollowing out of payout rules be the cause for alarm or for celebration? At a minimum, we think that honesty, efficiency, and transparency all require that those who would celebrate the rule's demise should take the formal step of eliminating it, rather than relying on complex run-arounds that consume time and energy and undermine respect for the letter of the law. In addition, we believe that payout rules play an important role. As a result, we argue instead for reviving the payout rule in such a way that it fulfills its intended purpose. We would close down each of the loopholes we describe, and the chapter briefly details how that could be done.

The bulk of our discussion, however, will focus on the larger argument of whether payout rules are detrimental or valuable. We begin by examining arguments against the payout rule.

Critics have offered several arguments against payout rules. Two of these involve claims that payout rules actually reduce spending. In one version of this point, critics argue that legally mandated "floors" end up functioning as "ceilings," so that the 5 percent minimum actually reduces the spending of foundations that would have been willing to spend more annually. In another version, the argument is that donors dislike being told what to do with their money, and so respond to payout rules by donating less. Yet another argument holds that government-mandated spending rules undermine the purpose of the charitable sector, which is explicitly designed to turn decisions about how to spend some public funds over to private actors.

We argue that these claims are mistaken, in part by showing that they rest on factual premises that are likely incorrect. We draw on original empirical research based on hundreds of thousands of tax returns and other documents filed by private foundations. Using statistical analysis of these data, we find—contrary to the "ceiling" argument—that a 1981 reduction in the payout rate did not reduce spending among firms that were spending above the minimum. And, looking to a natural experiment involving state adoption of payout-like rules in the last decade, we find no evidence that such rules reduce donations—if anything, the opposite is true.

We then turn to consider the broader purpose of the payout rule. We see payout rules as a corrective for the natural tendencies of philanthropists and foundation managers to hoard money rather than spend it. Unlike the Congress that underwrites them all, philanthropists and their agents typically have only one foundation and/or one career. Unable to diversify away the risks of failure, they will predictably be far more averse to risk than their well-diversified congressional sponsor. Too, many natural human failings, such as biases in favor of the measurable (fiscal returns) over the abstract (charitable performance), and hesitancy in the face of complexity, tend to slow spending. While we acknowledge that there are other possible correctives, payout rules are the most time-tested, and none of the other options are clearly superior.

I. BACKGROUND

This section brings readers up to speed on the law and history of private-foundation regulation. Part I.A. briefly describes the tax treatment of charitable contributions, along with the generally accepted justifications for why these tax subsidies exist. Part I.B. reviews the private-foundation regime in particular and discusses the origin and rationale for the payout requirement.

A. Tax Incentives for Charitable Giving: Details and Rationales

Federal tax law provides several distinct benefits for charitable contributors. Among these are charitable-contribution deductions from income and estate taxes, exclusions from the gift tax and income tax on gifts of appreciated assets, and the ability to deduct the full fair-market value of non-cash property. By our estimates, these rules in combination can produce in excess of $7 million worth of return value on a $10 million gift.[4]

Why does Congress provide such generous tax benefits for charitable giving? The prevailing view is that subsidies make up for two market failures, one economic, one political. Despite our best intentions, most humans remain at least somewhat self-interested. We therefore are usually unwilling to pay fully for benefits that accrue to other people—what an economist would call "positive externalities." Many goods, once purchased by one person, provide additional spillover benefits to others, so that no one individual has an incentive to provide as much as would be ideal from a social perspective. Examples here include public parks, museums, and medical research. By offering tax benefits, Congress hopes that we can be motivated through selfish considerations to purchase more of the positive-externality goods, moving society closer to the level it would choose if not for the market's failure.[5]

Of course, taxing and spending is another way to cure market failures, and so the second failure that rationalizes charity is government failure. A single national government could meet the demands of the majority voter but would sometimes leave unsatisfied those who wanted more or different goods than the majority prefer. Subsidies for charity are, in essence, a version of private federalism, dividing the atom of sovereignty by handing over some of the federal budget for allocation by donors and the managers they hire. In an ideal world, this has the potential to promote diverse and pluralistic responses to the world's ills.

Congress has established a fairly dense set of rules governing which entities are eligible to receive subsidized gifts. These limits are aimed at ensuring that money goes to its intended purposes—generally, providing goods that the private market alone would struggle to deliver.[6] For example, an eligible organization must be organized and operated for one or more exempt purposes.

Congress also distinguishes among eligible organizations, most notably in the division between "public charities" and "private foundations." To simplify a bit, tax law defines a public charity as an organization that derives most of its revenues from a wide base of donors or charitable-service revenues, while a private foundation gets its money from just a few individuals. Schools, hospitals, and churches are always public charities no matter their financing. Because of this technical definition, many entities that mimic the structure and functioning of other philanthropic foundations are able to escape categorization as a "private foundation." Gifts to public charities are treated a bit more favorably than are gifts to private foundations. Private foundations must also comply with a slightly more onerous set of governance rules, and they pay a modest tax, a bit more than 1 percent, on their net investment earnings.[7]

More relevantly for our purposes, among the special rules applicable to private foundations is the requirement that they make regular distributions, or "payout." Each year, a private foundation computes 5 percent of the net value of its investment assets. It then has until the end of the following year to spend that amount on "qualifying distributions," which can include grants to other charities.[8] Failure to meet the deadline triggers a hefty penalty. Grants to other persons or entities are often permissible but require more red tape and justification. Administrative expenses also qualify, as we detail more in Part II.A.

B. The 5 Percent Rule and Its Origins

The private-foundation payout rule was first enacted in 1969 as a modification to the rules governing tax benefits for charitable giving. Up until the middle of the twentieth century, all charitable donations were treated the same for tax purposes, regardless of whether the charitable organization receiving the property received broad public support and was engaged in direct charitable work (such as operating a soup kitchen or running a museum, hospital or college) or whether it was privately funded and simply held donated funds for the eventual distribution to other individuals or organizations doing direct charitable work. There was a single rule that simply required that these organizations be "organized and operated for . . . charitable . . . purposes." However, the exponential growth of private charitable foundations, along with their use for political purposes and explicit and audacious marketing of private charitable foundations as tax shelters for the wealthy, brought congressional attention.

Congress was particularly concerned about the disconnect between the time of tax benefit for donors and the time of benefit for society. In the words of the Joint Committee on Taxation Bluebook, "As a result, while the donor may have received substantial tax benefits from his contribution currently, charity may have received absolutely no current benefit."[9] This concern was especially great at the time when, due to high tax rates, the tax benefits of charitable giving were even more beneficial than they are today.[10]

Congress was particularly sensitized to this issue by the development and acceptance of the concept of "tax expenditure" in the 1960s. At that time, Assistant Secretary of the Treasury Stanley Surrey developed the theory that tax preferences were functionally equivalent to direct government spending. The theory of tax expenditures has become well accepted and is used by the Congressional Budget Office in calculating the federal budget.[11] Applying the tax expenditure analysis, if a taxpayer were to receive a $5 million reduction in taxes for creating a $15 million private foundation, that was recognized as being functionally the same as if the donor contributed $10 million and the government contributed $5 million toward the creation of that private foundation.[12] Once the deduction is seen as a substitute for direct spending, it is not surprising that Congress began to ask what the public was receiving in exchange for this significant *current* "expenditure" of public resources.

The first proposals considered ensuring that charitable funds would be put to use in a timely manner by limiting the life of private foundations to a term of twenty-five or forty years. Although term limits were ultimately rejected, Congress did enact provisions designed to assure distribution of at least a portion of the private foundation's assets. The first rules, enacted in 1954, did not require specific payout of funds, but instead provided that a private foundation could lose its tax-exempt status if its accumulation of income was "unreasonable in amount and duration." This rule had little practical effect as the standard was too vague, and the penalty—loss of exempt status—was so draconian that it was rarely imposed.

As a result of dissatisfaction with the rule against the accumulation of income, Congress was urged by Treasury to enact a rule regarding payout that would be more effective.[13] The proposed remedy was to impose a mandatory payout of all of a foundation's net income on a reasonably current basis.[14] Congress adopted a form of Treasury's proposal when it enacted the Tax Reform Act of 1969. As originally enacted, the payout rule required private foundations to distribute the greater of the private foundation's net investment income or 6 percent. However, this was eventually modified to the current rule that imposes a tax on private foundations that fail to spend at least 5 percent of their assets each year on their charitable purpose. Under this rule, our $10 million private foundation would be required to "pay out" at least $500,000 per year or else be subject to a penalty tax.

II. IS THERE REALLY A 5 PERCENT PAYOUT RULE?

The purpose of the 5 percent payout rule was to require private foundations to make regular distributions of their assets for charitable purposes. The common understanding is that private foundations meet their 5 percent pay-out obligations (i.e., make "qualifying distributions") by making grants to organizations that are actively involved in charitable activities (and indeed, these payments would qualify for meeting the payout rule.) However, the rules provided in the tax code are not so limited. "Qualifying distributions" are defined in section 4942(g) as meaning any amount paid to accomplish the organization's charitable purpose (including reasonable administrative expenses) or any amount paid to acquire an asset used to carry out its exempt purpose.[15]

As a result of this broad definition, in addition to outright grants to public charities, minimum distribution requirements can also be met by: (1) administrative expenses of the foundation, including salaries, which can go to family members; (2) making contributions to DAFs (from which there are no further payout requirements); and (3) making investments of the foundation's assets (even in for-profit companies) so long as the purpose is to fulfill the organization's charitable mission. Taken together, these rules provide ample opportunity for foundations to satisfy their 5 percent payout obligation without making any traditional grants to support charitable activities.

A. Administrative Expenses

A private foundation can meet its 5 percent payout requirement by paying salaries, trustee fees, and other administrative expenses. The only limitation on administrative expenses is that they be "reasonable and necessary." Once they satisfy that standard, there is no overall limitation on the total amount of administrative expenses that can qualify.

The result of this rule is that a significant portion of a private foundation's payout obligation can be met by salaries, rent, trustee fees, and travel expenses. The ability to credit these expenses might make sense for the largest private foundations with professional staffs, since the charitable work that these organizations are doing is primarily the administrative work of choosing and supporting grants. However, this rule allowing unlimited administrative expenses is more troubling in the context of small family foundations where a significant portion of the administrative fees is likely to flow to the donor's family and friends.[16] Thus, to return to the example of our $10 million foundation, it is possible for most or all of the $500,000 payout requirement to be met by paying salaries to the donor's children, maintaining a fancy office space, and paying travel expenses for annual meetings in exotic locales.

In part to address these concerns, in 2003, bipartisan legislation proposed adjustments to the administrative expenses provision.[17] The proposed legislation would have prohibited operating expenses, like rent and salaries, from qualifying as distributions for purposes of the 5 percent payout rule.[18] However, the legislation did not pass—meaning private foundations can continue to include administrative expenses within qualifying distributions to meet the 5 percent payout rule. More recently, the bipartisan Accelerating Charitable Efforts ("ACE") Act was introduced in both the Senate (in June 2021) and the House (in February 2022). This bill would prohibit foundations from meeting their 5 percent payout requirement through paying salary and travel expenses to family members or by making contributions to DAFs.[19]

The problem of administrative expenses being used to satisfy payout requirements is particularly prevalent with respect to smaller private foundations. Using data from charities' Form 990 tax returns, we calculated the relationship between administrative expenses and foundation size. We plot firms' overhead ratio, or share of expenses devoted to administrative costs, on the *y* axis, and log firm assets on the *x* axis. As figure 12.1 shows, there is a strong negative relationship between firm size and overhead ratios: small firms spend more on overhead. Among the smallest 15 percent of private foundations, more than a quarter of firm spending is administrative costs.

B. Donor-Advised Funds

Donations to public charities qualify for the 5 percent payout rule. Typically, public charities are those organizations, like universities, hospitals, churches,

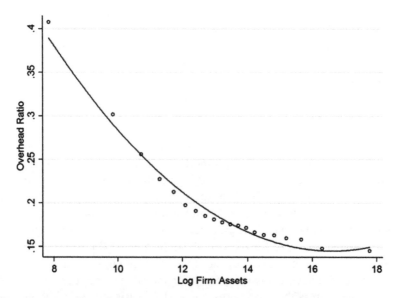

Figure 12.1   Overhead Ratios by Firm Size at Private Foundations, 1989–2012. *Source*: Data from Core-PF Cumulative File, 2013. Overhead ratio = share of administrative expenses over all expenses. Hollow circles are 20 bins of mean firm-year assets. Dollar values in 2013 dollars. Solid line: quadratic best fit line. N: 1,237,088.

food banks, museums, and other organizations engaged in direct charitable activities. Applied this way, it is easy to understand how Congress believed the payout rule would assure that private foundation assets were put to current charitable use.

However, the term public charity is not limited to those organizations engaged in direct charitable work. It also includes grant-making institutions—like community foundations—provided the organization receives broad public support.[20] Thus, private foundations can also meet their payout obligations by making distributions to community foundations and other publicly supported grant-making organizations.

This exception originally did not raise many concerns because the ultimate spending decisions over community foundation funds were made by the managers of the community foundations. There was every reason to believe that spending decisions would be based on the interests and needs of the community being served.

However, community foundations promoted a vehicle that would prove to be very effective in attracting charitable dollars (even if less effective in getting funds to the local community): the DAF. In order to accomplish the tax goals of giving the donor a current charitable donation, contributions to DAFs are structured as outright gifts to the sponsoring organization (in this case, the community foundation). But the understanding of the parties is that donors, or their designated agents, are given ongoing de facto control over the investment and spending of donated assets. In this way, DAFs function like charitable checking accounts. The sponsoring charity legally owning the funds agrees not to spend them on their charitable mission and instead keeps them in a segregated account awaiting instructions from the donor.

DAFs are not themselves separate legal entities, and a donation to a DAF at a community foundation (or any other public charity) is treated identically to a donation to the community foundation's general-purpose fund. The effect of this rule is that a private foundation can legally meet their 5 percent payout rule by making contributions to a DAF, even if the contributions remain in the DAF in perpetuity.[21]

Thus, in our above example, if a private foundation is funded with $10 million, it can fully meet its payout requirement by distributing $500,000 each year to a DAF and there are no further payout rules applicable to this fund.

The popularity and use of DAFs exploded beginning in 1991 when the investment company Fidelity created the first so-called "commercial" DAF sponsor—Fidelity Charitable. Although Fidelity Charitable adopted the structure of a community foundation, the organization did not purport to stand for any particular community or charitable purpose—other than the creation of DAFs. Commercial DAFs provided donors (and in this case private foundations) with maximum ongoing control over their contributed assets (provided that the legal documents governing the relationship did not grant donors certain key aspects of legal control, such as the right to reclaim the donated assets).

This ability to avoid payout rules by making a contribution to a DAF is difficult to justify in light of the temporal logic of the payout rule. Although it is understandable why some private foundations might *want* the flexibility afforded by DAFs, this is different from whether this rule is a good policy.

C. Program-Related Investments

PRIs represent the latest expansion of the concept of payout. PRIs enable private foundations to meet their payout requirements by using a variety of different financial instruments, including investing in for-profit enterprises. As explained in one article geared to practitioners: by using PRIs, private foundations can "serve as venture capitalists by providing seed capital to domestic and foreign for-profit companies, use all manner of creative financial structures (debt, equity, or a combination of both), and take it all into account as 'qualifying distributions' for the year."[22] Like administrative expenses, the concept of PRIs is not without justification. The contours of the concept have become so elastic, however, that depending on how they are structured, PRIs can allow private foundations to expand both their own assets and also the wealth of for-profit companies and their shareholders.

PRIs affect payout rules in two ways. First, the full value of a PRI can be used to satisfy a private foundation's 5 percent payout requirement. Second, in calculating what that payout requirement is, existing PRIs are not counted as part of the foundation's assets used to calculate the 5 percent payout requirement. For example, a private foundation that has total assets of $10 million, of which $6 million is invested in PRIs, need only distribute 5 percent of $4 million in order to satisfy its payout requirement. In addition, it can do so by making an additional PRI of $200,000. If a private foundation were to invest all of its assets in "program-related investments" it would have no further payout obligations.

Given the powerful effect of PRIs on payout requirements, it is particularly important to circumscribe the definition of what constitutes a PRI in such a way that it limits the exception to its intended purpose. Nonetheless, the trend in the law has been to significantly liberalize the scope of PRIs with little attention to the issues that they might raise.

Based on the legislative history, the original concept of PRIs included such investments as low- or no-interest loans to needy students or funds for low-income housing and urban renewal.[23] Each of these investments fits comfortably within the notion of funds spent for charitable purposes. However, in recent years, changes to the regulations have made clear that the concept of PRIs has been significantly expanded to include a wide array of traditional investment assets, including equity stakes in for-profit companies.

PRI is a complex issue because these investments can accomplish significant current good. However, because the requirements around PRIs are so lenient, PRIs can also be used simply to divert the foundation's resources into long-term investments that provide no meaningful current benefit and allow the foundation to otherwise avoid the 5 percent payout requirement.

Under the rules, investments must meet three requirements to be treated as a PRI.[24] First, the investment's primary purpose must be to accomplish one or more of the foundation's charitable purposes. To do this, it must both significantly further the foundation's charitable purposes and not have been made but for that achievement. Second, income production must not be a significant purpose for making the investment. Third, the investment must not be for lobbying or other political activities. These standards provide very little assurance that the PRI will accomplish a meaningful charitable purpose, as meeting the definition of PRIs is largely dependent on the subjective mindset of the foundation managers.

While payout rules are still technically operative, their effect has been significantly undermined by the ability of private foundations to meet payout requirements through administrative expenses, contributions to DAFs, and PRIs. As a result, payout rules no longer provide assurance that any private foundation funds will be committed to current charitable use.

Given how easily payout requirements can be circumvented, where do we go from here? Two choices are worthy of consideration: first, abandon the fiction of payout. Over the years, many arguments have been put forth that payout rules are a bad idea. Given the lack of effectiveness of the 5 percent payout rules, perhaps it is time to reconsider these arguments. The second alternative is to keep the payout rules and revise them in such a way that they fulfill their purpose.

We believe the second alternative is a better way to go.

III. SHOULD PAYOUT REQUIREMENTS BE ABANDONED?

One possible response to the disconnect between legislative intent and reality discussed above is to abandon the payout rules. There are a set of by-now familiar arguments against payout rules and we will review these arguments here.

A. Floors Are Ceilings

It's sometimes argued that setting minimum payout distributions could perversely reduce spending among firms that would otherwise have been inclined to spend more than the minimum amount.[25] All the available evidence suggests, though, that this claim is a myth. Further, it may well be confusing cause and effect.

To examine the floor/ceiling question, we assembled data from approximately twenty-five years of federal tax returns filed by private foundations. Where possible, we also merged these data with information gathered from the Foundation Directory, a publication of the Foundation Center.[26]

We do find that many foundations report that their mean payout ratio over the five-year period ending with their tax return is almost exactly the 5-percent minimum. However, we also found that the majority of foundations pay more than that, and in some cases quite a bit more. One feature jumps out immediately to explain the difference in payout behaviors: the presence of living donors. In the early years of our data, for which we have available information from the Foundation Directory on whether an organization has still-living supporters, we are able to plot separately payout rates (which we hand-compute) for firms with zero and one or more living donors. Figure 12.2 summarizes the result.

Payout rates among firms with living donors are considerably higher than payout rates of firms without, with living-donor foundations spending more than 10 percent on average in most years.[27] We obtain essentially identical results when we group firms by whether the organization has received any donations in the prior five years. We then use this metric as a way of identifying firms that likely have living donors in the tax-return data. We plot separate average reported payouts for the two groups, as shown in figure 12.3.

Here we see that, indeed, firms without any recent gifts spend, on average, the 5-percent minimum. But other firms average more than double that rate—and that average is omitting "flow through" firms that spend all or nearly all of their revenues each year.

We also can use the Foundation Directory Data to investigate whether changes in the law in 1976 and 1981 affected payouts. Between 1969 and 1976, the minimum required payout was 6 percent. From 1976 to 1981, it was the greater of 5 percent or the foundation's net investment income. After 1981, it settled into the modern 5 percent floor. If the "ceiling" hypothesis were correct, then firms that historically were spending more than the floor should have reduced their spending when the floor dropped. While predictions about 1976 are ambiguous, since they depend on the firm's investment returns, the 1981 change unambiguously dropped the cap for at least some firms.

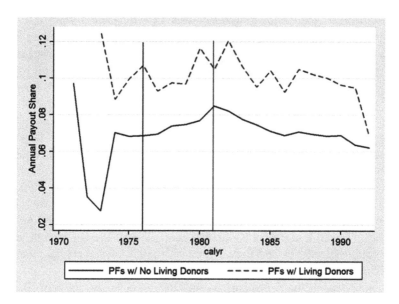

Figure 12.2 Payout Rates at Foundations with and without Living Donors, 1970–1990.
Source: Data from Foundation Directory. Payout is computed as expenditures/expenditures + assets.

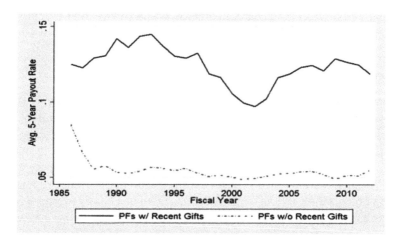

Figure 12.3 Mean Reported Payouts for PF with/without Recent Gifts.

Even a casual inspection of figure 12.2 suggests that there is little evidence the 1981 change reduced spending among the group of high-spending firms. As expected, the group of low-spending firms trends downward a bit after 1981, consistent with the theory that these firms aim to spend as little as possible.

We further conduct regression analysis in which we formally test the impact of the 1981 changes on firms that we calculate were spending above the floor at that time. These estimates are necessarily imperfect because we lack investment return data in the Foundation Directory sample, and so have no accurate measure of the floor facing firms before 1981. We can, however, compare the effects of 1981 on firms with living donors against those without. On average, 1981 increased the payout ratio among living-donor firms by about 1.5 percentage points relative to deceased-donor firms, and this result is highly statistically significant.[28] To emphasize, this was a year in which the floor unambiguously declined. If payout floors ever serve as ceilings, we see no evidence of that in our data.

If the payout requirement isn't a ceiling, why do so many firms cluster at 5 percent? Because it's a floor. These are all firms that would, presumably, spend even less if they could. For example, the average payout among the wealthiest colleges and universities is around 4.4 percent, according to NACUBO.

Another reason the 5-percent payout rate might be attractive to firms is because it has long been held up as the supposed ideal spending rate. Deep and Frumkin refer to 5 percent as "tradition," though they don't explain how to reconcile this tradition with the 6 percent rule enacted in 1969.[29] Gene Steuerle reports that Congress adopted 5 percent because it was told by industry experts that was the standard. In other words, it was industry practices that drove the 5 percent rule, not vice-versa.[30]

B. Payout Rules Could Reduce Giving

Another common argument against minimum payout requirements is that they may tend to reduce giving. The theory here, we assume, goes something like this. Some donors may simply prefer to have their funds spent very slowly. Others may fear that minimum payouts might threaten to end the viable life of the foundation prematurely, as the more a foundation spends each year, the more likely it is that a dramatic drop in asset values could render the organization at least temporarily unable to meet basic overhead needs. In effect, the payout is like a tax, forcing donors into spending they would prefer not to authorize. Thus, donors with preferences for perpetual life will be discouraged from donating if their donations are subject to spending rules.

One important point to note immediately is that these claims omit an important basic feature of tax economics. Taxes often bring both substitution effects and income effects, and at times the two are in conflict. It is true that, if payout rules are a tax, donors may perceive the value of a dollar put into a foundation as being less than it would be without the payout rule, encouraging them to seek out alternative uses of their funds. That is the substitution effect. But this point cuts in two directions. There is also an income effect. If donors want their firm to be perpetual, and it is subject to a payout rule, they may overcome the risk of catastrophic loss by putting more money into the foundation.

This is almost the exact tradeoff ordinary taxpayers face when thinking about how best to provide for their retirement in the presence of an income tax. On the one hand, the fact that there is a tax means that less of our labor effort will go into our own bank account. That should discourage labor. On the other, if our financial planner gives us a target dollar amount we need to hit to live comfortably in our AARP years, we actually have incentives to work harder as the tax rate goes up. Despite decades of debate and empirical investigation, economists have not been able to show which of these effects is more important to workers' decision-making.

To test our skepticism against real data, we examine the impact of a real-world policy experiment with payout rates. Of the fifty jurisdictions that adopted the Uniform Prudent Management of Institutional Funds Act (UPMIFA), about a dozen also enacted an optional percent soft cap on foundation spending.[31] The cap provision, section 4(d) of the Uniform Act, imposes a rebuttable presumption that any managers authorizing their firm to spend in excess of 7 percent of net assets in a given year are acting imprudently. While of course the cap is not the same as a floor, it has similar features. If donors prefer longevity, and fear that unconstrained managers might spend too fast, they should respond to the cap by donating more.

Our basic research design is what is known as a "difference in differences" regression. We compare affected foundations in states that adopted a cap against affected foundations in other UPMIFA-adopting states, while controlling for basic fiscal variables, year, state, and a set of time trends.[32] We summarize the results in table 12.1.

In brief, we find no evidence that donors like caps. If anything, we find some modest evidence that they dislike caps. Donations to foundations in capped states on average fall relative to donations to foundations in other UPMIFA states, but this effect is not measured very precisely. The 95 percent confidence interval ranges from a 10 percent decline to a 1 percent increase. We can say with some confidence in this estimation that caps do not increase donations by any notable amount. Our results are essentially unchanged if, as in column two, we weight our analysis by the value of firm assets.

Again, our argument is that these results are probative of the debate over whether payout rates on net affect donations. We find no evidence that donors value rules that tend to slow rates of spending. A lower payout requirement, like a cap, tends to slow spending rates. It is possible that donors do not view these two policies as equivalent, of course, but there is no obvious theoretical reason why that would be so.

Table 12.1   Effects of UPMIFA Spending Caps on Log Donations

VARIABLES	(1)	(2)
Capped Year?	–0.0490	–0.0460
	(0.0294)	(0.0309)
UPMIFA	0.0545**	0.0540**
	(0.0225)	(0.0241)
R-squared	0.091	0.086

Notes: Fixed-effects OLS regressions with firm fixed effects. Coefficients reported with (standard errors) clustered at the state level. Trusts are omitted. Regressions include controls for firm expenditures, assets, liabilities, investment return, officer compensation, and age; state and year fixed effects; and linear and quadratic state by year trends. Column two: weighted by mean firm assets. N: 568,124. **: statistically significant at the 5% level. Data from Core-PF Cumulative File, 2013.

C. Government Should Not Pick Charitable Winners and Losers

Yet another argument we frequently encounter against a minimum payout requirement is the suggestion that it contravenes the basic neutrality principle that underlies support for the charitable sector. That is, one of the defining goals of the nonprofit sector is to pursue policies the government wouldn't choose, or at least to try out approaches governments won't. To the greatest extent possible, then, government regulators should strive to take no position on the choices charities make.

While we (mostly) embrace this ideal,[33] we don't think it has anything to do with the payout rule. Indeed, as one of us summarizes elsewhere, one core rationale for the payout rule is exactly that government is *already* favoring foundation savings over foundation spending.[34] Briefly, the idea is that prevailing tax rules, by allowing donated assets to yield tax-free growth, offer a larger effective subsidy the longer a firm holds donated assets. If anything, payout requirements are a step back toward neutrality.

Even if the tax system were not already distorting the timing of charity, payout requirements would make sense as a correction to the failure of individual private decisions about timing to reflect the overall public good. We address this point in more detail in the next Part.

Lastly, mandatory payouts help to alleviate a fundamental tension in the structure of the estate tax deduction for charity. One of the two key goals of the estate tax is that it reduces concentrations of dynastic wealth. It was thought that a charitable-contribution deduction was consistent with this aim, since money turned over to charity presumably is freed of the dynasty's influence. Obviously, that is a problematic assumption in the case of ongoing family foundations.

In the absence of payout rules, the strain of managing this tension would have to fall entirely, and we think unsustainably, on secondary rules for foundation conduct. Many of the technical rules now governing foundations are, at bottom, half-measures aimed at reining back in the power of family foundations to serve as ongoing centers of dynastic influence. For example, private foundations are limited in their ability to own large blocks of corporate stock and face higher barriers than other charities in their dealings with politics, with donors, or with other insiders. All these rules cause undesirable side effects, impose compliance costs even on non-dynastic foundations, and are the subject of frequent gaming. If foundations had no payout obligations, the pressures we observe now would, we suspect, also grow dramatically.

D. Intergenerational Equity and the Value of Future Spending

The last three arguments we've covered criticize payout rules as such. That is, those who level these critiques may well accept the notion that charity today is superior to charity tomorrow, but object to the way in which payout rules govern that choice. Another potential argument is that foundations do better to spend their money in the future, and government should not stand in the way. This claim is not particular to payout rules and could apply equally to any effort to govern how philanthropy behaves over time. We have dealt with these arguments at greater length elsewhere,[35] but here we'll try to briefly summarize the state of the debate.

One rationale for spending in the future is intergenerational equity. It's sometimes said that future beneficiaries have just as great a claim on a foundation's resources as those around today. To argue for spending sooner, this argument goes, would be to value present lives over future lives.

We have no quarrel with intergenerational equity, but equity can sometimes demand spending today instead of tomorrow. If we all agree that our goal is to deliver the greatest total benefit to the world, whenever the beneficiaries may be born, we still have to ask what spending pattern produces the greatest value. Spending now can generate benefits for the future, too.

Indeed, as we've discussed this issue at a series of conferences, we've found a remarkable degree of consensus on this question. At the end of the day, nearly all participants agreed that the spend-save decision is, in a sense, a simple one. For each additional project a foundation might fund, it should ask: Would the total current and future "social return" on this project be greater or less than the "fiscal return" the foundation can get from simply investing the funds? If the social return is bigger, it should fund another project. If not, save the money for another day.

It's critical, though, that foundations account for *all* the social returns from current spending. Foundations should account for the possibility not only of direct long-term social returns (for instance, the economic growth that results from successful early childhood education programs) but also the indirect informational benefits to governments and other organizations that arise from studying every new grant. Few modern institutions are as well-positioned as foundations to coordinate and learn from policy experiments, and this is an opportunity that should not be left at the wayside.

Then, too, foundations must be sure to count the costs of saving for the future. The familiar problems of dead-hand control and agency costs snowball over time. We've shown that society, and the foundation sector, are both growing steadily richer over time.[36] Assuming diminishing marginal returns from wealth and from charitable spending, saving a dollar for the future means, on average, that dollar will likely go to less critical needs. Foundations also are not as informed about the ideal timing of direct service expenditures as the service providers themselves; holding back funds means that timing depends on the less-informed judgment of foundation managers.

Payout opponents sometimes argue that future spending will instead be more valuable than spending today because the future may bring greater needs or better solutions and keeping organizations fiscally sound holds together a valuable team of experts to meet those needs and apply those solutions.

However, these arguments confuse perpetual organizations with perpetual gifts. That is, all of these benefits are available for a foundation that spends all its available money today and then raises new money to distribute tomorrow. If a given foundation has trouble raising new money, a rival organization could hire away a successful team. Further, from the government's perspective, each foundation is just one line in its vast portfolio of investments in the foundation sector; there is always new future money available to meet future needs and to exploit future innovations.

One possible exception to this "portfolio" argument is that the charitable sector may be an especially useful place for society to try to save money during good times in preparation for future recessions. Unfortunately, data show that foundations do not actually increase, and often have moderately decreased, their spending during past recessions.[37] With some reforms, law could do more to encourage counter-cyclical foundation spending, but even so this would be an argument for relatively short-term savings, rather than perpetual endowments.

IV. WHY PAYOUT?

The various holes we've described in the web of the payout rule would not be trouble if payout were only a relatively unimportant policy. However, we think payout rules are central to the project of government-supported philanthropy.

Payout rules are a corrective. Philanthropic organizations, and those who manage them, are systematically biased against spending and in favor of accumulation. Some of these biases, as we've already noted, are the result of government policy, while others derive from the predictable incentives of managers and common human tendencies. Because these errors affect others, and because government is an important financial supporter of philanthropy, there is a strong government interest in helping to overcome these systematic failures. Even if not all preferences for delay are "errors" from the perspective of the foundation's controllers, these preferences may still depart from the optimal rate of spending from a social or policymaker perspective.

We'll argue in this part that faster spending has a number of important advantages that may not be obvious to the supporters and managers of individual firms. After explaining the social point of view, we explore the incentives of donors and managers to spend slowly and cautiously.

This same mismatch between the risks faced by investors and the risks faced by individual firms is commonplace in the for-profit world, and there it has standard solutions. For example, for-profit firm managers are often compensated with stock and stock options, in order to encourage them to take the kinds of big risks that diversified shareholders would prefer.

For now, payout rules are the best approximation the philanthropic sector has for this kind of incentive pay. That is, payout rules help to more closely align the social point of view with the point of view held by donors and managers. It would be interesting and worthwhile, though, to consider whether there are closer approximations of incentive pay for the philanthropic world. For now, we will settle for defending payout rules.

A. The Social Point of View

We can think of Congress, or any other policymaker whose resources lend support to the charitable sector, as a diversified investor. Congress places bets on thousands of philanthropic organizations. Some of those bets will pay off, and some will fail. In general, Congress will leave the best choice of projects up to each philanthropy. But, to the extent that individual firms may tend to systematically make choices that would reduce the overall social payoff, Congress may want to take steps to discourage such choices.

One key difference between Congress and individual firms, we'll argue, is risk aversion. As a large and diversified investor, Congress is essentially risk neutral. Whether any given foundation continues or goes bankrupt makes little difference, unless the collapsing firm were to take with it some valuable firm-specific investments that can't readily be transplanted elsewhere. Furthermore, Congress can predict, based on historic trends in giving, that there will be a stream of future money flowing into the philanthropic sector. For every bet that fails, another new wager is available.

This implies that, like the classic diversified investor, Congress actually wants each individual firm in which it invests to be risk-seeking. The potential payoff from one giant success is far more rewarding than a series of safe, mediocre outcomes.

For stock-market investors, these returns are in the form of dollars, but for Congress, the return is often in the form of information. Foundations are uniquely positioned to provide data and to guide experiments on social policy. Stunning policy successes can quickly be copied and adapted for use around the country or around the globe. Even information about daring failures provides valuable information for future experiments.

Congress may also prefer for firms to be risk-seeking with their budgets as well as their project choices. The more projects Congress and fellow foundations can observe, the better the chances are of finding the best approach to a given policy problem. Even relatively safe and familiar projects, such as funding for quality pre-K education, can provide useful information about the ongoing viability of a policy approach or reveal which operating charities are now in the best position to deliver good results. Congress therefore benefits from having more projects overall.

To be sure, foundations can also spend money in ways that provide minimal information: building more lavish offices or paying to wipe the dust off an Old Master. Not all spending generates informational spill-overs, but holding the share of information per dollar spent constant, more spending equals more information. Further, a foundation expanding its current project portfolio may well increase the amount of information generated per dollar, as many projects may have otherwise failed to get funding exactly because they are risky.

And indeed, these approaches can be risky for individual firms. Finding and funding bold policies can be expensive and may endanger the reputational capital of an individual firm. A serious policy setback might discourage staff and lead to an outflow of talent. The more a firm spends, and the lower its reserves, the more likely it is that an ill-timed downturn will leave it unable to meet current expenses. The next two sections explore in more detail sources of risk aversion for donors and firm managers.

B. Donors

Donors may prefer accumulation over spending for a variety of familiar reasons. We have covered this ground elsewhere and so our summary here will be brief. First, as Dan Halperin has shown, tax policy strongly encourages accumulation.[38] By exempting investments from tax when they are held by a foundation or other giving vehicle, but not when held by the donor, the tax system strongly encourages donors to park assets inside a tax-exempt entity. In effect, the longer an investment is held by charity, the larger the government's contribution to the gift.

While some recent commentators have observed that the tax system's realization rule can provide similar benefits,[39] these claims neglect the fact that those benefits are only available to taxpayers who are locked into a single asset. That is, taxes are generally only imposed on asset gains at the time of sale or other disposition, allowing assets to grow tax-free until sale. But this tax benefit is of course only available to owners who do not, say, sell an underperforming asset to acquire a new one. We should expect that, at the margin, investors will suffer these kinds of lock-in costs equal to any tax they might have incurred. Thus, the foundation or DAF alternative is an important cost saver. One of us has found evidence that donors are willing to suffer significant loss of control over their gifts in order to hold gifted assets in tax-free entities.[40]

Accumulation inside a donor-directed 501(c)(3) organization, such as a foundation or DAF, also allows donors to retain considerable control over their assets after already having claimed a charitable-contribution deduction for giving them away. Donors may value the power, prestige, and name recognition of controlling an ongoing stream of dollars.[41] As Halperin observes, the combination of tax advantage with personal use is a powerful incentive for the delay.

Current law further permits private foundations to continue to enrich and empower a donor and her heirs. Heirs can be paid a "reasonable" salary for serving as board members, be furnished with fairly lavish offices, and be reimbursed for board meetings in exotic locales. A foundation can additionally continue to exert substantial control over the family business, such as by leveraging the block of stock held by the foundation into board seats or employment as a senior executive at the firm. Some well-planned entities, such as the Milton Hershey School, have been able to retain complete ownership of their business through loopholes in the private-foundation rules.[42]

Psychological factors may additionally tend to discourage donors from spending quickly. Making complex decisions is mentally and emotionally taxing. In the face of such decisions, even experts can tend to procrastinate or take easy mental shortcuts.[43] Perhaps for those reasons, we also tend to favor outcomes that are easily measured over those that are more abstract or subject to interpretation.[44] In other words, donors may tend to prefer wealth accumulation over spending because they are human: letting balances grow is easy to see and doesn't take much effort, while making grants is time-consuming, challenging, and often delivers highly abstract rewards.

C. Foundation Managers

We can see many of the same factors at work for foundation managers. They too may prefer the easy and the measurable over the difficult and the abstract. For instance, one survey reports that managers favor accumulation because they can see it.[45] While many managers are undoubtedly motivated by a desire to do good, outside their preferred sphere they may not take fully into account the consequences their decisions might have for others. For example, not all managers will strive to fail spectacularly in ways that will provide useful lessons for others.

Managers also are unlikely to be totally ignorant of their own self-interest. Foundation employment is good, steady work. The manager's reputation is a personal asset that she cannot easily diversify. Thus, it's in managers' self-interest to take few risks with the finances or reputation of their organization. This is even more evident for managers with close ties to for-profit operations that can profit from holding assets under management, such as in the commercial DAF industry. Reputation and personal reward can also be tied to accumulation. In our data, foundations with larger endowments pay their officers more, on average.

CONCLUSION

In short, we believe that payout rules are worth preserving. Without some nudge from government, private foundations and their supporters would tend to reap tax benefits now but spend later, if ever. That reluctance could shortchange both present and future. And none of the supposed side effects of payout rules have any evidence to support them.

This brings us back to the possibility that under current rules private foundations can escape or finesse payout rules. Families can satisfy a payout requirement by paying themselves salary or handsome travel reimbursements, by distributing assets to another holding ground such as a DAF sponsor, or by making financial investments with enough "good intent" to qualify as program-related.

We therefore would tighten up on all these rules. To take what we see as the easiest first, foundations should not be allowed to pay salaries or reimburse for office expenditures or travel for anyone closely related to their initial supporters. In practice, the result of this rule might well be to shutter many small family foundations, with the assets distributed instead to DAF sponsors. Given the very high expense-to-grant ratios at small foundations, and the minimal added value those administrative expenditures likely deliver, we view that as a welcome result.

Next, a distribution from a private foundation to a DAF should not count for purposes of "payout" unless they are held in the DAF for only a short term. This exception could be modeled after the current rule allowing short-term set-asides for capital projects.

Finally, we think that the rules governing PRIs are worthy of closer scrutiny. While it might make sense to provide generous exceptions from the jeopardizing investment rules for investments entered into for a charitable end, we believe that we should be more careful when it comes to allowing investments to count for purposes of payout. Given the natural tendency for donors and managers to want to accumulate rather than spend foundation assets, we should be mindful of rules that make it too easy to displace grant-making with "investments for good."

With these rules and principles in place, we believe tax law would better balance two urgent needs: those of the future, but also those of the present day.

NOTES

1. "Nonprofit Organizations; Total Financial Assets Held by Private Foundations, Level," FRED Economic Data St. Louis Fed, https://fred.stlouisfed.org/series/BOGZ1FL164090015Q.

2. Now, some of the technicalities. The payout requirement is based on a share of each firm's "non-charitable use" assets; office buildings or other property actively used in the firm's operations are not part of the denominator. Firms can meet the payout requirement by making eligible expenditures within one fiscal year, so that in essence the rule requires that the foundation spends in year two at least 5 percent of the non-charitable use assets it held in year one. An accessible overview of private foundation rules can be found in Bruce R. Hopkins, *Nonprofit Law Made Easy* (Hoboken, NJ: John Wiley & Sons, 2005), 65–70.

3. During the pandemic in 2020, there were multiple efforts to reform the 5 percent payout rule, including the Emergency Charitable Stimulus proposal associated with the Patriotic Millionaires and the Institute for Policy Studies, and the establishment of the Initiative to Accelerate Charitable Giving, a coalition of philanthropists, leaders of major foundations, and scholars, which Ray Madoff, a coauthor of this chapter, helped to found. See "About Us," Initiative to Accelerate Charitable Giving, https://acceleratecharitablegiving.org/about/.

4. The first benefit is an income-tax deduction. Setting aside some technical detail, a charitable-contribution reduces the donor's taxable income, which in turn saves her an actual number of dollars equal to the donation amount times her "marginal" tax rate, which is the rate she pays on the last dollar of income. For instance, since the current top tax rate is 37 percent, a $10 million donation reduces a donor's tax paid by $3.7 million.

In addition, two separate rules combine to provide extremely favorable treatment for donations of property that have appreciated in value since acquired. First, although taxpayers usually must include such gains in income when property is "sold or otherwise disposed of," donations to charity do not trigger this rule—in technical lingo, a donation is not a "realization event." Second, and subject to some important exceptions, donations of property provide a charitable-contribution deduction in the amount of the full fair-market value of the property. This combined treatment violates the otherwise nearly universal tax principle that taxpayers cannot take deductions in excess of the amount of after-tax dollars ("basis") they have invested in an asset, resulting in negative effective tax rates in some cases. (In the case of donations to private foundations, however, donors can only claim the fair-market value deduction if the property is publicly-traded stock; though donors can still exclude the value of built-in gains from taxation.)

Finally, charitable contributions are not subject to the gift tax and also reduce the estate tax. At current Estate & Gift tax rates of 40 percent, this produces $4 million of savings on a $10 million gift.

Taken together, then, a donor who establishes a private foundation with a new $10 million contribution of appreciated, publicly-traded stock can save up to $7.4 million in current and expected taxes. The initial donation creates $3.7 million in income-tax savings. Assuming that none of the value of the stock has yet been taxed, its transfer saves the donor another 20 percent × $10 million = $2 million in potential capital gains taxes. And that $10 million will neither be taxed at the time of donor's death nor subject to the gift tax. Assuming estate taxes are only being saved on the value of the contributed assets net of taxes that would have been paid (which would be $4.3 million assuming the donor had paid the additional $3.7 million and $2 million in taxes), this would still save an additional $1.7 million (40 percent of 4.3 million). Taken together, the creation of a $10 million private foundation could save the donor (and effectively cost the government) up to $7.4 million.

5. Mark P. Gergen, "The Case for a Charitable Contribution Deduction," *Virginia Law Review* 74 (1988), 1396–407.

6. Because the rationales for charity are thoroughly explored elsewhere, we omit a detailed discussion. See e.g., Brian Galle, "The Role of Charity in a Federal System," *William and Mary Law Review* 53, no. 3 (2012).

7. 26 U.S.C. § 4940 (2019).

8. Foundations can also, with IRS permission, save up over multiple years for a single large grant. 26 U.S.C. § 4942 (2012).

9. J. Comm. on Internal Revenue Taxation and the Comm. on Finance, 91st Cong., *Summary of H.R. 13270, The Tax Reform Act of 1969* (Comm. Print 1969); Comm. on Finance, 89th, *Treasury Department Report on Private Foundations* (Comm. Print 1965).

10. The highest marginal rate was 77 percent in 1969, compared to 37 percent in 2019.

11. Cong. Budget Office, *The Distribution of Major Tax Expenditures in the Individual Income Tax System* (2013).

12. William McBride, "A Brief History of Tax Expenditures," *The Tax Foundation Fiscal Fact*, no. 391 (August 2013), http://taxfoundation.org/article/brief-history-tax-expenditures. Beginning in 1974 Congress required that these tax expenditures be recorded annually as part of the federal budget. See Stanley Surrey, "Federal Income Tax Reform," *Harvard Law Review* 84, no. 2 (1970), 352–408.

13. Comm. on Finance, 89th, *Treasury Department Report on Private Foundations* (Comm. Print 1965).

14. This remedy proposed that private non-operating foundations must expend all net income by the end of the year following the year such income is received, including ordinary investment income and short-term capital gains. J. Comm. on Internal Revenue Taxation and the Comm. on Finance, 91st Cong., *Summary of H.R. 13270, The Tax Reform Act of 1969* (Comm. Print 1969).

15. Excluded from this are contributions to organizations controlled by the foundation or a disqualified person with respect to the foundation and contributions to private foundations. 26 U.S.C. § 4942 (2012).

16. Sloan C. Wiesen, "Foundation Alms for the Rich," *National Committee for Responsive Philanthropy* (2003), https://www.ncrp.org/files/rp-articles/PDF/RP-Fall2003-Foundation_Alms_for_the_Rich.pdf.

17. Charity Aid, Recovery, and Empowerment Act of 2003, S. 272, 108th Congress (2003); Charitable Giving Act of 2003, H.R. 7, 108th (2003).

18. Ian Wilhelm and Brad Wolverton, "Pushing Grant Makers," *Chronicle of* Philanthropy, May 15, 2003.

19. "King, Grassley Introduce Legislation to Ensure Charitable Donations Reach Working Charities," Sen. Angus King press release, June 9, 2021, https://www.king.senate.gov/newsroom/press-releases/king-grassley-introduce-legislation-to-ensure-charitable-donations-reach-working-charities.

20. A charity is treated as receiving broad public support if it receives at least one-third of its support from the general public (defined as individuals who have provided less than 2 percent of the organization's support). Ray Madoff, Cordelia Tenney, Martin Hall and Lisa Mingolla, "Charitable Giving," in *Practical Guide to Estate Planning* (Wolters Kluwer CCH, 2013).

21. Some sponsoring organizations have policies to encourage or require regular distributions. But a private foundation seeking to defer ultimate distribution can freely shop for a DAF sponsor without such policies.

22. Ofer Lion and Douglas Mancino, "PRIs—New Proposed Regulations and the New Venture Capital," *Taxation of Exempts* 24, no. 3 (September/October 2012), 3.

23. According to the Bluebook: "The Act makes it clear that a program-related investment—such as low-interest or interest-free loans to needy students, high risk investments in low-income housing, and loans to small businesses where commercial sources of funds are unavailable—is not to be considered as an investment which might jeopardize the foundation's carrying out of its exempt purpose (since such an investment is classified as a charitable expenditure.) To qualify as program-related, the investment must be primarily for charitable purposes and not have as one of its significant purposes that of deriving a profit for the foundation." J. Comm. on Internal

Revenue Taxation and the Comm. on Finance, 91st Cong., *Summary of H.R. 13270, The Tax Reform Act of 1969* (Comm. Print 1969).

24. Exemption for Program-Related Investments, 26 C.F.R. § 53.4944-3(a) (2012).

25. Akash Deep and Peter Frumkin, "The Foundation Payout Puzzle," in *Taking Philanthropy Seriously: Beyond Noble Intentions to Responsible Giving*, ed. William Damon and Susan Verducci (Bloomington: Indiana University Press, 2006), 189, 202.

26. We thank Ben Marx for sharing his scans of historic Foundation Directories with us.

27. Our estimates may slightly overstate payout ratios, especially at firms with lower payout rates. We cannot observe which, if any, expenses would not count as qualifying expenses under the Tax Code in the Foundation Directory Data.

28. Full results of these regressions are available on request.

29. Deep and Frumkin, "The Foundation Payout Puzzle," 194.

30. C. Eugene Steuerle, "Distribution Requirements for Foundations," *Proceedings of the Annual Conference on Taxation* 70 (1977): 424.

31. The Uniform Law Commission has collected state enactment dates for UPMIFA on their website, https://www.uniformlaws.org/committees/community -home?CommunityKey=043b9067-bc2c-46b7-8436-07c9054064a3.

32. Much more detail on the construction of our data set and the coding of the UPMIFA and cap variables is set out in Brian Galle, "Why Do Foundations Follow the Law? Evidence from Adoption of the Uniform Prudent Management of Institutional Funds Act," *Journal of Policy Analysis and Management* 36, no. 3 (2017): 532–56.

33. For qualifications see Galle, "The Role of Charity in a Federal System."

34. Brian Galle, "Pay It Forward? Law and the Problem of Restricted-Spending Philanthropy," *Washington University Law Review* 93, no. 5: 1150–51.

35. For example, in Galle, "Pay It Forward?" 1175–76.

36. Galle, "Pay It Forward?" 1175–76.

37. Galle, "Pay It Forward?" 1179; Renée A. Irvin, "Endowments: Stable Largesse or Distortion of the Polity?" *Public Administration Review* 67 (2007): 450–51.

38. Daniel Halperin, "Is Income Tax Exemption for Charities a Subsidy?" *Tax Law Review* 64 (2011).

39. For example, see John R. Brooks, "The Missing Tax Benefit of Donor-Advised Funds," *Tax Notes* 150, no. 9 (2016), 1013. Brooks also notes that tax benefits can be minimal because they are captured by investment managers, a point with which we have no dispute.

40. Brian Galle, "Valuing the Right to Sue: An Empirical Measure of Nonprofit Agency Costs," *Journal of Law and Economics* 60, no. 3 (2017).

41. Louis Kaplow, "Utility from Accumulation," NBER Working Paper No. 15595, *National Bureau of Economic Research* (December 2009), https://www.nber .org/papers/w15595.

42. Schools are automatically treated as public charities under the tax code, even if their funding and governance are in essence those of a private foundation.

43. For a review of the evidence, see Kelli Alces and Brian Galle, "The False Promise of Risk-Reducing Incentive Pay: Evidence from Executive Pensions and Deferred Compensation," *Journal of Corporation Law* 38, no. 1 (2012): 53–100.

44. A useful discussion in the charitable context is Gerhard Speckbacker, "The Use of Incentives in Nonprofit Organizations," *Nonprofit and Voluntary Sector Quarterly* 42, no. 5 (2012): 1006–25.

45. Deep and Frumkin, "The Foundation Payout Puzzle," 189.

Selected Bibliography

Abdur-Rashid, Khalil. "Financing Kindness as a Society: The Rise and Fall of the Waqf as a Central Islamic Philanthropic Institution." *Journal of Muslim Philanthropy and Civil Society* 5, no. 1 (2021): 49–69.

Abrahamson, Eric. *Beyond Charity: A Century of Philanthropic Innovation.* New York: Rockefeller Foundation, 2013.

Adam, Thomas. "From Waqf to Foundation: The Case for a Global Integrated History of Philanthropy." *Journal of Muslim Philanthropy and Civil Society* 4, no. 1 (2020): 55–73.

Arnold, John. "The Slow-Moving Philanthropic Status Quo." *The Wall Street Journal*, December 22, 2020.

Ascoli, Peter M. *Julius Rosenwald: The Man who Built Sears, Roebuck and Advanced the Cause of Black Education in the American South.* Bloomington: Indiana University Press, 2006.

Berman, Lila Corwin. *The American Jewish Philanthropic Complex.* Princeton, NJ: Princeton University Press, 2021.

———. "Donor Advised Funds in Historical Perspective." *Boston College Law Forum on Philanthropy and the Public Good*, 1 (Oct 2015): 17–21.

———. "How Americans Give: The Financialization of American Jewish Philanthropy." *American Historical Review* 122, no. 5 (December 2017): 1459–89.

Bishop, Matthew, and Michael Green. *Philanthrocapitalism: How the Rich Can Save the World.* New York: Bloomsbury Press, 2008.

Bloch, Ruth H., and Naomi R. Lamoreaux. "Voluntary Associations, Corporate Rights, and the State: Legal Constraints on the Development of American Civil Society, 1750–1900." In *Organizations, Civil Society, and the Roots of Development*, edited by Naomi R. Lamoreaux and John Joseph Wallis, 231–90. Chicago: University of Chicago Press, 2017.

Brilliant, Eleanor L. *Private Charity and Public Inquiry: A History of the Filer and Peterson Commissions.* Bloomington: Indiana University Press, 2000.

Brody, Evelyn. "Charitable Endowments and the Democratization of Dynasty." *Arizona Law Review* 39 (1997): 873–948.

Brown, Peter. *Through the Eye of a Needle: Wealth, the Fall of Rome, and the Making of Christianity in the West, 350–550 AD*. Princeton, NJ: Princeton University Press, 2012.

Buchanan, Neil. "What Kind of Environment Do We Owe Future Generations?" *Lewis & Clark Law Review* 15, no. 2 (2011): 339–67.

Carnegie, Andrew. "The Gospel of Wealth." In Andrew Carnegie, *The "Gospel of Wealth" Essays and Other Writings*, edited by David Nasaw. New York: Penguin, 2006.

Colinvaux, Roger. "Donor Advised Funds: Charitable Spending Vehicles for 21st Century Philanthropy." *Washington Law Review* 92 (2017): 39–85.

Collins, Chuck, Helen Flannery, and Josh Hoxie, *Warehousing Wealth: Donor-Advised Charity Funds Sequestering Billions in the Face of Growing Inequality*. Institute for Policy Studies, 2018. https://inequality.org/research/new-ips-report-warehousing-wealth/.

Cordelli, Chiara and Rob Reich. "Philanthropy and Intergenerational Justice: How Philanthropic Institutions Can Serve Future Generations." In *Institutions for Future Generations*, edited by Axel Gosseries and Iñigo González, 229–44. Oxford: Oxford University Press, 2016.

Cullman, Lewis B., and Ray Madoff. "The Undermining of American Charity." *New York Review of Books*, July 14, 2016.

Daniels, Alex. "Grant Maker Dilemma: Spend More Now or Protect Shrinking Endowments?" *The Chronicle of Philanthropy*, April 1, 2020.

Epstein, Richard A. "The Temporal Dimensions in the Law of Property." *Washington University Law Quarterly* 64, no. 3 (1986): 667–722.

Fishman, James J. "The Private Foundation Rules at Fifty: How Did We Get Them and Do They Meet Current Needs?" *Pittsburgh Tax Review* 17, no. 2 (2020): 247–96.

Fleishman, Joel L. *Putting Wealth to Work: Philanthropy for Today or Investing for Tomorrow?* New York: PublicAffairs, 2017.

Francis, Megan Ming. "The Price of Civil Rights: Black Lives, White Funding, and Movement Capture." *Law and Society Review* 53, no. 1 (2019): 275–309.

Fremont-Smith, Marion R. *Governing Nonprofit Organizations: Federal and State Law and Regulation*. Cambridge, MA: Belknap Press of Harvard University Press, 2004.

Frumkin, Peter. "The Long Recoil from Regulation: Private Philanthropic Foundations and the Tax Reform Act of 1969." *The American Review of Public Administration* 28, no. 3 (1998): 266–86.

———. "He Who's Got It Gets to Give It." *Washington Post*, October 3, 1999. https://www.washingtonpost.com/archive/opinions/1999/10/03/he-whos-got-it-gets-to-give-it/7ebc1804-7f9a-42c9-a8a8-3a7a34c811fa.

Galle, Brian. "Pay It Forward: Law and the Problem of Restricted-Spending Philanthropy." *Washington University Law Review* 93 (2015): 1143–1207.

Hall, Peter Dobkin. *Inventing the Nonprofit Sector and other essays on Philanthropy, Voluntarism, and Nonprofit Organization*. Baltimore, MD: Johns Hopkins University Press, 1992).

Hansmann, Henry. "Why Do Universities Have Endowments?" *The Journal of Legal Studies* 19, no. 1 (January 1990): 3–42.

Hemel, Daniel, and Joseph Bankman. "Should Foundations Give Now or Later? There is No Right Answer." *The Chronicle of Philanthropy*, June 17, 2020.

Katz, Stanley M., Barry Sullivan, and C. Paul Beach. "Legal Change and Legal Autonomy: Charitable Trusts in New York, 1777–1893." *Law and History Review* 3, no. 1 (Spring 1985): 51–89.

Kavate, Michael. "Inside the Foundation Payout Debate: How Crisis and Opportunity Are Forcing Change." *Inside Philanthropy*, June 19, 2020. https://www.insidephilanthropy.com/home/2020/6/19/for-decades-foundations-have-given-the-minimum-required-that-may-be-changing.

Kimball, Bruce, and Benjamin Johnson. "The Inception of the Meaning and Significance of Endowment in American Higher Education, 1890–1930." *Teachers College Record* 114 (October 2012): 1–32.

Klausner, Michael. "When Time Isn't Money: Foundation Payouts and the Time Value of Money." *Stanford Social Innovation Review* (Spring 2003): 51–59.

Kramer, Larry. "Philanthropy Must Stop Fiddling While the World Burns." *Chronicle of Philanthropy*, January 7, 2020. https://www.philanthropy.com/article/philanthropy-must-stop-fiddling-while-the-world-burns.

———. "Foundation Payout Policy in Economic Crisis." *Stanford Social Innovation Review*, January 4, 2021. https://ssir.org/articles/entry/foundation_payout_policy_in_economic_crises.

Kulish, Nicholas. "Giving Billions Fast, MacKenzie Scott Upends Philanthropy." *The New York Times*, December 20, 2020.

Lechterman, Theodore M. *The Tyranny of Generosity: Why Philanthropy Corrupts Our Politics and How We Can Fix It*. New York: Oxford University Press, 2021.

Lowrey, Annie. *Give People Money: How a Universal Basic Income Would End Poverty, Revolutionize Work, and Remake the World*. New York: Crown, 2018.

MacAskill, William. *What We Owe the Future*. New York: Basic Books, 2022.

Madoff, Ray D. *Immortality and the Law: The Rising Power of the American Dead*. New Haven, CT: Yale University Press, 2010.

Mill, J. S. "Educational Endowments." In "Report on Commissions on Education in Schools in England, Not Comprised within Her Majesty's Two Recent Commissions on Popular Education and Public Schools." *Parliamentary Papers* 28, no. 2 (1867–1868): 67–72.

Miller, John J. *A Gift of Freedom: How the John M. Olin Foundation Changed America*. San Francisco, CA: Encounter Books, 2006.

Nasaw, David. *Andrew Carnegie*. New York: Penguin Press, 2006.

O'Clery, Conor. *The Billionaire Who Wasn't: How Chuck Feeney Secretly Made and Gave Away a Fortune*. New York: PublicAffairs, 2013.

Ord, Toby. *The Precipice: Existential Risk and the Future of Humanity*. New York: Hachette Books, 2020.

Ostrower, Francie. *Limited Life Foundations: Motivations, Experiences and Strategies*. Washington, DC: Urban Institute, 2009.

———. "Perpetuity or Spend-Down: Does the Notion of Lifespan Matter in Organized Philanthropy?" *Nonprofit Quarterly*, March 31, 2016. https://nonprofitquarterly

.org/perpetuity-or-spend-down-does-the-notion-of-lifespan-matter-in-organized -philanthropy.

———. *Sunsetting: A Framework for Foundation Life as Well as Death*. Washington, DC: Aspen Institute, 2011.

Parks, Dan. "Coronavirus 'Rapid Response' Funds Proliferate as Threat Grows." *Chronicle of Philanthropy*, March 11, 2020.

Proscio, Tony. *Harvest Time for The Atlantic Philanthropies 2011 - 2012: Focus, Exit, and Legacy*. Duke Sanford School of Public Policy, 2012.

Reich, Rob. *Just Giving: Why Philanthropy is Failing Democracy and How It Can Do Better*. Princeton, NJ: Princeton University Press, 2018.

Renz, Loren, and David Wolcheck. *Perpetuity or limited lifespan: How do family foundations decide?* New York: Foundation Center, 2009.

Rockefeller Philanthropy Advisors and NORC at the University of Chicago. *Strategic Time Horizons: A Global Snapshot of Foundation Approaches*. Chicago: Rockefeller Philanthropy Advisors and NORC at the University of Chicago, 2020.

Rosenwald, Julius. "The Burden of Wealth." *Saturday Evening Post*, January 5, 1929.

———. "Principles of Public Giving." *The Atlantic Monthly*, May 1929, 599–607.

Simes, Lewis M. *Public Policy and the Dead Hand*. Ann Arbor, MI: University of Michigan Law School, 1955.

Soskis, Benjamin. "To Be Young, Rich, and Philanthropic." *HistPhil*, January 11, 2016. https://histphil.org/2016/01/11/to-be-young-rich-and-philanthropic.

———. "Norms and Narratives that Shape US Charitable and Philanthropic Giving." *Urban Institute Research Report*, March 2021. https://www.urban.org/research /publication/norms-and-narratives-shape-us-charitable-and-philanthropic-giving.

Táíwò, Olúfémi O. *Reconsidering Reparations*. New York: Oxford University Press, 2022.

Thelin, John R., and Richard W. Trollinger. *Time is of the Essence: Foundations and the Policies of Limited Life and Endowment Spend-Down*. Washington, DC: Aspen Institute Program on Philanthropy and Social Innovation, 2009.

Thompson, Janna. *Intergenerational Justice: Rights and Responsibilities in an Intergenerational Polity*. New York: Routledge, 2009.

Troyer, Thomas. "The 1969 Private Foundation Law: Historical Perspective on Its Origins and Underpinnings." *The Exempt Organization Tax Review* 27, no. 1 (January 2000): 52–65.

Valentini, Laura. "On the duty to withhold global aid now to save more lives in the future." *Ethics & Global Politics* 4, no. 2 (2011): 654–64.

Villanueva, Edgar. *Decolonizing Wealth: Indigenous Wisdom to Heal Divides and Restore Balance*. Oakland, CA: Berett-Koehler Publishers, 2018.

Wall, Joseph Frazier. *Andrew Carnegie*. New York: Oxford University Press, 1970.

Wolf, Clark. "Contemporary Property Rights, Lockean Provisos, and the Interests of Future Generations." *Ethics* 105, no. 4 (1995): 791–818.

Wyllie, Irvin. "The Search for an American Law of Charities, 1776–1844." *The Mississippi Valley Historical Review* 46, no. 2 (1959): 203–21.

Zunz, Olivier. *Philanthropy in America, A History*. Princeton, NJ: Princeton University Press, 2012.

Index

Deep, Akash, 248

Development of Philanthropy Act (1987), 188

Diana, Princess of Wales Memorial Fund, 190

digital data, 26, 156; digital institution building through, 167–68; digital outsourcing of, 166–67; discontinuities of, 157–58; foundations and, 158–62; infrastructure for, 168–69; legal constructs for, 169–70; licensing for impact in, 162–64; as nonrival, 157–58; open access and open data as program strategy with, 164–66; open files in, 160–61; as open-source, 169, 172; perpetual foundation and, 158; redefining perpetuity with, 169–72; studying sector to influencing impact of, 162; tax records in, 159–61; trusts for, 172

digital resources, 25–26; considerations for, 156; forms of, 155

donor-advised funds (DAFs), 11; commercial, 243–44; digital data impacting, 161; five percent payout rule and, 242–44; Jewish Communal Fund as, 22; payout rules and, 29–30, 255, 257, 259n21; regulation of, 17–18, 35n49; rise of, 17–30, 56; tax considerations for, 139–40; timeliness and, 17–30

donors, 1; as cause-neutral, 153; engaged living major, 14–15; intent of, 28, 200–201, 208; living, 199–200, 210n15, 210n17, 246, 247, 248; payout rules and, 254–55; private foundations and, 254–55

Duke, James Buchanan, 48

Duke Endowment, 48

ECBI. *See* Eyberg Child Behavior Inventory

education: endowments to, 3; GEB for, 8; higher, 3, 85; OER for, 162; in South Africa, 226, 231

effective altruism, 18, 25; cause-neutral donor in, 153; changing opportunities in, 143–46; choice-worthiness in, 142; cost-effectiveness in, 143–46; definition of, 137, 153n1; further work in, 152–53; future weakness of will in, 140, 153n5; getting better knowledge in, 146; income change considerations in, 143; investment returns in, 147–49; loans for, 138, 153n4; major considerations for, 142–49; minor considerations for, 139–41; opportunities and knowledge in, 151; present generation valued more highly in, 142–43, 154n10; qualitative framework for, 149–52, *150*; self-interest in, 141; social return in, 147–48; special relationships and values in, 151–52; tax considerations in, 139–40; timing for, 137–39; uncertainty in, 141; value-aligned resources in, 144; values changes in, 146–47; "watch then pounce" strategy in, 145; what's more neglected in, 140

80, 000 Hours, 153n1

Einstein, Albert, 229, 234n23

Electronic Frontier Foundation, 162

Elizabethan Statute of Charitable Uses, 2

Embree, Edwin, 72

Endecott, John, 44

endowments, 1–2; of Carnegie, 87n12; dangers of, 3; in France, 187, 191–92; to higher education, 3; Jewish federations against, 22, 78–79; Jewish philanthropy through, 75–76, 80–81, 85; legal definition of, 3; in post–World War II years, 79, 87n12; as unmitigated good, 75

equality of opportunity, 23; in democracy, 100; ICTs and, 100–101, 103–4; *versus* inequality of opportunity, 135n55

About the Editors and Contributors

EDITORS

Ray Madoff is a professor at Boston College Law School specializing in tax law. She is the cofounder and director of the Boston College Law School Forum on Philanthropy and the Public Good.

Benjamin Soskis is a senior research associate at the Urban Institute's Center on Nonprofits and Philanthropy. He is a frequent contributor to the *Chronicle of Philanthropy* and the coeditor of *HistPhil*.

CONTRIBUTORS

Helmut K. Anheier is a faculty member of UCLA's Luskin School of Public Affairs and professor of sociology at the Hertie School in Berlin, Germany. His research centers on civil society, nonprofit organizations, and philanthropy. He is the founding editor-in-chief of the journal *Global Perspectives* (https://online.ucpress.edu/gp). He received his PhD from Yale University in 1986, held a chair of sociology at the Max-Weber-Institute in Heidelberg, centennial professor at the London School of Economics and Political Science, senior researcher at the Johns Hopkins University, and associate professor of sociology at Rutgers University.

Lila Corwin Berman is a professor of history at Temple University, where she holds the Murray Friedman Chair of American Jewish History. She is the author of *The American Jewish Philanthropic Complex: The History of a Multibillion-Dollar Institution* (2020).

Lucy Bernholz is a senior research scholar at Stanford University's Center on Philanthropy and Civil Society and director of the Digital Civil Society Lab. Bernholz is the author of numerous articles and books about philanthropy, policy, and technology, including *How We Give Now: Philanthropy by the Rest of Us* (2021) and coeditor of *Philanthropy in Democratic Societies* (2016).

Miranda Perry Fleischer is a professor of law at the University of San Diego School of Law and the Richard and Kay Woltman Professor in Finance. Professor Fleischer's research focuses on the interaction of distributive justice and tax policy relating to charitable giving, wealth taxation, and redistribution to the poor. She has published numerous articles and book chapters on those subjects and is frequently quoted in the press on issues related to charitable giving and nonprofit law.

Brian Galle is a professor of law at Georgetown, where he writes on tax policy, nonprofit law, and quantitative studies of the nonprofit sector.

Stanley N. Katz is a Princeton University legal historian who specializes in the study of philanthropy and civil society, and who retired from what used to be the Woodrow Wilson School at Princeton in July 2019. He received the National Medal for the Humanities from President Barack Obama in 2010.

Theodore Lechterman is an assistant professor of philosophy at IE University in Madrid. His research investigates what democracy demands from emerging economic and technological practices. He is the author of *The Tyranny of Generosity: Why Philanthropy Corrupts Our Politics and How We Can Fix It* (2022).

William MacAskill is an associate professor in philosophy and senior research fellow at the Global Priorities Institute, University of Oxford. He is the author of *Doing Good Better* (2015) and *What We Owe the Future* (2022).

Francie Ostrower, PhD, is a professor at the University of Texas at Austin in the LBJ School of Public Affairs and College of Fine Arts, director of the Portfolio Program in Arts and Cultural Management and Entrepreneurship, and senior fellow in the RGK Center for Philanthropy and Community Service. She is a principal investigator of the multi-year *Building Audiences for Sustainability: Research and Evaluation* study, commissioned and funded by The Wallace Foundation, and has authored numerous publications on philanthropy, nonprofit governance, and arts participation.

Tony Proscio has been a consultant to foundations and major nonprofit organizations on strategic planning, evaluation, and communication. His clients have included the Ford, Robert Wood Johnson, Kresge, Rockefeller, and F. B. Heron Foundations, the Atlantic Philanthropies, and the United Nations Secretariat. From 2013 to 2019 he was associate director of the Center for Strategic Philanthropy and Civil Society at Duke University's Sanford School of Public Policy.

Sandra Rau is a public policy professional who works at the intersection of the German public and philanthropic spheres. She has consulted for large and small philanthropic foundations, including Bertelsmann Stiftung and Vodafone Stiftung Deutschland gGmbH and currently works with one of the largest German statutory health insurance funds as a policy adviser on public health. She holds a Master of Public Policy from the Hertie School of Governance in Berlin.

Rob Reich is a professor of political science and, by courtesy, of philosophy at Stanford University. He is the co-director of the Center on Philanthropy and Civil Society, the author of *Just Giving: Why Philanthropy is Failing Democracy and How It Can Do Better* (2018) and the editor, with Chiara Cordelli and Lucy Bernholz, of *Philanthropy in Democratic Societies: History, Institutions, Values* (2016).